from Lancaster County

The Regional Church of Lancaster County
www.theregionalchurch.com

God Stories

© 2006 by The Regional Church of Lancaster County
Lancaster, Pennsylvania, USA
www.regionalchurch.com

ISBN: 0-9760387-1-4

Printed in the United States of America

Art by Kristen Oberly, grade 7
Ephrata Middle School

Dedication

This book is dedicated to the people of
Lancaster County, Pennsylvania.

Acknowledgments

Thank you to the many contributing authors who made this book possible.
Edited by Mark Ammerman, Karen Boyd, Cindy Riker, Becky Toews, Kim Wittel and Keith Yoder. House To House Publications Team: Karen Ruiz, Sarah Sauder, Carolyn Sprague and Jane Nicholas.

Cover photos and design by Chelsey Bollinger, grade 12, Warwick High School.

Content for each week's "Pray for Lancaster County" prayer focus is adapted from the *Transformation Prayer Guide* and used by permission of Prayer Transformation Ministries.
www.prayertransformation.com

Introduction

Welcome to this offering of inspirational meditations from authors in Lancaster County. Through our **fellowship** together as authors and readers, we will grow in our love for the body of Christ in Lancaster County.

Together, one day at a time, we will be a part of the fulfillment of the prayer of Jesus in the Garden of Gethsemane before His crucifixion. He and His Father agreed in their longing that those who believe in Christ as the Son of God will be one (John 17:20–23). Such oneness is a witness to the world that Jesus was sent by the Father. To that end we have gathered—in one volume—testimonies from hundreds of Lancaster County Christians. All speak of the goodness of the one great God we serve.

In the pages that follow are personal stories that show God at work in our lives: they will inspire our faith. Each month is introduced with art created by students from the region: they will encourage us in creative expression of our abilities. Some meditations are life lessons forged in experiences with God: they will prepare us to take steps of trust and obedience in a life-style of **worship**.

Weekly we will shape our region through prayer. As our voices and hearts harmonize with each theme for prayer, we will align our region with the principles by which communities are transformed in godly ways. Each theme is a specific application of how Jesus taught His disciples to pray: *Your kingdom come, Your will be done on earth as it is in heaven.* Agreement between heaven and earth is **partnership** with God in prayer for our region. Let us also bless the authors of these daily meditations.

Welcome to **fellowship**, to **worship**, and to **partnership**—as one. Together, let us honor the two Great Commandments (Mark 12:28–31), the Great Prayer (John 17:20–23), and the Great Commission (Matthew 28:18–20) of Jesus Christ the Lord.

—*Keith Yoder*

Keith serves as chair of the Regional Council of the Regional Church of Lancaster County.

January

God's Word, A Treasure

"Open my eyes that I may see wonderful things in your law."
Psalms 119:18

Throughout our years of missionary service in Brazil, South America, my husband Norm and I learned to appreciate the Word of God as we never had before. Additionally, we were often impacted by the way simple folks treasured the Bible and believed it implicitly!

A poor, little old grandmother started attending our church services. She told us that she had spotted an ad for a Bible in a discarded newspaper. Although she had never before heard of the Bible, she knew she wanted one. In simplicity she talked to God and told Him she would work to earn a Bible. We would gladly have given her one, but she insisted on keeping her promise to God. Little by little her savings grew until she finally was able to purchase the much-desired Book. She returned to us, joyously clutching her Bible. "Now you must pray for my eyes so I can read my Bible," she stated matter-of-factly.

We were astonished to learn that this lady had sacrificed so much to buy a Bible that she could not read. Even strong glasses would not help her terrible eyesight. Nevertheless, we prayed with her. Surely it would be God's will for this dedicated woman to be able to read His Word.

Very little time passed before this tiny lady was back at our house! Her eyes had improved miraculously, and she now was able to read her treasured Bible. In fact, she was not only reading the Word, but memorizing it too. Soon, this humble little grandmother who had hardly any schooling began teaching others the Word of God which she had hidden in her heart.

Lord, Your Word is precious! I want to be more committed to hiding its truth in my heart.

Betty Charles and her late husband Norm, co-founded Abundant Living Ministries, a Christian marriage and family counseling organization, Lititz.

Photo by Alicia Weaver, grade 9
Living Word Academy

Alvino's Bowl

"...he will be a vessel for honor, sanctified and useful for the Master, prepared for every good work." *2 Timothy 2:20–21*

A mong the few wedding gifts for which I remember the givers, one is a very simple plastic bowl, "Alvino's bowl."

At about twenty years of age, I enjoyed teaching a class of inner-city second graders. Alvino came to class. He was totally disruptive, constantly drawing the attention of the entire class to his antics. Reprimands didn't alter his course or slow his speed. I admit I held secret hopes that it was a once-and-done visit.

The next Sunday he was even more hyped and disruptive, any slight inhibition from newness removed. What to do? With my best teacher voice, I told the rest of the class to sit still and told Alvino to come with me. As I walked to the door, with Alvino sauntering behind me, I cried out to the Lord, "Help me. Show me what to do." Getting down, I looked into deep, dark brown eyes and saw... terror. My heart melted. As I gently hugged his thin, rigid shoulders I said, "Alvino, Jesus loves you. I love you. Please, can you help me by being quiet and listening so everyone in the class can hear?" He nodded solemnly.

The transformation that took place was miraculous. From that day on he was my best student, adoring and tender.

When Al and I were married, Alvino's gift was a plastic bowl. For forty-one years I have used it for salads or chips, never without thanksgiving for God's miracle-working love and a quick prayer for Alvino.

Father, Your love makes me a vessel of honor. Use me to serve in any capacity in Your house. Amen.

Ruth Ann Stauffer most recently served as prayer coordinator for Teaching the Word Ministries. She and her husband Al serve the body of Christ in OASIS Streams Ministries, an associate ministry of TTWM.

A Shield of Love

"For you bless the godly, O Lord, surrounding them with your shield of love." *Psalms 5:12 (New Living Translation)*

It had been an unusually long workday and I was ready to relax. I knew that if the traffic was light, I would have just enough time to get home by 9:00 p.m.—the time I told my husband I'd arrive.

But my drive was peppered with obstacles. First, a truck crept up a long hill in a no-passing zone. Next, a disabled vehicle blocked my lane at the crest of a hill. Then the railroad crossing bars dropped just as I approached the tracks. Trying to quiet my impatience, I reminded myself that maybe God had a purpose for the delays.

Within two miles, I saw the flashes of emergency vehicle lights. Intensely focused emergency personnel surrounded a badly-battered car and its occupant. I prayed for the occupant and said, "Lord, thanks for my safety." Immediately another thought ran through my mind, "Yes, but there could always be another accident down the road."

A mile later, my heart sank. Emergency vehicles were arriving at another accident scene that had obviously happened only minutes earlier—the exact time I would have been passing by unless my trip had been altered by the numerous delays.

Tears ran down my cheeks, as I suddenly understood the Father's heart of God in a new way. I had thanked Him for being my Provider. But I hadn't understood until that point that He was also my Protector, who daily shielded me with His love.

Father, thanks that You shield me every moment of each day. I can trust that what happens today has passed through Your Father's heart of love for me.

Kati French, a recent widow, is a mother and grandmother and serves as executive director at Susquehanna Valley Pregnancy Services.

God's Art Project

"Your people will rebuild the ancient ruins and will raise up the age-old foundations; you will be called Repairer of Broken Walls, Restorer of Streets with Dwellings." *Isaiah 58:12*

In the fall of 2003, God gave me a treasure…not a treasure that most people would want, but one that had my name written all over it. The treasure came packaged as a condemned house that I bought from the city for $1,500 on the 500 block of Manor Street, Lancaster City. As work began on the house, I realized that it was going to take even more work and money than I originally thought to fix it up. Instead of getting discouraged by this, God seemed to speak to me that this was His "art project" and that those of us working on the house were His instruments to create it.

Slowly the old house seemed to transform before our eyes. Taking the old out and replacing it with new was so rewarding. All around us it seemed like others were being encouraged by the "hope" that they saw in the project as well. I even got my cousin to put a fake stone facade on the front, which put the finishing touches on the home.

Prophetically, I believe that this "art project" of God's speaks to an area of Lancaster City that desperately needs to know that nothing is "hopeless to God" and that He is a God that loves to redeem old things and make them new. Come, Lord Jesus!

Dear Father, Thank You that You use us, Your kids, to paint "Your art projects." What a privilege to partner with You to see the old become new on Manor Street. May this home be a beacon that shouts out "YOUR HOPE" to a neighborhood that needs to hear and receive Your Message. You are a RESTORER…You are a REDEEMER, and we worship You.

Jonathan Groff lives with his family on Filbert Street, Lancaster City. He works construction and helps give leadership to an emerging house church network.

Stopping for the "One"

"[Jesus] had to pass through Samaria...[He] sat down beside the well...there came a woman of Samaria to draw water...."
John 4:4–7 (Revised Standard Version)

Often a missionary to Mozambique has taught that to save them all, you must "stop for the ONE." It was a Wednesday night and Ann was on her way to church. As she was getting into the car, a woman was walking past her house, and seeing the "For Sale" sign, asked why it was being sold. Ann immediately heard in her heart, "stop for the ONE." She quickly put her things into the car, closed the door, and moved to where the woman was standing. They talked for over half an hour and Lottie shared a very private pain. Being from a foreign land, she had never learned to read English and it seems that no one ever took the time to teach her. Ann followed the prompting and offered to help.

In the ensuing months, Lottie would come by Ann's home (still not sold) and the Lord gave simple instructions to help her read.

Recently, after weeks of not seeing her, Lottie came for a short visit. There was a "knowing" that it was her time. The gospel was shared and with gentle tears, she asked Jesus to forgive her sin and come to live inside her heart. A new sister had been "born again!"

When she got up to leave, Lottie hugged Ann and exclaimed, "I just know this is why your house hasn't sold." Ann's heart gives God all the glory. His divine delay in selling her house became a divine appointment for her!

Heavenly Father, so many times we are rushing to our appointments, services, meetings, and we miss opportunities to share Your love. Thank you for teaching me to "stop for the ONE"...and giving a wonderful example of what happens when I do. Thank you for keeping my house from selling so that "one" of Your daughters could come home and read the Word as well!

Diana Oliphant serves abroad with Global Missions of The Worship Center, Lancaster.

Our Ever-Present God

"Haven't I commanded you? Strength! Courage! Don't be timid; don't get discouraged. God, your God, is with you every step you take." *Joshua 1:9 (The Message)*

Since I was a little girl, I have struggled with "tummy aches." By the age of 15, I was diagnosed with ulcerative colitis. It was a blow. My parents struggled with feelings of guilt that somehow it was their fault. Insurance companies denied me life insurance. Various medications were tested. Some helped; some caused side effects that were especially distressing for me as a teen. I felt like damaged goods: but deep down, I trusted God for my healing.

Fast forward 15 years to the year 2004. After having neglected my health during college and young adulthood, I finally got back into the routine of checking in with the specialist and taking my medication. Although I had accepted the disease as a part of my life, I continued to hope for a miracle. My parents were warriors on my behalf, constantly beseeching the church family to remember me in prayer. Occasionally, my father would suggest I pursue the option of surgery. It terrified me.

In the late summer of 2004, some routine testing revealed pre-cancerous cells developing. This time, when the surgery was brought up, I recognized that it was time for the healing I had hoped for. After two miraculous surgeries to remove my large intestine and reconstruct my digestive system...I feel like I have never felt before. I have received my healing. God is so good. All of my needs were met in abundance during recovery. I have never felt so loved by my family, church, or co-workers. The verse that I have highlighted was one given to me by a friend prior to the surgery.

Lord, I ask for the courage to trust in You through all of life's trials. Thank You for Your constant presence in my life.

Stacey Gagne is office manager at FM 90.3 WJTL in Lancaster.

Bursting Forth From Heaven!

"Oh, that you would burst from the heavens and come down! How the mountains would quake in your presence!…When you came down long ago, you did awesome things beyond our highest expectations. And oh, how the mountains quaked! For since the world began, no ear has heard, and no eye has seen a God like you, who works for those who wait for him!" *Isaiah 64:1, 3–4 (New Living Translation)*

If the very mountains created by God would quake in His presence, imagine how our hearts would tremble at a glimpse of His glory! If the Lord burst forth from the heavens and became fully present in our midst, everything would change instantly. Our concerns in this world would quickly fade as we stood breathless, awestruck, and over-whelmed. We would suddenly realize that our expectations have been far too low, and that God's power and presence can bring even nations in humble submission before Him. As this passage indicates, God works for those who wait for *Him*—for *His glory* to be revealed! May we turn our hearts toward Him and pray with hope and expectation, waiting for nothing less than His very presence among us.

Pray for Lancaster County is our weekly prayer focus for the individuals, families, churches and communities of our region. Please carry this emphasis in your heart and your prayers throughout the week.

God and a Box of Cereal

"And my God will meet all your needs according to His glorious riches in Christ Jesus." *Philippians 4:19*

Jehovah-Jireh. God, our provider. This is easy to proclaim when all is well and His supply is evident. When things are tough, however, that's when we see God's special provision. A number of years ago I found myself in a situation where my faith-based ministry salary was running low. My paycheck was short due to a lack of support. I was concerned. I paid my bills one night and found that I now had only 16 cents left in my bank account. The car had half a tank of gas, the cupboard a box of cereal, and the refrigerator a carton of milk. The next paycheck was two weeks away. Okay, Lord, now what?

I showed up at work the following morning to learn that we had committed "last minute" to a week-long multimedia outreach at a festival in northern California. It was an incredible opportunity that clearly God was orchestrating. No one else was available to go with Doug, a fellow worker, so I was asked to make the trip despite having just returned from a long tour. When God opens a door, how can you say "no"? While on tour, all of my expenses were covered. Upon return, other co-workers, without knowing of my situation, invited me over for lunches and dinners to learn about the incredible week of outreach. I didn't miss a meal, and the half a tank of gas stretched until the next pay day. God supplied *all* of my needs.

Heavenly father, thank You for Your abundant provision in my life. Forgive me when I fail to recognize that "every good thing bestowed" comes from You and You alone (James 1:17). Help me to rely more fully on You and to be content regardless of my situation or circumstances (Philippians 4:11-12). Amen!

Brad Hoopes, an ordained minister, serves as Director of Development at Dayspring Christian Academy, a Principle Approach school utilizing America's classical, biblical model of education.

Remember Who You Are

"For we are God's workmanship, created in Christ Jesus...."
Ephesians 2:10

Remember who you are, and don't spend all your money in one place." As parents, I'm not sure why we got in the habit of repeating this advice; nevertheless, the oft-reiterated phrase never failed to elicit a few rolled eyes as our kids left the house. Two of our children are now adults, leaving one teenager still getting the sage advice as she walks out into the dramas of adolescence. On reflection, it probably was better advice than we knew...

Remember who you are. An 18th century rabbi named Zusha said, "If they ask me in the next world, 'Why were you not Moses?' I will know the answer to that question. But if they ask me, 'Why were you not Zusha?' I will have nothing to say." God created only one of you. Don't pretend to be someone else. As a Christian, you are a unique child of God, a friend of Jesus, one with Him in Spirit, forgiven of your sins, complete in Christ, free of condemnation, complete in the good work He started in you, appointed to bear fruit, God's workmanship. You can do all things through Christ who gives you the strength. When we know who we are in Christ, our behavior begins to reflect our true identity.

Don't spend all your money in one place. One of the fruits of the Spirit is self-control. It is an important aspect not only of managing money but of how we approach life. An attitude of giving keeps us from becoming greedy and self-centered. Our son started supporting a Compassion child in his junior year of high school and has continued to do so through the sparse finances of his college years. Money matters so often are matters of the heart that are tied up in our values, choices, relationships and self-worth.

Lord, help us to rest in who we are in You and approach today with a generosity of spirit.

Karen Ruiz is the editor of House to House Publications, Lititz.

January 10

A Mighty Foothold

"And don't sin by letting anger gain control over you. Don't let the sun go down while you are still angry, for anger gives a mighty foothold to the Devil." *Ephesians 4:26–27 (New Living Translation)*

The tension in the room was tangible, suffocating all common sense. My wife and I lay on our bed. The only light came from the dim glow of a street lamp outside our bedroom window. The argument we were having had long strayed from its original point. What could have been a healthy dialog, quickly became angry, violent words. Our breathing was heavy as we laid facing away, disgusted at each other's company. Minutes passed, as we both lay wide awake in our dark room.

"Get out of here!" my wife exclaimed. I looked toward the doorway, where I expected to see a child out of bed. No one was there.

"She better not be talking to me," was my thought as she spoke again. This time, the statement was proceeded by, "In the name of Jesus…." The hairs on the back of my neck stood up. I scanned the room. As she shouted a few more times, I prayed in silence. Something lifted without me saying a word. She explained that she noticed an oily darkness on our wall growing and spreading as we argued. At first, she chose to dismiss it as a figment of her imagination. When we stopped speaking and instead let the anger fester, she finally recognized what her eyes were seeing. The dark oily substance was feeding from our anger and growing rapidly! Then she understood it to be a demonic presence.

We apologized and asked God to forgive us. This episode demonstrated the spiritual reality of the scripture found in Ephesians. Many are unaware of what transpires in the unseen dimension of the spirit when God's word is disregarded.

Lord, let sensitivity to Your Word provoke us to righteousness.

Jamie Centeno is an elder at In The Light Ministries and a field director with Lancaster Teen Haven.

Praying Through the Battle

"For our struggle is not against flesh and blood, but against the rulers, against the authorities, against the powers of this dark world and against the spiritual forces of evil in the heavenly realms." *Ephesians 6:1*

I was scheduled to go to Banda Aceh, Indonesia, to help with tsunami relief, and more importantly, to show the love of Christ to a people who have been weighed down by the yoke of Islamic fundamentalism.

As the day drew closer, it seemed as though a huge load was trying to crush me. There was the usual hustle and bustle of getting ready that precedes a two-week trip, but there seemed to be more stressors emotionally. A longtime patient was killed in a violent car crash, another patient of twenty years died suddenly, there were conflicts at church, my father-in-law became critically ill, and there were more things to finish than I had time for. I also wondered if I was going into an ugly hostile situation in Indonesia, given the reported hatred of Americans.

I was feeling oppressed and depressed. As I made the long trip, I realized Satan doesn't like it when we're doing God's work! The trip was bathed in prayer, and we had a great time ministering to the needs of the people we met. They were warm and receptive and we felt that the love we were showing was making a difference. Satan had one more shot, however. While I was sorting medical supplies, several boxes fell on my head. I got home to find that I had pain, spasm, numbness and weakness in my arm—a significant pinched nerve! After much prayer, God healed the nerve and gave me back my health, joy and peace, and I understood more clearly the spiritual battle the Lord had won from all that prayer!

Lord, help us to see the battle around us and depend on Your strength to fight the evil one.

Chip Mershon, M.D. is a physician at Cornerstone Family Health Associates, on the board at Water Street Rescue Mission, and an elder at Lancaster Evangelical Free Church.

January 12

Rapid Angels

"He will give His angels [especial] charge over you to accompany
and defend and preserve you in all your ways...."
Psalms 91:11 (Amplified Bible)

We knew we were in trouble as we headed into the rapids.
The raft before us was up against the rocks and we were
aimed right for them! It was like slow motion as our raft
went vertical and overturned at the top end of the rapids. As we went
down the narrow passage, the raft was on top of us and we couldn't
come up. I saw people struggling to surface, and then I saw a bright
light. It seemed like I was being carried, but not by the fast-flowing
water. It was more like being carried protectively. The next thing I was
aware of, I was holding onto a rock in a quiet jetty below the rapids. I
later realized that, although I had ridden down the rocks of those rapids
out of the raft, I had no bruises, scrapes, or cuts even though I lost my
helmet and a shoe. Clinging to that rock, waiting for the river guides to
rescue me, I remembered that earlier that morning I had declared Psalms
91 for my family and myself. I had been rescued by the Lord.

God is gracious in all His ways and faithful to fulfill His word!

*Father, thank You for angels that do Your bidding. Thank You for the
angel of protection that You sent to the river that day. Keep us mindful
of Your promises, and expectant for all You will do in Your love for us.
Open our eyes to see the angels.*

Lauren Charles, along with her husband, Keith, serves as director of
the Healing Rooms of Lancaster City.

January 13

Weak People

"But we have this treasure in jars of clay to show that this all-surpassing power is from God and not from us." *2 Corinthians 4:7*

Six months after having heart surgery and a complication with medication, I began to experience low mood, high anxiety and sleeplessness. The diagnosis was clinical depression. All of this was a totally new experience for me. The recovery from depression was a process that took several months.

In addition to serving as pastor of Manor Church, I am also the director of Roxbury Holiness Camp, a ten-day teaching and preaching camp meeting. As we came together for the 2004 camp meeting, the members of the planning committee urged me to tell my story of depression and recovery at camp. So I did. In an evening service I gave a simple, ten-minute testimony about my depression—what it felt like and how God helped me out of it—which was a combination of prayer, medication, counseling, exercise, diet...and waiting.

After the service was over, there was a line of people waiting to talk with me. Each one told of an experience with depression that they or a family member had. Unfortunately, many of them had been given unhelpful advice by well-meaning Christians—advice such as, "All you need is prayer," or "If you just try harder, you can snap out of this." My experience of multiple elements in the healing process was a great encouragement to these people.

In my 26 years of serving as director of the camp, it seems that the thing I did that touched people most deeply was to tell about a time when I was weak, and the situation looked impossible—and then to tell about God's faithfulness in that very situation. God delights in using weak people and impossible situations.

Heavenly Father, help us to be honest about our needs and weaknesses so that we can receive Your help and power.

John Hawbaker is senior pastor of Manor Church (Brethren in Christ) located south of Mountville.

January 14

The Firestorm of Divine Grace

"'The time will come,' says the Lord, 'when the grain and grapes will grow faster than they can be harvested. Then the terraced vineyards on the hills of Israel will drip with sweet wine! I will bring my exiled people of Israel back from the distant lands, and they will rebuild their ruined cities and live in them again....'" *Amos 9:13–14 (New Living Translation)*

The prophet Amos saw a time coming of complete healing and restoration of the land and of God's people. Imagine fields overflowing with grapes and grains in such abundance that the harvesters cannot keep up. In terms of spiritual harvest, envision masses of people eagerly seeking the fullness of God. Imagine broken-down, desolate cities restored to places of safety and bustling commerce. Think of the joy of families healed, and relationships overflowing with love, honor, and respect. This kind of abundance can only come as the fulfillment of God's promises for hope and healing. This kind of revival and transformation is already happening in many places around the world. Could it be that we will soon enter into what is called "the firestorm of divine grace"? May it be so, Lord—even *today*!

Pray for Lancaster County is our weekly prayer focus for the individuals, families, churches and communities of our region. Please carry this emphasis in your heart and your prayers throughout the week.

January 15

Spiritual Diets

"Enter through the narrow gate. For wide is the gate and broad is the road that leads to destruction, and many enter through it. But small is the gate and narrow the road that leads to life, and only a few find it." *Matthew 7:13–14*

I've struggled with weight all my life. I admit that a lot of commercials pique my interest when I see someone took this pill or ate that diet food. According to the National Eating Disorders Association, the diet industry is a $40 billion industry, which is amazing considering 95% of all dieters will regain their lost weight within 1–5 years! It doesn't take a genius to know that good weight loss takes time and effort by a long-term discipline of eating right and exercising.

We can fall into similar traps in our Christian walk. Satan tempted Jesus and he tempts us, too. What kind of "spiritual diets" does Satan tempt you with? Is there a quick fix to having a closer walk with the Lord? I believe that spiritual maturity, like losing weight, takes time and effort. We must continually read God's Word and implement it into our daily lives.

Jesus tells us to go through the narrow gate. The Message interprets this as "don't look for shortcuts to God." Don't get discouraged by the narrow gate. Be bold and stand up for your faith, even when it feels like everyone around is doing something else. Your reward is in heaven!

Lord, give me strength and endurance to stay on the narrow path. When I feel alone on this path, remind me that You are there and You will always walk alongside me. Don't let me fall into temptations of "the easy way," but help me to stay my ground, knowing that my reward is more than I can imagine.

Lyndell Thiessen is a member of DOVE Christian Fellowship Westgate in Ephrata. She is serving as a missionary with her husband, Bruce, in Fortaleza, Brazil.

"Phil, we are sorry..."

"There is neither Jew nor Greek, slave nor free, male nor female, for you are all one in Christ Jesus." *Galatians 3:28*

It was 1960, when a fellow student (who later became my wife) and I were seniors at a Lancaster County high school. One highlight of that year was our class trip to Washington D.C.

At the end of this day, after touring much of our nation's capital, there was a dinner waiting for us at a special restaurant in the city.

Now we had a fellow black classmate, but we hardly noticed his color, because he was our friend and comrade. As we pulled up to the restaurant and stopped, we all stepped out of our coach-bus with the exception of our friend, Phil. He would not be allowed to dine with us at a place like this.

We were so unaware at this stage of life of these realities, socially and culturally. We were country folk and this kind of prejudice was not practiced among us. However there was a sadness that went to the core of our spirit, one that remains within us to this day every time we tell this story.

But we succumbed to the way things were at that time and salved our consciences with, "What can we do?" And we haven't ever seen him after that year!

We both look back on this experience and want to weep each time it comes to our minds: "Why did we not stay out in that bus with him; what would it matter how this would affect us?" We want to rush to him and say, "Phil, we are so sorry, we wish we could do this event all over again and embrace you in your own right. Will you forgive us?"

Father God, this sin was really against You. Will You forgive us? Please, wherever our friend is at this moment, comfort him and draw him close to Yourself, in Jesus' name, Amen.

LaMarr and Naomi Sensenig serve as spiritual parents and intercessors.

Fear God

"So the Lord commanded us to observe all these statutes, to fear the Lord our God for our good always and for our survival, as it is today." *Deuteronomy 6:24 (New American Standard)*

In the spring of 2003, we asked the middle school art teacher to come to a Concert of Prayer for our school district and share how we could best pray for students. She said that she felt the number one problem for students was that they had no fear of God. She then passed out laminated bookmarks with these two verses: "There is no fear of God before their eyes (Romans 3:18)" and "Fear the Lord, you His saints, for those who fear Him lack nothing (Psalms 34:9)."

I still have my bookmark. I thank God for that godly Christian teacher and for the insight the Lord gave her for each of us that night. As I've pondered the gravity of those words, I've also thought of the alternative in Scripture. "The fear of man brings a snare (Proverbs 29:25)." But the fear of God brings wisdom, honor, and warning of evil (Proverbs 9:10, 31:30, 16:6). The list goes on.

How, then, do we grow in the fear of God? Regularly acquaint ourselves with how awesome and fearsome He is. Job 38 and Isaiah 40 contain great thoughts of our God. "Who has measured the waters in the hollow of His hand and marked off the heavens by the span (Isaiah 40:12)?" Scripture is filled with verses on the fear of God. Search for them. Meditate on them. Then pray along with me, "Establish Thy Word to Thy servant as that which produces reverence for Thee (Psalms 119:38)."

O Father, forgive us. We are a home, a school, a county, a nation that does not fear You. We ask for Your mercy and grace and help in this. May we "fear You while the sun endures and as long as the moon throughout all generations (Psalms 72:5)."

Ellen Gingrich serves with Donegal Moms In Touch.

Hold Loosely

"The weapons we fight with are not the weapons of the world. On the contrary, they have divine power to demolish strongholds. We demolish arguments and every pretension that sets itself up against the knowledge of God, and we take captive every thought to make it obedient to Christ." *2 Corinthians 10:4*

The ministry I am a part of was spending considerable time before the Lord praying that we become less and He become more. It was a powerful time for us individually and corporately. During this time, I was approached to consider a possible move within the ministry. My initial reaction was to say "no." I believed that I was right where the Lord intended me to be, and I felt no desire to make a change. Quickly there was conviction in my spirit over the word "I." "I believed." "I desired." Where was God in that? I asked a friend in the ministry to pray with me as I sought the *Lord's* will in this decision. While we prayed, He made it clear to me, without doubt and with peace, that I was to make the change. That weekend I attended a women's conference and decided to ask the Lord for confirmation. During a quiet time in his Word, He did just that.

In honesty, it took time for me to accept the coming change. It took nine months for all to be in place for the move. Just enough time for the Lord to birth within my spirit a sense of excitement and eager anticipation for what lay ahead. At this writing, the move is just three weeks away. He has given me more than a glimpse of the blessings of obedience, and I feel certain it is only the beginning.

Dear Lord, forgive me for my short-sightedness. Thank you for Your grace. I praise You!

Kathy Zubik is the director of the Lebanon Pregnancy Clinic and former director of the Lancaster Pregnancy Clinic, all part of Susquehanna Valley Pregnancy Services.

Desperate Dependence

"…we were under great pressure, far beyond our ability to endure, so that we despaired even of life. Indeed, in our hearts we
felt the sentence of death. But this happened that we might not
rely on ourselves but on God, who raises the dead."
2 Corinthians 1:8–9

S ometimes life overwhelms us and we feel like we can't endure.
This is where I found myself as a young mother expecting my
second child. My alcoholic father suffered a stroke and needed
someone to care for him. My husband and I felt that the Lord was
asking us to take him in. He was an unbeliever and through the years
had caused me significant emotional pain, but I was eager to obey the
Lord because I regularly prayed for my father's salvation.

The situation was difficult as my father's frustration was unleashed
on me, and he battled with depression. Following the birth of my second child, the responsibility of the children and my father began to
overwhelm me and I, too, spiraled into depression. I began to feel, as
Paul states in these verses, "the sentence of death on my life." It felt as
if God had abandoned me after my willingness to obey Him.

As I cried out to God in desperation, He showed me that at times
He allows us to experience seasons of great pressure so that we might
learn to rely on Him instead of ourselves. I began to see that as a child
of an alcoholic I had learned to "survive" pain and difficulty by being
strong. Now I had come to the end of my own ability so that I might
learn to rely on Him. God's goal isn't to make us stronger people but
rather to cause us to see our own weakness and learn to depend on Him
in all circumstances.

P.S. My father accepted Christ three months before passing away.
God is good!

Heavenly Father, help me learn how to rely on You in all circumstances.

Jackie Martin is a prayer ministry leader and teacher.

Perseverance Against All Odds

"...suffering produces perseverance...character...hope. And hope does not disappoint us...." *Romans 5:3–5*

A story that has greatly encouraged me to persevere is that of Adam Taliaferro. Adam, whose ambition since he was 6 years old was to play in the National Football League, won a scholarship to play football at Penn State. Not only was Adam a star athlete, he was also an honors student, a humble and well-liked classmate. In 2000 he played for Penn State as a true freshman. But his career ended abruptly when, in the last minutes of the game against Ohio State, Adam received a severe spinal cord injury. The odds that he would ever walk again were three out of one hundred. But Adam didn't give in to self-pity or despair. He believed he would walk again. And so did his parents.

Prayer vigils were held on campus and in Adam's room. One night in particular Adam's dad, trying to fight discouragement, cried out to God for some kind of sign. At 1:00 a.m. he received a call from the hospital...Adam had slightly moved his foot. It was the first movement of any kind since the injury. Overwhelmed with tears, Mr. Taliaferro and Adam's mom rushed back to the hospital where they joined Adam in thanking Jesus for giving them that hope.

Eventually, Adam's progress picked up, and through the intensity of physical therapy, he began showing improvement not just month-to-month, but week-to-week and day-to-day.

On September 1, 2001, less than a year after his injury, and contrary to all the doctors' predictions, Adam led his Penn State team onto the field before a sellout crowd of 109,313 people who all stood to their feet to honor him.

Father, there are times in life when we just feel like hanging up our uniforms. Please help us not to quit. Teach us how to persevere through our suffering, and on the other side, find a hope that doesn't disappoint.

Becky Toews leads the women's ministry at New Covenant Christian Church.

January 21

Kingdom Fruit -Bearers

Pray for Lancaster County

"I am the true vine, and my Father is the gardener. He cuts off every branch in me that bears no fruit, while every branch that does bear fruit he prunes so that it will be even more fruitful...I am the vine; you are the branches. If a man remains in me and I in him, he will bear much fruit....This is to my Father's glory, that you bear much fruit...." *John 15:1–2, 5, 8*

Jesus desires that we bear much fruit, but to do so we must be connected to Him as the true Vine. In the process of becoming fruitful, we are warned that we will be pruned so that we will bear more abundant fruit. Although pruning can seem painful in the moment, it is for our ever-increasing growth. He also warns that the dead branches will be cut off because they are useless to His kingdom. It is ultimately by our overflowing fruit that God is honored here on earth. Pray that true transformation will begin with your own intimate connection to Jesus, the Vine. Invite God to do the necessary pruning in your heart—in order to bring Him honor and glory!

Pray for Lancaster County is our weekly prayer focus for the individuals, families, churches and communities of our region. Please carry this emphasis in your heart and your prayers throughout the week.

Our Unfailing Supplier

"But my God shall supply all your need according to His riches in glory by Christ Jesus." *Philippians 4:19 (New King James Version)*

In 1990, we started our first long-term mission assignment. We traveled to Hua Hin, Thailand, to start a school for missionary children. We raised our own funds, including airfare. The cost of living in Thailand was very reasonable. Our family of five could make it on about one thousand dollars per month. At the end of our second term, we needed our monthly thousand plus twenty-seven hundred dollars for return airfare. We were planning to go home in March and needed to buy our plane tickets by the end of February.

We didn't have half the money we needed for airfare, and our February income was only two hundred and fifty, the lowest amount during our stay in Thailand. We bought our plane tickets by credit card, trusting that God would bring in the rest of the money.

In the natural, it didn't look good, because the total gifts that had come in amounted to thirteen hundred dollars. We flew back to the U.S. and took two days to settle in. The third day home I called our banker who handled our finances while we were overseas. I asked him what our balance was. He replied that it was twenty-seven hundred dollars—exactly what we needed to pay off our credit card!

God taught us a valuable lesson: He would meet our needs no matter what the circumstances looked like. He also provided a job for us for three months managing a thrift store until we left for our next assignment in Puerto Rico.

Father God, we acknowledge You as our Jehovah Jireh, the great provider. Just as You did for Abraham and Isaac, You provide our resources before we reach our hour of need. Thank you for the riches You give us through Your son, Jesus.

Mike and Liz Ingold are founders of the Barnabas Ministry (encouraging and strengthening missionaries), a satellite ministry of Petra Christian Fellowship, New Holland.

Flawed Vessels

"But we have this treasure in clay jars, so that it may be made clear that this extraordinary power belongs to God and does not come from us." *2 Corinthians 4:6–7 (New Revised Standard Version)*

When Joy and I vacationed in Ireland, she said she wanted to buy a chimney pot, a decorative extension for chimneys. I reminded her that they are big, heavy, and sooty! We looked for days with no success, and then spotted some at a hardware store. We bought one, as did our friends. We wrapped them up and checked them as "luggage."

On the way home, the pots were dropped once or twice. When we unwrapped it, ours had a gazillion pieces broken off. I glued it back together with epoxy, and it serves as a planter. Most of the cracks face the wall!

That chimney pot is ordinary earthenware, cracked, and glued— but it tells of a wonderful trip to Ireland, a bold trip home, and connection with friends.

God has lit up the world with the treasure of His grace. While we put treasures in special containers in safe places, God puts His treasure in us ordinary clay jars! We're cracked pots, all of us. Our flaws show; anyone can see God's repair lines. But we hold a great story and a bold adventure that connects us with others. God's reasons are ingenious: when people see the Light, they have to know it comes from God and not from us!

Lord, sometimes I'd like to be decorated and attractive. But You have made me ordinary for Your purpose. Make it clear to someone today that everything extraordinary is really You and not me. Amen.

Kent Kroehler is senior pastor at First United Methodist Church in Lancaster.

January 24

Be Imitators Of God

"Be imitators of God, therefore, as dearly loved children and live a life of love, just as Christ loved us and gave himself up for us as a fragrant offering and sacrifice to God." *Ephesians 5:1–2*

As a family physician, I almost daily hear comments from my patients that are humorous and sometimes profound. Recently an eighty-five year-old gentleman and his wife came for a checkup, and he stated that he was going to retire from his part-time job at Wal-Mart. I asked him what he will do with all of his time, and he quickly replied, "I will have wild love!" His wife and I roared with laughter.

The Lord reminded me that He wants us to be "wildly in love" with Him whether we are still children or are in the twilight years of our lives. Revelation 3:15 talks about the church in Laodicea as being lukewarm—neither hot nor cold such that "I am about to spit you out of my mouth."

John Eldridge wrote a book several years ago called "Wild at Heart" which has inspired many of the men in my church to be more passionate in their relationship with God. This has subsequently carried over to their marriages, families and other mentoring relationships.

Also, a favorite chorus that we sing by Matt and Beth Redman echoes, "…I'll stand in awe of You. Yes, I'll stand in awe of You. And I'll let my words be few. Jesus, I am so in love with You."

God is calling us to cultivate the relationship with Himself so that we can agree with the writer of Song of Songs 2:16, "My beloved is mine and I am His."

Father, I pray that I would have a deeper, intimate, even wild at heart kind of love with You. Remove all of the barriers that block that relationship from blossoming. As Your Word says, I truly desire to live a "life of love" totally sold out to Jesus.

T. Scott Jackson is a physician at Crossroads Family Medical Center.

Spirit Feed!

"Trust in the Lord, and do good; dwell in the land, and feed on His faithfulness." *Psalms 37:3 (New King James Version)*

Now is the time to put your house up for sale and it will sell quickly." Those were the words I heard in my spirit while at work. That evening Fran and I discussed this opportunity the Lord was giving us to move from a large house, which no longer served our purpose, to a smaller one. Monday morning the realtor arrived for us to set our asking price, sign the papers and put our house on the market. That afternoon he had a couple look at it, and later that same day he returned with a cash down-payment and a firm offer to buy at our price for cash. This buyer did not need a mortgage! You read correctly—in one day the house was marketed and sold! We moved 30 days later.

We had been praying, asking the Lord for wisdom as to what to do about our housing situation. Then the Lord answered with a specific word of direction. Over the years His answers to my prayers keep rolling in. Now this answer was added to my *feed list* of His faithfulness.

My list is composed of directions and answers received which meet three criteria. The instructions received in my spirit:

- Are in line with what the Bible teaches.
- Will be accompanied by a sense of peace and thankfulness in my life.
- Meet with the confirmation of my spouse and/or those affected by what my decision will be.

Let's feed on His faithfulness as answers to our prayers come. Because of the "feed list" our trust and expectations of Him cause us to dwell securely where we live, work and interact with others.

Lord, may we remember Your loving answers to us in the past, feed our spirits on them and trust Your mighty hand to guide us.

Richard Armstrong serves on staff at The Worship Center as assistant director of Global Ministries.

Faithful God

"The eternal God is your refuge and dwelling place and underneath are the everlasting arms...." *Deuteronomy 33:27 (Amplified Bible)*

We are living an adventure that is truly beyond what we could dream or imagine! God has taken us from a tame and manageable course with a comfortable life, and has redirected us into a brand new area that we know nothing about.

It is as if we stepped off a cliff into a free fall where we would be caught by the Lord or crash. And we've realized that God doesn't allow us to crash if we are trusting Him, hearing His word, and walking into what He calls us to, even if it's "over the edge" and beyond our experience.

We have seen God set our course one step at a time in unfamiliar territory. We have seen Him bring divine appointments and supernatural connections. We've seen Him establish prayer support and bring words of confirmation from His heart. We have seen God release favor that can only come by His hand and give wisdom that is beyond our knowledge. We've experienced God opening doors of opportunity and providing finances from the most unexpected places.

We believe He's asked us, "Will you go?" As we've answered, "Yes," He's shown Himself faithful in every aspect of the adventure.

God is about advancing His kingdom. As we will walk with Him and work with Him, we are experiencing the adventure of our life!

Father, thank you for Your promises to never leave or forsake us, to direct our path, and to give wisdom when we ask in faith. Thank You that Your promises are true and You are faithful to fulfill each one. We fix our eyes on You, and we set our hand in Yours. We look with expectation at all You are bringing to pass and we say, "Thank you for the adventure!"

Keith Charles is a marketplace minister, and with his wife, Lauren, serves as director of the Healing Rooms of Lancaster City.

God's Amazing Provision

"'If you can?' said Jesus. 'Everything is possible for him who believes.'" *Mark 9:23*

It has been said that the first year of marriage is the hardest. I have found that it's not so much hard as it is a test of faith. Here's a case in point.

My husband, Shawn, and I got married in October 2004. Then in January of 2005, I had arthroscopic surgery on my left knee, due to a skiing accident that had happened a year ago. Numerous people, including the doctor's assistant, believed that because it was a preexisting injury it would probably not be covered by my insurance policy. So we began to pray.

In April, we got the papers from the insurance company. And what I had feared came true. I looked through the piles of bills that I thought I was going to have to pay. It came to approximately twelve thousand dollars!

I panicked. I thought God had not answered our prayers. For a few days after that, I was depressed and wondered how we were going to pay for it. We got together with my parents later that week, and they looked over the papers. They soon discovered that I had been mistaken. Those bills were just copies of what the insurance company had paid! The surgery had been covered!

I relate this experience to Abraham and Sarah. Shawn had a peace that God would provide, just like Abraham believed that God would provide a son in his old age. I was like Sarah, and basically scoffed at God and said, "Yeah, right!" Later that evening I felt God saying to me, "Jenn, you prayed that I would provide. Why didn't you trust and believe I would?"

Father, forgive us when we don't believe, when we lose our trust in You. Help us to remember Your loving care for Your children. Amen.

Jennifer Paules-Kanode is a writer, a part-time DJ on WJTL 90.3FM, and an English as a Second Language instructor.

God's Intended Normalcy

"And the name of the city from that time on will be: The Lord is there."
Ezekiel 48:35

The sovereign Lord revealed to Ezekiel an exact description of a restored Jerusalem. He gave detailed measurements of the city gates, along with names according to the tribes of Israel. But the final description is actually the greatest distinguishing characteristic of the city. The restored Jerusalem was to be known from that time on as "The Lord is there." It was a city to be marked profoundly by the presence of the Lord. The fact that the Lord's presence was the greatest identifier of the city is in reality God's *intended normalcy*.

In the heart of God, the desolation that infects our cities and whole regions today is unusual; it is not His intended desire. God's heart is that His presence be real and manifest in every aspect of society. Perhaps we need to readjust our understanding of normal. In this world there will never be a "perfect" society: however, we can set our sights and prayers on God's *intended normalcy* being the identifying mark of our communities.

As you pray, allow the Lord to examine and re-identify what you assumed to be God's *intended normalcy* for your life, church and the city where you live.

Pray for Lancaster County is our weekly prayer focus for the individuals, families, churches and communities of our region. Please carry this emphasis in your heart and your prayers throughout the week.

They Are Precious in His Sight

"Even so it is not the will of your Father which is in heaven, that one of these little ones should perish." *Matthew 18:14*

In years gone by, I confess that I was not a great supporter of short-term missions trips because I thought that a few weeks to another country was more like a sight-seeing trip than an opportunity for ministry. About eight years ago, our then twelve year-old daughter, Lydia, asked to go to Russia with a Josh McDowell ministry team. She had always had a heart for orphans, and since some friends of ours were going on the trip we gave her permission to go. On the last day of her two-week trip, she was allowed to go to an orphanage near Moscow, and she made friends with a little girl named Anya. Lydia came home and announced that she believed we should adopt Anya. I thought, "How sweet. Now let's get back to reality."

Lydia did not give up on Anya, and to make a very long story short, we adopted Anya. We found out in the process that she had an older sister, Masha, and we adopted Masha as well. Since then, my wife Lisa has taken up Lydia's calling to work with orphans, and over the past several years she has been involved in getting about twenty-five children adopted into homes in the United States.

So, from one short-term missions trip lots of wonderful things have happened. It's a good thing God is in charge, as His vision is so much broader than mine.

Lord, thank you that You are concerned about people that I would never consider. Thank you especially since I may be one of those people.

Joe Troncale, M.D. is the medical director of the Caron Foundation, an addictions treatment center. He is a member of Petra Christian Fellowship in New Holland.

The Tug of God

"Jesus answered and said to him, 'Truly, truly, I say to you, unless one is born again, he cannot see the kingdom of God.'" *John 3:3*

Wow! Imagine having two birthdays! Would that mean you get twice the cake, twice the ice cream, twice the presents, twice the candles, and twice as old? I am one who attended church regularly all my life. I was baptized and joined the church in my teenaged years. I typically got involved in church and its ministries when it suited me. However, God did not always take first place in my life. Actually, I am not sure He took second, third, or fourth place either. There were other things to take care of—basically, the treasures that this world has to offer. I praise God that I was involved in church enough that there was a sensation of God constantly tugging at me.

Then, on May 24, 1996, I attended a Promise Keepers rally in Washington DC with a group of men from the church. On Friday night the speaker spoke about being born again. He asked the burning question, "Do you know the date that you were born again, born into the kingdom of God? Do you have a 'born again' birthday?" I realized at that point that I had no idea. That God-tugging sensation returned. God was pulling at me, saying: "I want all of you, Tom, not just part of you. Follow after *Me*." I went forward that night to give "all" of myself to God. A couple of years later God led me into youth ministry, through seminary, and into pastoral ministry. God has *never* left me. On May 24, 1996, at the earthly age of thirty-five I became born again.

Praise God for the church that allowed me to be constantly reminded of God. May the Spirit of God be equipping the church to continue the work of leading people to Jesus Christ that more and more may be born again into a saved life through Jesus Christ our Lord.

Tom Weber is the pastor at Akron Church of the Brethren.

The Vision Will Come

"Then the Lord answered me and said, 'Write the vision and make it plain on tablets, that he may run who reads it. For the vision is yet for an appointed time; but at the end it will speak, and it will not lie. Though it tarries, wait for it; because it will surely come, it will not tarry, Behold the proud, his soul is not upright in him; but the just shall live by his faith.'" *Habakkuk 2:2–4*

Habakkuk needed to hear from God, so he set himself up on a high tower to wait for an answer. God told him to write the vision down plainly so everyone would understand it. I believe we can learn from this example. First of all, Habakkuk decided he was going to "set himself up." He was determined to wait on God. Second, Habakkuk was obedient to follow the instructions God gave him. God then encouraged him to wait patiently until the vision came to pass.

What is the vision God has instructed you to do? What are some of the things the Lord has been impressing you to do for Him? Have you written it down? I believe one reason why God instructed Habakkuk to write everything down was to keep it as a reminder to him and to keep it alive until it actually came to pass. This applies to us today. It is right there in front of us, helping us to stay in faith and in thanksgiving to God. Then if hard times come, threatening to snuff out the vision, we will not be discouraged and give up because we have been putting our faith to work.

Father, thank you for the vision You have for my life. I purpose to write it down. Make it clear so I can run with it. Thank you for bringing it to pass at the appointed time.

Sherlyn Smucker serves and ministers alongside her husband, pastor Sam Smucker, at The Worship Center in Lancaster.

Februar

February 1

Just Being There

"When Moses' hands grew tired, they took a stone and put it under him and he sat on it. Aaron and Hur held his hands up—one on one side, one on the other—so that his hands remained steady till sunset." *Exodus 17:12*

I don't recall hitting the brakes. With a sickening crash, my car slammed into the fallen tree that blocked the dark road. The impact threw my vehicle into the other traffic lane and head-on into an oncoming car. My body smashed forward into the dashboard, and my face bent the steering wheel.

I had scraped together money for my first car, a 1969 Camaro. It wasn't much of a muscle car, but it had all the 1970s accents, shag carpet, mag wheels and 8-track tape player. None of that mattered as I pulled myself out of the mangled wreck. Suddenly I realized I couldn't speak, and I collapsed on the hard, rain-slicked roadway.

I recall the distant ambulance siren and waiting for what seemed like hours until finally its red flashing emergency lights reflected off the wet pavement next to me. As I was lifted into the ambulance, I heard a familiar voice. It was my cousin Bob, insisting that he ride with me to the hospital that was nearly ten miles away. Bob had arrived at the accident scene and immediately recognized my car. There was nothing medically Bob could do. He simply took that long ride to the emergency room with me, holding my hand as I struggled to breathe.

The encouragement of a friend's presence calmed my spirit. Am I such a friend to those who are suffering? Does my presence help people breathe more easily, grieve more thoroughly, suffer more courageously, and heal more completely? Sometimes just being there is spirituality at work. If we think our presence means nothing, we underestimate the life-changing influence of simply holding someone's hand.

Dear God, help me to sit quietly beside those who suffer. Amen.

Dave Witmer is a church planter and musician, and serves with HopeNet Fellowship of Churches.

Art by Kelly Kreider, grade 9
Lancaster Mennonite High School

February 2

He Cares

"Cast your cares on the Lord and he will sustain you." *Psalms 55:22*

Over the years I have discovered that when God begins teaching you something new from His Word, you will be tested on those principles...sometimes sooner than you would expect.

Two months before Carol and I married, we bought an old house. The house had been converted into a duplex in the early 1970s. The tenants that lived in the side that we wanted had trouble finding a new apartment. With the pressure on, Carol and I had to find an apartment of our own since we didn't want to live in my van.

We quickly realized that the cross-town apartment we rented was much nicer than the house we owned! Since the rent of our tenants paid for the rent of our apartment, this seemed like a nice money-making opportunity until I got laid off from work. Then winter arrived and the tenants started complaining about the heat.

The main part of the house had to be set at 75° just to get the converted side up to 65°. I contacted a plumber friend, who informed me that it would cost about $700 that I did not have. That night I lay in bed trying to figure a way of solving the dilemma. Finally, God was able to burst through my anxiety and remind me of what I had been learning for the past two weeks. I repented and fell asleep almost immediately, probably from sheer exhaustion.

The next morning, I woke up, drove across town, knocked on the door of the "hot" side. I reached down to a radiator, turned the valve the whole way off and then slightly back open. The temperature between the two apartments balanced to within half of a degree of each other. God had a better plan and it didn't cost a cent.

Lord, remind me to cast my cares on You at all times, because You care for me.

Hank Rogers is the financial administrator of DOVE Christian Fellowship International.

The Real Thing

"Jesus answered: 'Watch out that no one deceives you. For many will come in my name, claiming, "I am the Christ," and will deceive many.'" *Matthew 24:4–5*

One day in the late 1800s, my grandmother had some errands to run so she left the family farm for several hours while her hired help, a young woman, finished baking bread and other chores. When grandmother returned, she asked the hired girl if she had anything for lunch. "I ate some of your delicious blackberry jam on a piece of the bread I just baked," the girl responded.

"Blackberry jam?" quizzed grandmother. "I don't have any blackberry jam."

"Sure you do," the hired girl said. "It is on the shelf in the cellar way."

Grandmother went to see for herself and gasped, "That's not blackberry jam, it's a forgotten jar of dark molasses, and it's full of big black dead ants!"

They both burst into laughter when the girl admitted, "Oh, and to think I chewed them up real good!"

The hired girl was so sure she had the real thing. It is amazing how our minds (and taste buds, it would seem!) are easily fooled. During the nine decades that I've been on this earth, I've learned that I must evaluate things based on how they measure up to what the Bible says is true. The only source of absolute truth is what God reveals in His Word because it serves as a filter for discerning truth.

Lord, today we commit to seeking the truth, living the truth and believing the truth as we allow Your Word to transform us.

Charity Heller is ninety years old. She served with her husband, Parke, pastor emeritus of Hammer Creek Mennonite Church, and also taught Sunday School for many years.

Pray for Lancaster County

God's Heart for Renewal

"Never again will you be called the Godforsaken City or the Desolate Land. Your new name will be the City of God's Delight and the Bride of God, for the Lord delights in you and will claim you as his own." *Isaiah 62:4 (New Living Translation)*

The very heart of God is always for restoration and renewal. We see it with each new season of the year; we see it in how He restores and renews those who come to Jesus Christ by faith in His finished work on the cross. Restoration is His desire for families, churches, and entire cities and regions.

Why? Because it is in the very nature of who God is. In the first verses of Isaiah 62, Isaiah says he will not keep silent until God accomplishes His work of renewal and restoration, righteousness, and salvation. Isaiah prays with fervency as he cries out to God for his city. God's heart is exactly the same for *your* city.

Pray for Lancaster County is our weekly prayer focus for the individuals, families, churches and communities of our region. Please carry this emphasis in your heart and your prayers throughout the week.

Patience in Reaping

"And let us not lose heart in doing good, for in due time we shall reap if we do not grow weary." *Galatians 6:9 (New American Standard Bible)*

Jesus became my Savior during the Gulf War. One Tuesday night an old friend telephoned. We talked politics and he listened to my ranting about the war. After twenty minutes, Brian stopped me cold when he said, "But Keith, it is all in the Bible." That Saturday I purchased a new Bible and began reading the book of Luke. On Sunday, I gave my life to Christ.

Eight months later, I met Brian at his church for Sunday worship, my first time in church since becoming born again. As I walked toward the church sanctuary, a couple I recognized from my childhood neighborhood greeted me. When I reintroduced myself to them, they nearly flipped!

Herb and Doris held Good News Bible Clubs in their back yard during the summer. I had attended the club when I was ten years old. I remember being in their back yard with many other neighborhood children, doing arts and crafts and listening to stories. As I reintroduced myself, I told them of my recent conversion. And as only God could orchestrate, Herb and Doris told me that they were starting a new believers Bible study in their home in the next few weeks. They invited me to attend.

I faithfully attended these studies for over a year. My hunger for God's Word increased and I received a great desire to serve Him. In September of 1993, I enrolled in Bible college and graduated in the spring of 1996. After graduation, God placed me here in Lancaster County serving him in a variety of ways.

Father, may we be blessed to see the fruit of our labors. Thank you for everyone who plants and waters. Thank you for everyone You placed along my path.

Keith Hahn is an elder at New Hope Bible Fellowship Church and a staff member of Lancaster Youth Network of Churches.

Help for the "Spatially Challenged"

"I will instruct thee and teach thee in the way which thou shalt go: I will guide thee with mine eye." *Psalms 32:8 (King James Version)*

Those words have a special meaning for me because I have no sense of direction. For most of my adult years I struggled with this lack of ability, often saying to my husband, "I think I'm a reasonably intelligent person; why can't I read a map?" I instinctively turn the wrong way, whether exiting a room, a building or a parking lot. I really am "spatially challenged"!

My most vivid experience of having to rely on God's help and direction was when I traveled, alone, to Scotland to be with my daughter shortly after she gave birth to her second child. This meant taking a bus to the New York airport, getting on the right plane, changing planes in London, and so on. On the return trip my flight was delayed five hours, causing me to miss my transportation back to Lancaster, requiring an overnight stay in New York, and finding train travel back home.

In all of this, I was never frightened and I didn't get lost! Not a big deal to most people, but a very big one to me! I've never been more aware of God's protecting and guiding presence, especially in Grand Central Station when I was struggling with my luggage and a wonderful African American man appeared, seemingly out of nowhere, like a guardian angel, and carried my bags for me. I quickly learned he was a brother in Christ. I readily recognize that today's verse goes much deeper than reading a map or finding one's way out of a store, but I also know that my heavenly Father knows my frailties and meets my daily needs, mundane though they may be!

Dear Father, thank you for Your guidance and protection, and for Your Word, which is a lamp to my feet and a light to my path.

Sylvia Hollinger serves as administrative assistant to her husband, Paul, at WDAC-FM, and is editor of WDAC's Program Guide.

Mending Broken Pieces

"And we know that in all things God works for the good of those who love him, who have been called according to his purpose."
Romans 8:28

On the job, I work in fiberglass repair. How someone ends up at my shop is usually a unique story. Maybe a truck's fender was damaged by a deer or an accident happened on icy roads. A boat may have hit some rocks or was in a storm and needs repair. Sometimes normal wear and tear on a vehicle requires fiberglass work to strengthen it. I work on new things as well as older models.

I can take broken pieces and bond them together, reconstructing the truck hood or boat hull. With several steps of sanding and painting, the damage disappears. If the work is done properly, it is stronger than the original.

We can go through hard knocks in life. A storm may have taken us by surprise. A broken heart or dented pride leaves us needing the healing touch of the Lord. Maybe poor choices in others' lives leave us scattered. The damage may not have even been our fault. God can take the broken pieces, however the damage was done, and reconstruct something beautiful.

It takes patience to work through the different stages of repair. Give the Lord time as He works on your heart and life. God may use others in the process, like I use my trusted suppliers. Some of my customers are delighted to see a finished project, surprised at how well it really turned out. Trust the Lord to complete the job with excellence.

"May the God of hope fill you with all joy and peace as you trust in him, so that you may overflow with hope by the power of the Holy Spirit (Romans 8:28)."

Dear Lord, grant us wisdom and patience as we go through life. Help us trust You every step of the way. Amen.

Carl Mohler is a Sunday School teacher at Ephrata Mennonite Church.

Prison's Open Door

"...where the Spirit of the Lord is, there is freedom. All of us...seeing the glory of the Lord...Are being transformed into the same image from one degree of glory to another...." *2 Corinthians 3:17–18*

Tammy, are you guilty of the abortion you had?" the leader of the Post Abortion Bible Study asked.

"I guess I'm not," I stammered. She then read to us from Beth Moore's book *Praying God's Word.* The author likened people living with shame and guilt to someone living in a prison cell with the door wide open. We have been granted a pardon from the King, but we stay in that prison cell feeling unworthy because we believe all the lies that are written on the walls about us.

As this was being read to us, God gave me a vision of myself sitting on a hard, dirty bench in my cell with my head hanging down, not knowing that there was a door, let alone an *open* door. As I was hearing the words being read, I lifted up my head and looked at that door; it was open! I stood up and took a few steps toward the door. I stood at the threshold of the door looking out into a colorful, bright world.

When the leader finished reading, I took that last step outside of my cell. I turned around and looked back—one last time—into that dark cell I had lived in for so many years. I would never go back into that cell, and I declared, "I am not guilty! I am free!" The weight of all my guilt and shame had been lifted from me. Since then my life has completely turned around and I am living in the assurance that God is with us always.

Dear Father, thank you that You never give up on us and long for us to be with You, living in Your glory, grace and love.

Tammy Gibson is a secretary at Salem United Methodist Church in Manheim and co-facilitates the Post Abortion Bible Study at Susquehanna Valley Pregnancy Services.

February 9

Speak, Lord

"My message and my preaching were not with wise and persuasive words, but with a demonstration of the Spirit's power."
1 Corinthians 2:4

As a psychiatrist I was trained to talk to people for hours and years, if necessary, to bring about change. Several years ago I became a psychiatrist in a prison setting, where I needed to see 5-6 people per hour. How could I make any difference beyond the medications which I adjusted? I prayed, "Dear Jesus, would You please demonstrate what You can do?"

One day I spent five minutes with a young woman facing life in prison for being an accomplice in a murder. I determined rather quickly that she did not need medication. She said she was a Christian but I did not feel that I could connect with her spirit in such a short time.

In desperation I said, "Oh, Jesus, speak!" I then said to her, "It may sound strange, but give me any number that comes to your mind between 1 and 150." She said "3." Then I said, "Before asking you this, I prayed and asked God to speak to you through one of the 150 Psalms."

I then read Psalms 3 from my Palm Pilot. As I read she began to weep. She said, "That is my life." A week later she reported that as a result of this encounter she cried all night and recommitted her life to Christ. Since then she has grown mightily in the Lord and has guided others to Christ.

I have seen God speak to persons using this approach dozens of times since then. I minister for years and use many words and see limited change. But in a moment God can change a life if I give Him the space to work.

Dear Father, forgive me for filling up all the space with my wisdom. Help me to make more space for You to work.

Enos Martin, M.D., bishop in New Testament Fellowship of Mennonite/Anabaptist Churches, also provides psychiatric care in several local prisons.

February 10

The Nudge of the Spirit

"'Have faith in God,' Jesus answered." *Mark 11:22*

It was my day off. One of our parishioners called to tell me about someone at her work place who was despairing of life. Perhaps I could contact this person. My wife and I were doing an errand that day which took us close to where the woman lived. We could make a contact that same afternoon. Should we? She didn't live close to our church. How many persons had we talked and prayed with over the years to no avail?

But the Spirit nudged us to at least call. The woman was surprised to hear from her friend's pastor the very next day after their conversation. She reluctantly said we could come. We visited with her, and she told her story of feeling that God never worked for her. For other people, yes. But God didn't answer her prayers.

We asked to pray together, and my wife prayed for release from the deep pain she perceived in the heart of our new acquaintance. We soon left, not knowing whether God had acted, yet sensing a brightening in the woman's countenance.

Weeks later our parishioner reported that the one we had prayed with seemed like a new person. She had seen God at work in circumstances in her life. Months later, there was more of the same. The woman we had prayed with was praying for others. God was doing his work of transformation by his Holy Spirit.

What if our friend from church had not made that phone call to us? What if we had given in to fears that God wasn't going to do anything and that we were too inadequate? But in our weakness, God was strong. We acted on less than a mustard seed of faith, and God produced a harvest. A changed life. And the weak faith of three Christian believers was strengthened by seeing God at work.

Father, let me always be attuned to Your call to intercede in the life of one who is in need of Your healing touch.

Jim Leaman is pastor at Groffdale Mennonite Church, Leola.

An Awareness of Our Emptiness

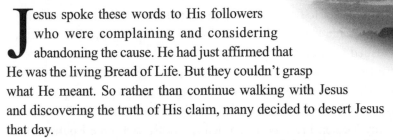

"The Spirit gives life; the flesh counts for nothing. The words I have spoken to you are spirit and they are life."
John 6:63

Jesus spoke these words to His followers who were complaining and considering abandoning the cause. He had just affirmed that He was the living Bread of Life. But they couldn't grasp what He meant. So rather than continue walking with Jesus and discovering the truth of His claim, many decided to desert Jesus that day.

But by abandoning Jesus, they soon learned that they could accomplish nothing apart from Christ. Their flesh counted for *nothing*. His closest disciples chose to stay with Him, and eventually they discovered that Jesus was the life He claimed to be. They went on to walk in the fullness of the kingdom of God here on earth. Likewise, we must empty ourselves of our own pride and ambitions, and invite the fullness of Christ to flow through us.

Pray for Lancaster County is our weekly prayer focus for the individuals, families, churches and communities of our region. Please carry this emphasis in your heart and your prayers throughout the week.

Cast Your Net On The Right Side

"[Jesus] said, 'Throw your net on the right side of the boat and you will find some....'" *John 21:6*

Wounded in ministry. A slap in the face with no warning of its coming impact and imprint on my life. Left with a loss of confidence and a security that disappeared because maybe God was withholding himself from me.

I returned to fishing, attempting to rediscover who I was in Christ—fishing with a net made of confusion, doubt and fear. For months, I wrestled with this net, wishing to be rid of it. I knew forgiveness toward the one who hurt me was the key to a restored relationship with my Master. Wearily I continued to forgive and kept casting my damaged net. I longed to see it filled with peace and a renewed confidence in my Master. Fresh despair filled my heart each time I pulled in the net, only to discover it remained empty and tattered.

After one night of futile fishing, Someone called to me from the shore. "This time, forgive as I forgave while on the cross. Then cast your net on the *right* side of the boat. I will fill your net with abundance of me." Hope was like a sunrise in my soul. It was the Lord! This time, I forgave as He forgave. I cast my net on the other side of this hurtful experience.

I came to shore, eager to be near him. Jesus knew I was coming hungry. It was time to break fast with him. My spiritual fast is over. As I continue fishing on the "right" side, my mended net is filling with His sweet presence.

Master, equip me to "fish" in an attitude of forgiveness towards others. Enable me to cast my nets on the "right" side so I may continually experience a fresh, abundant "catch" of You, Lord!

Teresa Siegrist is a pastor's wife and mother of three. She serves alongside her husband, Wes, at Erb Mennonite Church, Lititz.

Life Laid Down

"We know love by this, that He laid down His life for us; and we ought to lay down our lives for the brethren." *1 John 3:16*

Our son, Andrew, the third born of our eight children, joined the Marines in 2003 and served seven months in Iraq from July 2004 to February 2005. He normally rides standing in the open turret of a humvee. Though wounded in a roadside bomb that killed one of his sergeants in August 2004, Andrew is ready for his next expected deployment in November 2005.

Phyllis, a dear lady from our church, was dying of cancer before Christmas while Andrew was overseas. When my wife, Joyce, said she was praying for her healing, Phyllis said that she was prepared to go, and that she had asked the Lord to spare Andrew and take her. She died a few days later, just before Christmas.

When we told Andrew about her words and death in a phone call from Iraq on Christmas Day, he was very blessed. After asking the time of her death, he immediately got choked up. We later learned that at the same time Phyllis died, a huge bomb on the road next to Andrew's humvee failed to detonate fully, sparing him and his comrades. It was an unusual, homemade explosive device that looked like a large oval ball, loaded with nuts, bolts and other metal junk. While the initial explosion split the ball in two at its seam, the main bomb never went off.

Our lives are Yours, Lord, and we rest in Your hands. Amen!

Steve Cote has been pastor of Zion Church of Millersville since 1975 and is chaplain of the Millersville Fire Company.

February 14

Happy Hearts

"I have loved you with an everlasting love; I have drawn you with lovingkindness." *Jeremiah 31:3*

I have always enjoyed Valentine's Day. Something about all the red in the middle of winter brightens up the whole winter season. I like to bake heart shaped cookies (I save my baking steam until after the Christmas cookie rush). Sometimes I come up with my own cards, but I really like picking from the many creative cards available in the stores. I stuff my mailbox with outgoing cards in hopes of bringing a smile and encouragement to friends and family far and wide.

One year during my usual round of sweets and notes, I did not send a card to one particular friend I was getting to know. He sent me one. Later I found out he was disappointed he hadn't gotten one from me. He didn't even know about all the cards I sent out! Today that man is my husband and I make sure he gets his share of valentines.

This Valentine's Day, as you show love to others, in different ways, don't forget one important Person: Jesus Christ. Give Him your hopes and dreams, thanking Him for the many ways you see His love. His love for you is never ending. His thoughts toward you are more than the grains of sand.

Dear God, thank you for giving Your love to us every day. Open our eyes to see others around us who need to experience that love.

Sarah Sauder serves as the director of House To House Publications, Lititz.

February 15

Here Comes Another Storm

"...the boat was being swamped, and they were in great danger. The disciples...woke him saying, 'Master...we're going to drown!' He got up and rebuked the wind and the raging waters; the storm subsided, and all was calm." *Luke 8:23–24*

Every year coastal sections of the United States brace themselves for another hurricane season. Seasons like 2004, when four hurricanes devastated Florida, cause loss of life and billions of dollars in damage. Hurricanes are destructive and alter our world.

Not all storms are weather-related. Some begin with a visit to the doctor, others in heated conversations. Some develop at work through misunderstandings; some when rebellious teens ignore their parents'— and God's—counsel. Storms in our personal world can be just as destructive as those in the Atlantic.

What must we realize in this? Simply, there is one in the boat with us who can handle the storms. The Psalmist records what life can be like in a storm (Psalms 107:23–32). Souls can melt "because of trouble." People soon arrive "at their wits' end," and must "cry out to the Lord" in their trouble. What results? "He brings them out of their distresses. He calms the storm...guides them to their desired haven."

The disciples learned this in Mark 4:35–41. The Lord led them right into a storm (verse 35: "Let us cross over to the other side"). He stayed with them (verse 38: "He was in the stern"), and controlled it (verse 39: "Peace be still...and there was a great calm"). They learned that Jesus was no mere man, and could take control.

Often storms arrive one after another. Take courage; you are not alone. Cry out to the Lord and see Him work in your life. Then do as the Psalmist encouraged, "Give thanks to the Lord for His goodness...exalt Him...praise Him (Psalms 107:31–32)." As the songwriter said, "He's the shelter in the time of storm."

Lord, in my storms, may I realize You are with me and are able to protect me by Your strong power. Amen.

Robert Reid is the senior pastor of Calvary Monument Bible Church.

Hear From Heaven, And Forgive!

"Hear from heaven, Your dwelling place...and forgive."
2 Chronicles 6:21

Recently, I felt a numbness and coldness settling into my soul. I cried out to God. I meditated on scripture. I asked others to pray for me. And yet still I felt a hardness developing around me. What's going on inside of me? Why is this happening?

As I shared my struggle and questions with a spiritual counselor, I began to get in touch with some of the deep disappointments, pain, and weaknesses deep within. Success, controlling the outcome, trusting in my own efforts—these are hard things to let go.

Later that day, I read how Solomon, after building the temple, suddenly cried out, "But will God really dwell on earth with men? The heavens, even the highest heavens cannot contain You." Then Solomon prayed, "Hear from heaven, Your dwelling place, and forgive." Forgive? What an odd prayer request at this important moment of dedicating the temple of God! I usually pray, "Hear from heaven and give,"—not, "Hear from heaven and forgive."

Over the next few days, instead of rushing into my prayer requests, I began to pray, "O Lord, hear from heaven and forgive." In these quiet moments of surrender before God, I felt the ice surrounding my heart begin to melt. Could God actually be hearing from heaven? Is it possible that I am a dwelling place of God today?

And God responded: "If my people, who are called by my name, will humble themselves and pray and seek my face and turn from their wicked ways, then will I hear from heaven and will forgive their sin and will heal their land (2 Chronicles 7:14)."

Oh Lord, help us to humble ourselves, to pray, to seek Your face, to turn from our wicked ways, and to forgive as we have been forgiven. Amen.

Ron Zook pastors New Holland Mennonite Church with his wife Judy.

Unity is Awesome!

"But avoid foolish controversies and genealogies and arguments
and quarrels about the law, because these are unprofitable and
useless." *Titus 3:9*

When I first started in youth ministry, I was introduced to
other youth leaders in the area. They were mostly from different churches, and I didn't know how that would work.
Would there be any unity in the group? I quickly discovered, however,
that these brothers in the Lord were my most trusted allies. We didn't
argue or debate about theologies or philosophy. We prayed together,
laughed together and even cried together. It wasn't about competition,
but about joining together to win as many as possible to the gospel of
Jesus Christ. No one was better than the other but we all had a common
goal—to see Jesus move in our hearts and in the hearts of the lost and
hurting.

I praise God for allowing me to get to know such a wonderful group
of men. I have been truly blessed, and I know that if I had allowed the
devil to speak disunity or pride in my heart, I would have missed out on
wonderful friendships and ministry.

May we all join together to win as many as possible for Jesus. May
we stop the gossip and slander in our home churches and our communities. We have much work to do, and if we allow Satan to divide us we
will be a dim light in a very dark world. We must repent of the sin of
separation and ask God to bring together again His Holy Church.

*Jesus, I pray that You would unite Christians to be like-minded and
desire Jesus and His love. There is much work to do, and we need to
work together now to bring in Your awesome harvest.*

Mike Wenger is the director of TNT Youth Ministry.

Increased Appetite for the Things of God

"Taste and see that the Lord is good; blessed is the man who takes refuge in him. Fear the Lord, you his saints, for those who fear him lack nothing." Psalms 34:8–9

If our appetites go unchecked in terms of fleshly indulgences, they can drive us to obsessive thinking and unhealthy consumption. Whether it is an appetite for food, pleasure, or sinful activities, an appetite for the wrong things will take us on a path of ultimate self-destruction.

How much better to have a ravenous appetite for the things of God! If only we would be driven with a passion to taste the things of the Lord—to see that He is good and He fulfills all our needs. An increased appetite for God is an invitation for Him to come and fill our lives and communities with all that is good from above.

Pray for Lancaster County is our weekly prayer focus for the individuals, families, churches and communities of our region. Please carry this emphasis in your heart and your prayers throughout the week.

Called to Follow

"...Who am I, that I should go to Pharoah and bring the Israelites out of Egypt?" *Exodus 3:11*

My company had closed its offices, leaving me without a job. As I waited and prayed over the next several weeks, I began to feel a question in my soul about why I was not pursuing work with compulsive over-eaters. Even though I informally helped people with this all the time and had researched it for years, my answer was ready. Although it was my passion, I did not have my doctorate yet. Who was I to assume I could pursue this field without my doctorate?

The next week, I woke up to a song phrase "he realized what he was meant to do." Every morning, I woke up to the same phrase—"he realized what he was meant to do." I began feeling challenged. "You know that you are good at this, Tricia. Why are you going to do nothing with it until you have your doctorate? What are you waiting for?" The phrase continued entering my head without warning. Finally, I committed to doing *something* to pursue ministry to compulsive eaters. There was a blizzard, so I sent an e-mail.

I received a response and God began opening the doors for me to work with people with food problems. At the first door, He showed me the immensity of the need and the perfect fit for my knowledge and talents. Since then, an incredible number of opportunities have unfolded, even though I still do not have my doctorate. Each time, I say, "Who am I?" God says, "Only through my strength." Now I also say, "Where do I go next?" and "How will it work?" This I know: He has shown me what I am meant to do—and I will follow.

Dear God, help us to trust in Your strength and power instead of our own.

Tricia Groff, M.S. is a counselor at Crossroads Counseling Center, Lancaster and a cognitive therapist at ACADIA, Lancaster.

Sold!

"Now to Him who is able to do exceedingly abundantly above all that we ask or think, according to the power that works in us...."
Ephesians 3:20

Your house won't be easy to sell" These words were followed by legitimate reasons why we could expect a long wait until our house sold, perhaps up to a year or more. A neighbor's beautiful home hadn't sold for more than a year. Would ours be different?

God was calling us to move, and after diverse assessments, we took the matter to Him. We prayed and asked God what He would have us do. The answer wasn't one we were expecting.

We sensed we were to sell the home ourselves, not through a realtor. Of all our options, this seemed to be the most illogical one! We lived in a secluded wooded area. Who would notice our sign? However, we felt God gave us a listing price and so the process continued.

After putting our little homemade "House For Sale" sign in the front lawn, we asked God to bring the right buyer. We also prayed that we would not need to show the house repeatedly and the transaction would go smoothly. Within six days we had a signed contract! God answered our requests beyond anything we anticipated.

Interestingly, this scenario was repeated three months later with a home that family members had tried to sell for years. We were asked to sell it. We prayed and once again set out that small homemade sign. Within a couple of days we had a signed contract!

God desires for us to ask for and hear His strategy in each situation. As we hear His voice and step out in faith to obey it we will reap the fruit.

Lord, thank you for wanting to speak to me. Open my ears that I may better hear Your strategy for my situation. You can move mountains and You desire to do above all we can ask or think!

Lucinda Dise serves with her husband, Allen, senior pastor and elder of Newport DOVE.

My Provider

"...put their hope in God, who richly provides us with everything...." *1 Timothy 6:17*

Our utilities were soon going to be turned off because we didn't have enough money. I was 43 and going to seminary full-time while Judy was working full-time. We had surrendered our lives to Jesus Christ three years earlier. The Lord had brought much correction and healing to our lives, and His work was still in progress. We had two high school-aged boys at home. Our daughter's marriage was falling apart, so she and her two children were living with us.

The Lord had been doing wonderful things *in* us and *for* us. He led me to attend seminary, and He led us to a house that could accommodate all seven of us. Amazing! Blessed in so many ways, yet no matter what we did, we came up short of money.

One morning I was pouring out my heart to God, and I prayed, "Lord, we need $1,000 to get our bills caught up so we don't get booted out of this house. The checking account is empty. What are we to do?" In my spirit I clearly heard Him say, "Pay the bills." I knew that He was telling me to write the checks to pay the bills. By 8:30 a.m. I had them on the kitchen counter ready to take to the mailbox.

At 9:30 a.m. a friend called and asked me if I could come see him. I did so, and by 11:00 a.m. I was in his office. He said the Lord had put it on his heart two weeks earlier to give me some money, and he had forgotten to do so until today. He told the Lord that if I came to see him by noon he would give me a certain amount, and if it was after noon it would be half that amount. He then handed me an envelope with $1,000 in it!

Lord, You are my Provider. I place my hope in You!

Jim Meador is lead pastor at Willow Street Mennonite Church.

February 22

The Character and Influence of One Man

"Blessed is the man who fears the Lord, who finds great delight in his commands." *Psalms 112:1*

We all may choose what road our life will take and how we will influence the world around us. The choices we make go to the core of the foundation we build in the secret places of our lives when no one is looking. Are we allowing the Lord the freedom to build His Word and character in us? Or are we living a life that makes us look good and pleases others? Character is not built in one day, but over a lifetime.

> "To the distinguished character of a Patriot, it should be our highest Glory to laud the more distinguished Character of a Christian."
> —George Washington, Valley Forge

Almighty God, I yield thee humble and hearty thanks that thou has preserved me from the danger of the night past, and brought me to the light of day, and the comforts thereof, a day which is consecrated to thine own service and for thine own honor. Let my heart, therefore, Gracious God, be so affected with the glory and majesty of it, that I may not do mine own works, but wait on thee, and discharge those weighty duties thou request of me. Give me grace to hear thee calling on me in thy word, that it may be wisdom, righteousness, reconciliation and peace to the saving of the soul in the day of the Lord Jesus. Grant that I may hear it with reverence, receive it with meekness, mingle it with faith, and that it may accomplish in me. Bless my family, kindred friends and country, be our God and guide this day for His sake, who lay down in the grave and rose again for us, Jesus Christ our Lord, Amen.—Prayer of George Washington, May 2, 1778

Jeff Burkholder is chairman of the board of supervisors of Elizabeth Township (Brickerville).

Miracles Still Happen

"And the Lord stood with me and strengthened me, in order that through me the proclamation might fully be accomplished."
2 Timothy 4:17

These were the words my wife repeated to me daily as I lay in the intensive care unit, totally paralyzed on my deathbed, soon to see God. My life had changed at Christmas of 2001 when I was diagnosed with Non-Hodgkin's Lymphoma and Chronic Lymphocetic Leukemia. I received chemotherapy and passed with flying colors. I was in a partial remission that could last from a few to many years.

Then it hit. Precisely four weeks after that terrific report, I was on my deathbed. Physicians first called it a flu, then pneumonia, then a strange virus, parasite or fungus. No one knew what they were fighting, and four people prepared my wife for my death. "Twenty-four to forty-eight hours to live or die," someone announced. A physician agreed that only God or a miracle could save my life.

That verdict started a chain reaction of prayer throughout the church, community, and finally the country. Thousands of people prayed. God's church rallied and sought a miracle.

God intervened. Massive amounts of steroids were administered, and just in the nick of time, two days after the death sentence was given, the miracle arrived. Doctors shook their heads in disbelief. I was out of the intensive care unit within two weeks, back to preaching within a few more weeks.

Surely, God stood with me and is enabling me to continue proclaiming the gospel of Jesus Christ and to relive a story I have only heard about...for I was brought back because our people prayed. Praise the Lord.

Lord, may I always be reminded of what You have done for me and remember that nothing is impossible with God.

Pastor Ken Mingledorff has organized and served faithfully for 29 years at the New Holland Church of the Nazarene.

Don't Forget Any of His Benefits

"Praise the Lord, O my soul, and forget not all his benefits—who forgives all your sins and heals all your diseases."
Psalms 103:2–3

Christians would never forget the benefit of forgiveness. Why are we so quick to forget the benefit of bodily healing? We have no difficulty believing God *can* heal but are reluctant to declare that He *will*. I don't understand why at times I prayed for healing and saw no change. But like this Psalm says, I want to give praise to the Lord for the benefit I have received when He *has* healed me.

In 1983, I contracted hepatitis. Our doctor told me I would recover, but it usually took three weeks. The following day, a pastor came and prayed for me. I felt a surge of power, and by the next day I was back to normal. Several years later, a small cyst developed behind my ear. My doctor said it would need to be removed. That weekend at church I asked Curt to pray for healing. The next morning the cyst was half its size! I asked Curt to pray again, remembering that even Jesus had to pray twice for the blind man. Curt prayed again and within hours the cyst was gone. Last year I had another remarkable healing. I came home from a mission trip with an ear infection. Several doctors each tried to control the infection, but it always returned. Eventually, I lost all hearing in that ear. A specialist discovered the infection had moved into the mastoid bone. He said I needed surgery to remove the infected part of the bone. Several pastors gathered and anointed me with oil. When I returned from a two-week ministry trip, I went for another scan. The doctor couldn't find any trace of infection!

Father, I don't want to forget any of Your benefits. I am grateful for all the help of doctors but Lord, You are my ultimate physician.

Barry Wissler, senior pastor of Ephrata Community Church, leads HarvestNET, a resource ministry linking churches and ministries, and serves on the executive team of the Regional Church.

An Invitation for God to Come

"...You who call on the Lord, give yourselves no rest, and give him no rest till he establishes Jerusalem and makes her the praise of the earth."
Isaiah 62:6–7

Both the question and answer are very simple. When asked why God has come to various communities around the world and brought revival, the people can point to a single reason: *Because He was invited.* If we desire God to come to our communities and bring revival on all levels of society, then we must dedicate ourselves to call upon Him and invite Him over and over again—and give ourselves no rest until He is delighted to come! That means not only asking, but also offering a spiritual climate that is welcoming for His presence. If God has not answered with His powerful, transforming presence, then we must seek to understand what is holding Him back. There is no price too great to pay for His all-consuming presence. Even so, come Lord Jesus, come!

Pray for Lancaster County is our weekly prayer focus for the individuals, families, churches and communities of our region. Please carry this emphasis in your heart and your prayers throughout the week.

Delightfully Directed Details

"The steps of the godly are directed by the Lord. He delights in every detail of their lives." *Psalms 37:23 (New Living Translation)*

O ur vacation was truly a gift from the Lord and we enjoyed every moment. It was over too quickly. We found ourselves tearfully bidding our special friends good-bye and facing the part we dreaded most—the eleven to twelve hour drive home.

We headed out on the highway later than we had hoped. Packing final items, last-minute trips to the bathroom, and two unscheduled stops for needed items forced us to make needed adjustments. We decided to embrace the rest of the day as an adventure and asked the Lord to guide us.

There were the usual construction delays. Several times we consulted a map and adjusted our route. Near lunchtime, we were close to the town where we had lived early in our marriage and decided to stop, eat and reminisce. We enjoyed the meal and memories, then slowly made our way through town so the children could see our old apartment. As we approached, we asked the Lord to bless a neighbor with whom we had lost touch. Pulling into a nearby parking lot, we looked up and saw her walking toward our minivan. She was stunned as we jumped out calling her name.

She had spent the morning in prayer on a hill overlooking the region. At one point, she started to leave when she felt the Lord direct her to linger. She stayed until she felt released and started her walk home.

Our paths crossed at the perfect moment. Just a few minutes earlier or later, and we would have missed each other. As we met, we were all filled with delight—the Lord's and ours.

Lord, thank you for caring enough to direct the steps of my life. Help me remember today that I can trust You with the details and help me to share in Your delight.

Don Riker serves congregational, ministry and business leaders with Teaching The Word Ministries in Leola.

The Biggest Rush

"If you abide in Me, and My words abide in you, ask whatever you wish, and it shall be done for you." *John 15:7*

My class in wooden pole climbing consisted of twelve students. We require each individual to wear safety harnesses connected to an arrestor, which acts much like a seatbelt; if you fall, it locks and stops you in a matter of inches.

After two days of climbing, the poles are showing a good bit of wear, developing vertical splinters every time someone gaffs into them. Utility poles are pressure treated with a very harsh chemical that often gives the climbers a rash if they touch the pole, so they wear heavy gloves and long-sleeved shirts.

Tuesday afternoon, one girl's gaffs "cut out." Losing her footing, she instinctively bear-hugged the pole. Having no sudden drop, the arrestor didn't stop her fall and she slid all the way to the bottom.

It tore the sleeves off her shirt, leaving her arms with nasty cuts and large splinters. Now you must understand, linemen have the reputation of being a pretty tough bunch. This girl flatly refused medical attention, pulled the splinters out with her linemen's pliers and showed up the next morning ready to climb.

The Lord instructed me not to pray for her publicly, so I prayed for her that night in my personal quiet time. Wednesday at lunch one of the fellows loudly asked, "Clair, what's the biggest rush you ever got?" I said the biggest rush I ever got was praying for someone and watching God heal them right in front of my eyes. The room went completely quiet.

Thursday morning, the young lady walked up to the front of the class, pulled up her sleeves and her arms were completely clear. One by one, the students came to me after class wanting to get right with God.

Father, I pray that You would send out laborers into the workplace.

Clair Stauffer, author, inventor and businessman, is the director and founder of Refreshing Leaders Ministry.

February 28

His Precious Love

"And I pray that you…may have power…to grasp how wide and long and high and deep is the love of Christ…."
Ephesians 3:17–18

Two o'clock in the morning! It was one of those nights when I was awakened and there was no going back to sleep. I have come to recognize God's voice in that spirit alarm clock, so I got up and went to my worship corner. The next hour was a watermark experience for me spiritually. God's presence was more real to me in that early morning stillness than at any other time in my life. I worshiped, sang and wandered through Scripture. In the exhilaration of a specific answer to prayer and the wonder of God's presence, I asked Him, "Is there anything else You want to tell me?" His answer was not audible but it came with no less clarity. He simply said, "I love you."

It was so precious to me that in that intimate moment, when He had my full attention, the most important thing God wanted me to know was that He loved me. No instructions, no reprimands or suggestions for areas of my life that need improvement—just, "I love you." Scripture says that God loves me with the same love that He has for Jesus. That is huge! Ephesians 3:19 says God's love surpasses understanding. Romans 8:39 assures me that nothing can separate me from His love. Isaiah 49:16 tells me I am engraved on the palm of His hand. What else do I need to know? After that bedtime story, I slept soundly until morning.

Father, I delight in the ways You show me that You love me. Help me to flesh out Your love to others so they can experience it too.

Cindy Neff serves on the board of Susquehanna Valley Pregnancy Services.

66

*Trevor Good, grade 10, Homeschool
Brady Barley, grade 1, Farmdale Elementary School,
Hurubie Meko, grade 5, Locust Grove Mennonite School*

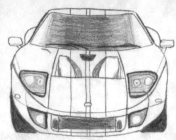

March

Ashes

"Therefore, I abhor myself, and repent in dust and ashes."
Job 42:6 (New King James Version)

In the church affiliation in which I was reared there was little attention given to symbols and icons of our faith. After moving to Lancaster County as a college freshman, my appreciation grew for other traditions within the Christian faith.

Seven years into my residence in this region, in our school one day I noticed that one of the volunteers had a smudge on her forehead. As a courtesy, I informed her of the fact saying something like, "There is a spot of dirt on your forehead." After she reverently explained that she had been to an Ash Wednesday service that morning, the embarrassment about that "spot of dirt" belonged to me.

The fastnachts or pancakes we enjoy on Shrove Tuesday (shriving or confessing sins) represent the cleansing of cupboards of all foods not to be eaten during Lent. The pastries and ashes symbolize cleansing our souls in preparation for a season of self-denial.

Ashes are a symbol of mortality. They help us remember that what God said of Adam is true for us. "For dust you are, and to dust you shall return (Genesis 3:19)." The Lord formed the first human being by breathing life into dust. Without the breath of God, human beings are nothing more than dust and ashes. Death comes to everyone.

Ashes are a symbol of penitence. Like Job's repentance above, ashes remind us of the original sin and of our need for genuine sorrow for our pride and sins.

Creator and Redeemer, without the breath of Your Spirit we are spiritually dead. Breathe in me new life for this day. Cleanse me from sin through Your sacrifice on the cross. Deepen my ability to be truly sorrowful for how the sins I commit dishonor You and wound others. I believe such sorrow will be turned into greater reverence and joy in the forgiveness of my sins.

Keith Yoder, founder of Teaching The Word Ministries, serves on the Regional Council of the Regional Church of Lancaster County.

The Big Picture

"If we endure, we will also reign with him...." *2 Timothy 2:12*

My dad was in his early fifties when he died. It was a time of struggle for me as I tried to make sense of what seemed like an untimely death. We had faithfully prayed. The elders of the church anointed him with oil. He felt he had a personal word from God that he would be healed. We stood with him in faith. We claimed the promises of Scripture. We thought God would surely heal him, but he died. I struggled to understand why and to resolve my inner conflict and disappointment with God and His promises. Out of this period of sorrow and struggle emerged a truth that has helped me when life doesn't make sense.

I have come to understand that some things that happen can only be understood in light of an eternal perspective. Some things have no present satisfactory explanation. The pat answers such as "it must have been God's will" just don't cut it.

The freeing truth is that these difficult things that happen in our lives have a direct bearing on preparing us to rule and reign with Christ in eternity. The things that don't make sense now and make it appear as if God hasn't honored His word are actually fulfilling an even greater fulfillment of those promises. I know that all of God's ways are just and right, so when life doesn't make sense I find a place of rest in knowing God's eternal purposes are at work. I then make the choice to trust Him. Someday I will see the big picture and I will understand.

Lord, when life hurts or doesn't make sense, help me to look beyond my pain and disappointment and trust Your eternal purposes at work in my life.

Lester Zimmerman is pastor of Petra Christian Fellowship, apostolic leader of the Hopewell Network of Churches and council member of the Regional Church of Lancaster County.

God's Call

"It was he who gave some to be apostles...and some to be pastors and teachers, to prepare God's people for works of service, so the body of Christ may be built up." *Ephesians 4:11–12*

In the summer of 1988 I sensed that God was calling me to pastoral ministry. God's call came suddenly, but clearly. At the time, I was finishing my college education, preparing to get married and planning my future and career very carefully. God had other plans! I did graduate from college and get married, but that call of God led me to take my college degree and new wife and move onto the campus of our denomination's seminary to prepare for ministry. We had no jobs, little money and few prospects. The only certainty we had was that God's calling and leading had brought us to that place. Therefore, He must be planning to take care of us. And He did. God provided for our needs in many miraculous ways through that time, and I entered pastoral ministry in 1993.

As I think back on that time in my life, I am uncertain as to whether that bold move was a great step of faith or youthful exuberance. It was probably a combination of both. What I am certain of is that God's calling and plan for my life and ministry was leading the way.

Responding to God's calling in my life has brought many joys and some hard times, too, but I have never once regretted it. God calls people into all kinds of service, not just pastoral ministry. The calling of God to service can be a powerful force in our lives and in God's kingdom, but it is up to us to say "yes!" to that calling and respond in faith.

Dear Lord, please grant me the wisdom to discern Your call and the courage to respond to it.

Rev. Kirk R. Marks is the pastor of St. Paul's Evangelical Congregational Church in Reamstown.

Choosing Brokenness

Pray for Lancaster County

"...This is the one I esteem: he who is humble and contrite in spirit, and trembles at my word." *Isaiah 66:2*

An unfortunate part of our human nature is that we resist the very things that God says He esteems in us. God is attracted to those who embrace brokenness. In fact, God *esteems* those who are humble and contrite. It is a simple principle: the more we put ourselves front and center, the less God can work through us. This is actually a form of idolatry because we are setting ourselves up as being better than God. What a contrast to the kind of person God is looking for—someone who will actually "tremble at His word." It is one thing to give intellectual assent to the idea of brokenness: it is another thing indeed to embrace those things that bring brokenness into our lives but once we understand that it is brokenness that draws the presence of God, how can we not embrace whatever will bring Him closer to us and to our cities?

Pray for Lancaster County is our weekly prayer focus for the individuals, families, churches and communities of our region. Please carry this emphasis in your heart and your prayers throughout the week.

March 5

Beyond Comprehension

"And the peace of God, which surpasses all comprehension, will
guard your hearts and your minds in Christ Jesus."
Philippians 4:7

I was lying in bed, way past midnight, wide awake. I was praying,
crying, and trying to listen, all at the same time. My emotions were
confused and my mind was stunned. I was having trouble compre-
hending what was taking place. My husband had died suddenly three
days before, and in the morning we were going to bury his body. There
was a terrible ice storm, and the wind was howling outside as the ice hit
the windowpanes in a rhythmic pattern. It was so harsh and cold.

God spoke to my heart that night, very simply and profoundly. He
told me He was in control. I drifted into a light sleep and awoke to face
one of the most difficult days of my life. The storm had subsided, leaving a coat of slippery ice on the roads. But despite the ice, family and
the body of Christ surrounded us with their support and love. It was a
day filled with celebration and rejoicing, as we celebrated the life of a
man who had lived for the kingdom of God and who now was face to
face with His Lord and Savior.

Several weeks later I was back to work and asking God for the
strength to go on. I was sitting at my desk crying, and in walked my
pastor's wife and good friend. She came just when I needed her, and
together we cried and prayed. She told me I could have the peace that
goes beyond comprehension, as she had experienced during the death
of her son. I told her I wanted that, and together we prayed. From that
day on, God's peace surrounded my heart and mind, exactly as His
Word promises.

*Dear Father, You are a God who doesn't lie, and Your Word is true.
Today I experience Your peace, despite whatever circumstances I am
facing. You are my peace.*

Nyla Martin is the director of Columbia Pregnancy Center, Columbia.

The Spirit of Sonship

"For you did not receive a spirit that makes you a slave again to fear, but you received the Spirit of sonship. And by him we cry, 'Abba, Father.'" *Romans 8:15*

All of my life I strove to do what was right because I felt I had to in order to be fully loved by God and others. I knew Jesus saved me from my sin, but I never felt I had a home, a place of unconditional acceptance. One day, my father revealed that he had been sent away from his family and home at the age of 12 to live and work on a farm. He said, "Those were some tough times, lonely times!" I felt that same way my entire life, lonely and striving for acceptance. This left me desperate for change in my life and in my father's life.

From that place of weakness and need, I received prayer for a revelation of God my Father's unconditional love for me. I came away knowing that God was indeed my Father. That's why Jesus came to lead me back to the Father. I knew that He loved me unconditionally no matter what—and he would never stop, ever. I knew that I had a home with my Father and Jesus in heaven, and I didn't have to strive for myself any more. I was now free to be a son and simply follow my heavenly Father's directions.

The next week I visited my dad in the hospital, and this man who had never shared his heart with me began saying things like, "I'm so glad you came to see me; I love you; I'm so proud of you." He had given his life to Jesus and had received an assurance that he was God's son in Jesus and had a home again. He was now free as the Father's son to be a loving father to his own children.

Father God, my heavenly Daddy, continue to overwhelm me with Your endless love!

Jere Mellinger, serves on the prayer and ministry team at Ephrata Community Church.

You're Fired!

"Trust in the Lord with all your heart and lean not on your own understanding; in all your ways acknowledge him, and he will make your paths straight." *Proverbs 3:5–6*

As a young believer and supervisor, I was faced with management's most difficult task—to fire an employee. He was young and smart, with great potential. Raised in a Christian home, he had abused drugs and alcohol and had been through rehab. Returned to work, he could not meet the probation requirements. I was obligated to terminate his employment.

I conducted the formal discharge meeting with this young man, his supervisor and union representative. As everyone was leaving the room, I felt prompted by that "still, small voice," telling me to pray for him. So, as this dejected, defeated and discouraged young man stood to exit, I asked for a private moment. This was not "standard operating procedure" and made no sense to my mind. Yet there we were in an empty corporate conference room when I took his hand and prayed. I affirmed his value as God's creation and interceded for deliverance, asking for strength and holy intervention.

Sometime later, I left that company and moved to Lancaster County. Several years passed and while on a visit back to that area, I was leaving a restaurant when I heard someone shout my name. I looked up to see that same young man that I fired years ago, hurrying across the parking lot with his wife and children. We embraced. I will never forget what he said: "George, I am in God now." He went on to tell me about his family, his career and his church!

Lord, let us always see the value of Your human creation and have a heart to hear Your voice and to act in obedience to Your Spirit, even when it doesn't make sense.

George Mobarak serves as vice president of development for Signature Custom Cabinetry in Ephrata.

God Turns the Page

"For I know the plans I have for you," declares the Lord, "plans to prosper you and not to harm you, plans to give you hope and a future. Then you will call upon me and come and pray to me, and I will listen to you." *Jeremiah 29:11–12*

It was the winter of 1987. I felt God was calling me to take a step of faith and move into an unknown future. The company I worked for was going through its annual down-sizing. I sequestered myself in my apartment to ask God what I was to do. I emerged from that weekend feeling that if the "incentive package" hit my department, I would leave the company. But just a few days later, I was asked to take a promotion. I wondered how that fit with the direction I felt I received earlier about leaving. I thought maybe this was God telling me to stay, so I accepted the new position.

Shortly after I did, the news came that my department would be included in the down-sizing, so off I went again for another weekend seeking God's guidance. The answer seemed the same; it was time to move on. When I told my boss, you could've knocked him over with a feather: he couldn't fathom how I could consider leaving with no job lined up. But I knew it was the right thing to do. And then, much to my amazement, three weeks later I had a job offer in Lancaster County. I put a deposit on a house, and was given a salary comparable to what I had before. It was as if God showed me the book of my life and He turned the page right in front of me to the next chapter.

Father, what step of faith are You asking me to take today? I pray You'll give me the courage to follow You and seek Your best for me in the next chapter of my life.

Deb Roggenbaum serves as director of development at Susquehanna Valley Pregnancy Services.

Send Me

"Don't be afraid, for I am with you. Do not be dismayed, for I am your God. I will strengthen you. I will help you. I will uphold you with my victorious right hand." *Isaiah 41:10 (New Living Translation)*

But God! How am I to oversee post-abortion ministry? I don't have any training! What am I to say? What if I make a mistake? Do I know anyone who has experienced an abortion?"

All these thoughts raced through my mind, and my heart hammered in my chest as I searched for an escape. My supervisor had just answered my innocent question, "Who will oversee the Post-Abortion Bible Study?" with her nonchalant response, "You will."

As I struggled to accept this new responsibility, the Lord reminded me of my sincere commitment made as a teenager. "Here am I. Send me." I had taped Isaiah 6:8b to my bedroom mirror and had avowed to obey my Lord in whatever He asked. God wasn't going to let me get out of this one!

A few months later, sitting across from two shame-filled post-abortion women, I ached as the pain they bore touched my heart. Compassion swelled in me and I knew that, despite my weaknesses and lack of professional training in this area, God would grace me with His love and train me to fight the injustice of abortion and its devastating aftermath.

Five years have passed, and each woman the Lord has brought into my life to encourage and love humbles and blesses me. I continue to be awestruck with the phenomenon of lives transformed by the Truth. My sincere commitment continues to be, "Lord, here I am. Send me."

Father God, thank you that You know the desire of my heart even when I feel fearful and vulnerable. Help me to trust You to provide everything I need to serve You and others with excellence.

Carol Weaver is the director of Post-Abortion Ministry with Susquehanna Valley Pregnancy Services. She serves on the pastoral team at Praise Dome Tabernacle.

Daily Bread...Specifically

"Give us this day our daily bread." *Matthew 6:11*

In 1979, I was a college student, going to school full-time and working full-time. I was far from home and, like many young people, barely scraping by. A family event was being planned that I so wanted to attend, and yet I knew I didn't have the financial resources to make the flight home and back, or the time to travel a slower way.

In my prayers, I so often asked God to "make my life easier," or to change my circumstances so that I could afford to live differently. But my pastor had recently preached a sermon series on the Lord's Prayer, and, for the first time, I understood "Give us this day our daily bread," in the context of asking God for what you need *specifically* and for *today.*

As I began asking God to provide a way for me to be with my family, I felt released from the burden of worry about my overall circumstances, and God's peace descended on me in a new way. Within a few days I heard from my grandmother, who told me she had taken out a savings bond for me some years before that had come due, and that perhaps I could use it for my trip home. I made my plane reservations and did make the trip, praising God for answering my prayer and for teaching me how to come to him as a child comes to her father.

One more thing: when I cashed in the savings bond a few weeks later, its worth was within one dollar of the cost of my ticket.

Heavenly Father, may I trust You with all my deepest needs, knowing that You are a good and loving Father, who delights in giving us bread!

Kim Wittel is director for Ministry Development with Love INC (Love In the Name of Christ) of Lancaster County, and is a member of St. Peter's Lutheran Church.

Pray for Lancaster County

March 11

Choose Not to Be Offended

"An offended brother is more unyielding than a fortified city, and disputes are like the barred gates of a citadel."
Proverbs 18:19

This proverb gives powerful insight into the forces at work when one is offended. Those who take offense are compared to a fortified city with walls and gates that cannot be broken down. If we commit to live according to the principle that God is drawn to holiness and humility, then a critical issue is the determination never to be offended.

The question for each of us (and not the *other* person) is, *Will I make the determination for the sake of unity and breaking of my own pride, that I will not be offended?* This cuts to the very core of pride, and pride is what God says He opposes. Pride is at the very heart of being offended. We must deal ruthlessly with our own sin and pride. Make the determination today that from now on, by the power of the Spirit of God, you will not be offended.

Pray for Lancaster County is our weekly prayer focus for the individuals, families, churches and communities of our region. Please carry this emphasis in your heart and your prayers throughout the week.

So This is What it Means to Be a Christian

"...I consider everything a loss compared to the surpassing greatness of knowing Christ Jesus my Lord, for whose sake I have lost everything...." *Philippians 3:8*

They were Ivy League-educated professionals, lived in a nice home, drove new cars and lived a comfortable life. Then God called them to a remote people, barely touched by the gospel. So they gave it all up and went.

God took them to a dirty, forgotten town. They found a decent apartment, but with no working elevator to their upper-level flat. Their kids, who once enjoyed a spacious yard filled with neighborhood friends, had no place to play outside, and their closest playmates were 30 minutes by bus. With the language barrier, a new diet, no western appliances, intermittent electric outages, leaky pipes, shopping only for as much food as they could carry, and no car—daily life became much more of a chore than it used to be.

When my wife and I had the opportunity to visit them, I remember thinking, "So this is what it means to be a Christian."

Then I thought about all I had *not* given up, and all that following Christ does *not* cost me in the West. I began to consider if there were not some things I could let go of for the sake of my Lord.

Our culture is defined by materialism and amusement. Christians should be defined differently, in part by what we give up. For example, maybe we need to consume less and give away more or cancel our cable so we can spend more time with our families and seeking God. Could that be part of what it means to be a Christian in the West?

Lord, You have blessed us abundantly, and we take it for granted. May we seek not a larger bank account or bigger home, but may we seek to eliminate the many distractions that sidetrack us from following You.

Representative Gibson C. Armstrong represents part of Lancaster in the Pennsylvania House of Representatives.

I Love You

"May the Lord make your love increase and overflow for each other...." *1 Thessalonians 3:12*

It was May 12, 1997, when cell phones had limited use. I was traveling to a job site one hour away and gave my wife a call. Before we hung up, we told each other, "I love you!" Little did I know those would be our last words to each other. It was only moments later that God called my wife to her eternal home. The words "I love you" have a whole new meaning for me today. Not only did those words give me good memories of the past but they also help me enjoy every day as I see how a few words can brighten our days.

Yes, the Lord has blessed me with another great wife. The words "I love you" come much easier, not only to my wife but also to other people around me. God has helped me open my eyes and see new opportunities to share with those who walk through the valley of weeping. He also has springs of living water to refresh us (Psalms 84:6). Why is it that those simple words "I love you" are so hard to say?

Lord help me to express my love to those around me as You have expressed Your love for us.

Glenn A. Hoover and his wife, Ginny, pastor at Carpenter Community Church.

Lord of the Hard Drive

"Call to me and I will answer you...." *Jeremiah 33:3*

One afternoon in February 1999, I was repairing a laptop computer for Ainde Wainzo, one of our national Bible translators in Papua New Guinea. After some tests, I determined that the hard disk drive was bad and could not be revived, so I called Ainde to discuss the problem.

Responding with typical Papua New Guinean calm, Ainde seemed fairly unruffled. But he did become concerned when he realized that some scriptures he had translated into his own language were stored on the dead hard drive and nowhere else. I told him I'd see if any of those files could be recovered.

Feeling somewhat pessimistic, I removed the hard drive from the laptop, and installed it in a test machine. I flipped on the switch, and heard the unwelcome clicking sounds that usually mean a hard drive is terminally ill. As I suspected, the message popped up on the screen: "Primary hard drive failure." I shut the computer off and began to pray.

"Father," I said, "You know that this hard drive contains the only copies of precious parts of your Word that Ainde has translated into his own language. Please, in Jesus' name, make it possible for me to retrieve them. The enemy has done so much to hinder this translation program. Lord, show Yourself powerful and victorious."

Once again, I flipped on the power switch. This time, my ears were greeted with a normal hard drive whir! In a few minutes, I was able to copy the desired files safely onto another disk. I then ran some diagnostic tests on the old drive, which verified that it had serious problems. In fact, that was the last time I was ever able to access the files containing the translated scriptures on that drive.

Father, remind me to welcome You into every situation today.

Nelson Blank and his family are missionaries with Wycliffe Bible Translators. They served in Papua New Guinea, and now serve at the Wycliffe Northeast office in Willow Street.

God's Grace is Sufficient

"...My grace is sufficient for you, for my power is made perfect in weakness...." *2 Corinthians 12:9*

B eing raised on a farm made me the farmer's daughter. Farm work was extremely difficult for me because of back pain. Many days and nights, I could be found crying from the pain. Not recognizing a reason for the pain, it was often viewed as laziness and stubbornness, My childhood days still bring tears to my eyes. Being the middle sibling of three, I seemed to get lost in my complaints. My childhood love for Jesus started to grow cold and indifferent.

At age 16, a physician diagnosed my pain as being born with a degenerative spine condition called Spondylitis and Scoliosis. This explained my days and nights of restlessness and pain. My wounds became scars. I felt so imperfect! When my pity parties became un-bearable to even myself, I knew it was only God who could make a difference.

I joined a Bible study on understanding God's love. When I was brought to the understanding of God's precious love for even me and how he suffered on my behalf, I knew I needed forgiveness for my attitude and lack of love. After all, God created me just the way I am, imperfections and all.

Since pain and I go everywhere together, I've decided we had bet-ter become best friends. I respect her and take care of her. Until God heals me, we will stay close. My attitude has made a big difference, and we get along most days. Perseverance, tenacity, and God's love for me has made all the difference.

Dear God, if my pain is not leaving, then it's Your precious grace I'm receiving. Thanks, God, for being my best friend and reminding me daily as I face each new day with pain. It's Your pain You suffered for me that keeps me able to continue on with Your plan for my life. Amen.

Dona L. Fisher is chairman of the National Day of Prayer and Change of Pace Bible Studies.

Transformed Through Tragedy

"...and by His stripes we are healed...." *Isaiah 53:5*

My father was drafted at 18 years old to fight in World War II. Even before his graduation from high school he was sent off to basic training and found himself on the fast-track to the battlefield of Europe. Even before he reached the shores of France and the conflagration of bloodshed and destruction on the drive into Germany, he confronted a situation that would be forever riveted in his memory. While in basic training he witnessed the electrocution of a friend and fellow soldier-in-training. To this day, to just see the man's name brings my dad to instant sorrow—a sorrow beyond anything I've ever seen in him. This tragedy changed him forever.

Tragic and calamitous events transform us. They either drive us to Christ and His healing, or they distort us and turn into miserable souls. Some souls lash out with blame and accusations, some run away emotionally, others cover up their pain, and—even worse—some souls use their place of authority to inflict judgment on others out of their own fears and self-condemnation, even to the point of abuse. It is staggering how a wounded or guilty individual can turn and pour out their emotional revenge on innocent souls. May Jesus have mercy on us.

Do you harbor bitterness, envy, and condemnation in your heart? Are you injuring others out of your pain? It's time to allow the crisis of Jesus' own sufferings and death to free you of your guilt and shame and sin. "By His stripes we are healed" is not just a slogan...it's a life transforming truth.

Lord Jesus, help us to receive the fullness of Your grace and forgiveness in our lives so that we may be able to forgive others also. Help us to be those who restore and heal, and not those who bring shame and condemnation. Amen.

Scott Lanser is pastor of New Hope Church in East Hempfield. He also serves on the staff of the Associates for Biblical Research.

Everything We Need

"His divine power has given us everything we need for life and godliness through our knowledge of him who called us by his own glory and goodness." *1 John 1:3*

When I first considered the invitation to contribute something to this devotional, I thought, "I don't have anything exciting to share." I am frequently presented with thoughts similar to this. I am not always immediately aware who offers them to me.

At one of our recent intercessor's prayer times, someone prayed that God will give us all a story to tell. All of a sudden, my inner eyes were opened to the miracle of salvation that God had done for me through Jesus Christ. If not for Jesus' intervention, Satan could have taken my physical life. I could be mentally ill. I could be alienated from my family and friends. I could be homeless. All of the above statements have a real life experience connection. However I want to call attention to the presence and power of God, not to what Satan wanted.

So you see I do have a story to tell. It is the witness to the faithfulness and mercy of our God. My whole life is a God story. And so is yours.

God used the power of His Holy Spirit, His scriptures, the body of Christ, my parents, family and friends. His resources are endless. To Him belongs the praise and thanksgiving.

Lord God how awesome is Your love! Will you allow me to work with You on behalf of others as my "thank you" to You?

Kathleen Hollinger is a mother, grandmother, great-grandmother and Prayer Ministry leader for ACTS Covenant Fellowship, Lancaster.

It's All About Obedience

Pray for Lancaster County

"In everything that he undertook in the service of God's temple and in obedience to the law and the commands, he sought his God and worked wholeheartedly. And so he prospered."
2 Chronicles 31:21

The Lord's Temple had been desecrated and defiled by King Ahaz. But his son Hezekiah had a different heart, and when he became king of Judah, he was obedient to make things right in the eyes of God. King Hezekiah ordered that the priests first purify themselves, and then that the Temple be purified and returned to a place of honor to the Lord.

Then people of the land were given the choice to follow in their own personal obedience. In the end, there was great joy in Jerusalem, a joy they had not seen since the days of Solomon. Because Hezekiah sought God wholeheartedly, scripture says very simply, "And so he prospered." It is said that man is impressed by activity, but God is impressed by obedience.

Pray for Lancaster County is our weekly prayer focus for the individuals, families, churches and communities of our region. Please carry this emphasis in your heart and your prayers throughout the week.

A Dream

"For my thoughts are not your thoughts, neither are your ways my ways," declares the Lord. "As the heavens are higher than the earth, so are my ways higher than your ways and my thoughts than your thoughts." *Isaiah 55:8–9*

Only two weeks after I asked Regina to marry me, we were on our way to Black Rock Retreat to get our engagement pictures taken. Regina began to share her wild dream from the previous night with me. Her dream went like this: "It was a hot summer day and we were in Africa. We were in a church building with hundreds of Mennonites, just talking and worshipping together. That was the extent of my dream, which I am sure had no significance for us."

I was shocked at her dream because only the week before I had picked up information on the Mennonite World conference in Zimbabwe, Africa. I realized the Lord was speaking and I should pay attention. Regina had no idea that the MWC was going to be held in Africa that year. We also found out about the "Holy Spirit in Mission" conference in Addis Ababa, Ethiopia.

We began to pray and make plans. We had to raise our own support of $6,500. The Lord provided more than enough to cover all of our needs. We were also planning our wedding for June, 2003, and our trip was to take place July 28-August 19.

Our trip to Africa was filled with many divine appointments. It was a foundational trip for us as a newlywed couple and we were able to see the Lord's hand at work throughout our time there. Even though it did not seem to make sense, the Lord was asking us to trust Him.

Father, I trust You to lead and guide my life. Reveal Your plans for us in dreams and visions. Speak, for Your servant is listening.

Eric Martin is a part of Gemeinschaft in Lancaster City and works for BrentMore Construction.

My Banner

"...the Lord is my Banner." *Exodus 17:15*

A s a young man I sought worldly passions. After twenty years and many mistakes, I came to the realization that the direction in which I was traveling was futile. At the age of 36 I found myself alone, broken.

One day while pondering my condition and remembering the biblical teachings of my youth, I began to beg God for a life with meaning. I realized that I was totally lost without Him.

Several months later, I met Peggy. We soon married and had a little boy named Thomas. Soon after Tommy was born, I found myself lost in a difficult area, while traveling for business. I was nervous and sought some comforting music on the radio. Instead, I came across Dr. James Boyce preaching from Exodus 17:11-12.

Although my life had clearly been changed before, something was still missing. Upon the conclusion of Dr. Boyce's sermon, I realized my daily need for Jesus in my life.

I began to read the Scriptures daily and often wondered about some of the folks I knew. Who would reach those still lost without Christ? Such questions, combined with a profound ongoing conversion experience, grew into a life-changing passion to reach others for the Lord.

Today, by His grace, I am an ordained minister of the gospel serving the Lord by offering biblical counseling to those who are hurting here in Lancaster, Pennsylvania.

Dear God, we are all Your creation, trying to survive in a fallen world which is destined for destruction. Outside of Christ Jesus and a constant reliance on Your Word through the Holy Spirit (Matthew 4:4), there is no therapy or instruction that can teach, correct, or answer our questions in our effort to fill the void in our hearts. Please Lord, change the hearts of those who do not yet know You that they too might find healing and salvation. In Jesus' name, I pray. Amen.

Rev. Thomas R. Miller is a biblical counselor.

My Household

"...Believe in the Lord Jesus, and you will be saved—you and your household." *Acts 16:31*

As a child we didn't attend church as a family. Instead, a big yellow school bus came for us four kids each Sunday morning. The bus wasn't from the local school but from the church closest to our home. The smile on my father's face is clear in my mind to this day. As we went out the front door to the bus, he'd lean further back in his chair with the Sunday paper waiting on his lap.

Thank God for the Baptists who sent that bus. During a Vacation Bible School when I was twelve, I gave my heart to Jesus. In no time, even as a young teenager, the call of God on my life to be a pastor emerged.

This call was not something that made sense to my family. But God had a secret weapon in our family. She stood about 5'1" tall. My father's mother knew Jesus well. Growing up, we mainly visited my father's family, since my mother's was many states away to the south. My grandmother literally prayed us into the kingdom. She is with Jesus now, having gone to be with Him just last year. But she saw almost her entire family of six children, sixteen grandchildren, and twenty-four great-grandchildren begin to attend church and come to Jesus one by one.

Recently my older brother (who is now also a pastor) and I had the opportunity to serve communion to my family. The service was outdoors in a beautiful setting by a pond. While my family communed together, a healing warmth came over me. As the sunshine poured through the trees, it was as if my grandmother was smiling down on us.

Never give up praying for your family. God keeps His promises. I know He has to me.

Dear God, thank you for adopting my family. Bless You, Father of our Lord Jesus Christ and for Your loving grace. Amen.

Jeff Snyder is senior pastor of Columbia United Methodist Church.

Hitchhiking

"...while he was still a long way off, his father saw him and was filled with compassion for him...." Luke 15:20

I had been hitchhiking north on Route 5 in California, standing with my thumb out in Redding for eight hours, before the station wagon finally stopped to pick me up. I was 21, had just returned to the States from my first tour of Vietnam as a Navy "CB," and was traveling up the coast to visit a friend. If I had known who was picking me up, I might have stayed out of the car.

He was a middle-aged man who looked normal enough until he asked if he could finish singing his song. It was some kind of old-time religion hymn. I recognized it from when I was young. This concert included banging a tambourine on his knee as he sang (and drove). When the concert ended, we proceeded to debate about God for hours, me arguing vehemently against Christianity. I wanted nothing to do with the religion I was raised in.

Finally, it was almost time for me to get out, as he was headed west and I planned to continue north. The man asked if I wanted to stay in the car and go to a Christian conference with him in Big Sur. Of course, I rejected this, relieved to be getting away from him. As we arrived at our parting intersection, I remember almost word for word what he said to me, "Young man, shortly I am going to let you out of the car and then I'm going to pray for you. And I'll soon forget about you, but you'll always remember me and what I've told you."

Thirty-five years later, as a Christian pastor, I still remember.

Father, thank you for Your mercy in the midst of our blindness toward You. May You use us to help open the eyes of others who have yet to see You.

Chip Toews pastors those awesome folks in New Covenant Christian Church.

Pregnant?

"As you do not know the path of the wind, or how the body is formed in a mother's womb, so you cannot understand the work of God, the Maker of all things." *Ecclesiastes 11:5*

My wife and I were thrilled by the discovery that we were expecting our first child! I realized the saying "We're pregnant" has great truth. Surrounding this discovery of life was a swirl of new thoughts and emotions concerning the growth and birth of our child. I quickly became captivated by the mystery of the womb. There was, without doubt, a child being formed, but with few immediate signs of growth. It would take the entire nine months of "secret" growth in the womb until we would see the birth of our child.

Are you pregnant with the things of God? Are His vision, desire, purpose and plan growing in the womb of your spirit? It's easy to doubt the progress and growth of God's mysterious ways when it's difficult to see their future completion.

From the moment we learned of our pregnancy, we were able to rejoice and celebrate the miracle. Over the term of the pregnancy, our hearts accepted, loved, and joyfully anticipated the birth—despite not knowing what the child would look like. If you find some of the new things that God is doing in your life a bit mysterious and wonder about their outcome, take a moment to consider the miracle of birth. Trust the Lord as He causes the new seed in your heart to grow. Allow the Lord to connect your heart with His heart through the entire season of new life. We will never be able to fully understand the works and miracles of the Master, but we can be confident that He is always doing a new and good thing in us.

Creator God, continue to birth in our hearts the desires and passions of Your heart.

Josh VanderPlate is a worship leader and had previously served as an associate pastor for five years.

March 24

Decisions

"For we are taking pains to do what is right, not only in the eyes of the Lord but also in the eyes of men." *2 Corinthians 8:21*

With each passing day, I'm faced with countless decisions on a personal and business level. At times, doing what is right becomes a painstaking task because the decisions I make can affect many people.

At one point in my career, I faced a decision that would affect numerous people. Depending on how the decision played out, I could have enhanced relationships or allowed a long-term negative effect to begin. Throughout the whole process, I was receiving counsel to act opposed to what my heart was feeling. I respected the advice but was uncomfortable with what they were telling me. I needed guidance from God, and through prayer I asked Him to show me what to do. I wanted to hear a specific person confirm what I knew was the right decision. He did call two days later. However, the "God thing" was that this person was part of the council advising me to do something I couldn't be at peace with! The gentleman, originally opposed to what I wanted from the beginning, told me to do what I knew was right in my heart. Only God can do that.

God is always concerned about the issues that trouble us and always willing to help when we ask. There is nothing too small or bothersome for Him.

When making a decision, these five things always guide me:

Look closely at the circumstances; gather information (go on a fact-finding mission); allow some time to pass (hasty decisions can be hurtful); pray; use intuition (make the decision based on what your heart is telling you).

Father, help us to include You in every decision we make.

Anne Beiler is the founder of Auntie Anne's, Inc. In 2005, Anne sold the international pretzel franchise to embark on the next chapter of her life.

Begin With *My* Heart

Pray for Lancaster County

"Search me, O God, and know my heart; test me and know my anxious thoughts. See if there is any offensive way in me, and lead me in the way everlasting." *Psalms 139:23–24*

R evival begins with a single, solitary decision. Am I willing to put my heart on the line with God, let Him examine it with the truth of His Word, and then take full responsibility for those things that offend Him? The temptation is to ask God to move quickly among the masses so that revival can be swift and seemingly effortless. But God is more interested in the transformation of the individual heart—and especially *your* heart!

As you learn to abide in God's presence and take the time to seek His heart for your life, you will find yourself being ushered into a glorious place with Him. Then God will create within you a yearning for others to experience His sweet presence, which will fuel your passion and prayer for corporate revival.

Pray for Lancaster County is our weekly prayer focus for the individuals, families, churches and communities of our region. Please carry this emphasis in your heart and your prayers throughout the week.

Abundant Life

"The thief does not come except to steal, and to kill, and to destroy. I come that they might have life, and that they might have it more abundantly." *John 10:10 (New King James Version)*

I was going through a time of feeling that my job was very mundane and that I wasn't experiencing "life" the way God intended. My heart's cry was, "God, it's time for a change. I want to see Your favor, blessing, and faithfulness in my life."

I was working second shift and during a late drive home, my car edged off the road. As I tried to swerve back, I lost control. My car went up over a bank, flew threw the air, and hit a telephone pole. It rolled three times before coming to a stop, landing upright.

Every part of the car was demolished except my seat. I remembered feeling like the car was flying, but something pressed against my chest, holding me down in my seat, even though I wasn't wearing a seatbelt. I cried out "God, where are You?" Immediately I heard him reply, "I'm right here," and peace came over me.

I realized God or an angel had held me in my seat to preserve my life. I started thanking God because I knew I could've died, but only sustained minor injuries.

God used the few weeks that I was off work to draw me closer to him. I was able to build a close relationship with my girlfriend, who later became my wife. Soon after, I was promoted at my job and I saw God's blessing and favor. God used the circumstances to say, "I haven't forgotten you. Not only do I want you to have *life*, but I want you to experience it more abundantly."

God, You have plans to prosper us, not to harm us, plans for hope and a future. We believe You for an "abundant" life.

Vern Martin is the manufacturing supervisor at a medical manufacturing plant, and serves as the prophetic administrator for Ephrata Community Church in Ephrata.

Heart to Home

"As for you also, because of the blood of your covenant, I will set your prisoners free from the bottomless pit. Return to the stronghold, you prisoners of hope. Even today I declare that I will restore double to you." *Zechariah 9:10–11 (New King James Version)*

Recently I was talking to a friend who was going through a very big transition that would change the life of her family. She said to me, "Did you ever notice how hope comes in underneath you and lifts you so that you can take faith by the hand once more?" This made me think of the scripture that talks about "faith being the substance of things hoped for, the evidence of things not seen (Hebrews 11:1)." So the basis of faith is hope. Our God is gracious to provide a kind of built-in response mechanism for us. I know that we sometimes feel hopeless, but He has not left us without hope. We just need to ask for it.

There was a particular time that I needed a promise. An answer that I was looking for seemed long in coming. So rather than despairing, I asked God for a promise. It was this one in Zechariah 9:10-11, and I realized for the first time that we as His children are "prisoners of hope"! Usually the word *prisoner* suggests in our minds a negative existence, a sense of bondage and restraint. But with God it is wonderfully free and secure!

To top off all this, He says, "I will restore double to you." In the New Living Bible it reads, "I will give you two mercies for each of your woes." Who of us wouldn't receive that?

Heavenly Father, teach us more how to live out of Your mercy and grace, so that we experience the truth You have given to us. In Jesus' name, Amen.

Naomi Sensenig with her husband, LaMarr, serve as spiritual parents and intercessors.

Direct Access

"Be anxious for nothing, but in everything by prayer and suppli-
cation with thanksgiving let your requests be made known to
God." *Philippians 4:6 (New King James Version)*

During the autumns of 2003 and 2004 my personal world was
expanded to include Romania by a short-term medical mission trip with Christian Emergency Relief Teams (CERT). I
always "knew" Christ's body is a global community but now my heart
loves other believers in Medias, Romania and vicinity.

Praise God there are many believers in Romania who are spreading the Good News of Jesus Christ. They are learning that there is a
God who loves them and that the Bible is God's love letter to them. The
lie is shattered that to access God they must pay the priest for prayers.
Access to Jesus is direct and for all! There is no need for money to
access God.

The joyful face of Vasile in 2004 is forever etched in my memory
as he came to the clinic and spoke of how his life was transformed over
the past year since his salvation. He praised God for losing his job as a
coal miner for twenty plus years because that was the only reason that
he came to the medical clinic in 2003 where he learned of Jesus and
accepted Him.

Vasile is the picture of Philippians 4:6. He is joyful at age forty-
seven despite living in poverty and with no pension. Since he cannot be
a coal miner, he bought one milk cow, and he sells milk to his neighbors for income. "God takes care of me. I would rather have eternal life
and know Jesus than have my job back." His wife does not yet know
Jesus but he says, "I know she will."

*Dear Lord Jesus, please help me to remember how priceless is direct
access to You, and help me to count my many blessings. Amen.*

Peg Waller is a cardiac and infusion RN. She has been leading a
Nurses Christian Fellowship Grad group in Lancaster for the past fifteen
years.

False Humility is Like False Christianity

"But when you do a charitable deed, do not let your left hand know what your right hand is doing, that your charitable deed may be in secret and your Father who sees in secret will Himself reward you openly." *Matthew 6:3–4 (New King James Version)*

"God opposes the proud but gives grace to the humble." *1 Peter 5:5 (New King James Version)*

The Pharisees seemed to be the most humble people in the ancient world. They prayed openly, fasted weekly, tithed one tenth of their money and put even many modern day Christians to shame with their life-style. Yet, Jesus pointed out that they loved the approval of men rather than the approval of God (John 12:42–43).

Today, false humility takes many forms.

How often do we think, "Lord, You see this money or time I'm giving toward ministry." Perhaps God is thinking, "I gave you that money and those gifts or talents so you can show your obedience to Me." We all like to be recognized or honored for our service. When we don't get recognized we ask why, as if it's owed us.

True humility is a quality that others recognize in us without us drawing attention to it. When you claim you have humility, you automatically void yourself of that quality. It is a privilege that God endowed us with certain abilities to use for His glory alone. It may mean avoiding the limelight and allowing someone else to get the credit for our contributions. What the Lord sees in secret, He will reward openly either in this world or the world to come.

Help me, Lord, to throw off any false humility in my life. Let me walk in true humility so that others may see Your hand in my life. Amen.

Eric Davenport is the owner of Davenport Design & Advertising and attends a local marketplace ministry Bible study through Faith Connections at Work, which is devoted to raising up workplace evangelists.

Power-Filled Calling

"For God did not give us a spirit of timidity, but a spirit of power, of love and of self-discipline." *2 Timothy 1:7*

After the death of my brother-in-law, business partner and best friend, I experienced deep grief and fear. Fear developed into a very negative self-talk pattern that took me to the edge of an emotional breakdown.

Due to his absence in the family business, I needed to step to the plate and take the leadership position of president and CEO. I began telling myself I was not adequate, I am neither smart enough nor educated. I am here only because my partner dropped out. I don't have the business skills and training. No one will follow me. I am indecisive. The list went on. Fear began to settle in like a dark cloud.

One day a gentleman came to my office offering to pray with me. This continued on a regular basis for over a year. The Holy Spirit began to break through, and it was revealed to me that God had called me to this position. I was to be a steward like the one found in Matthew 25:14-30. He began to teach me that He has given me a spirit of power, of love and a disciplined mind.

I was disciplined in many areas, but my negative self-talk was totally out of control. Once the Holy Spirit revealed this thought of being disciplined in my thinking, things began to change. The dark cloud began to lift. I got back on my feet and embraced the stewardship over this great calling God has given me. This calling has brought much fulfillment everyday.

Father, today I thank You for giving us a spirit of power, of love and a disciplined mind. Thank you that we no longer have to dwell in fear and timidity, but You are big in us and enable us to fulfill the calling to which You have called us.

Glenn Good is husband, father, grandpa and president/CEO of Quality Custom Cabinetry, New Holland.

His Word—Everyday

"The Sovereign Lord has given me an instructed tongue, to know the word that sustains the weary. He wakens me morning by morning, wakens my ear to listen like one being taught."
Isaiah 50:4

For much of my life I struggled with daily devotions. I would go through seasons of consistent Bible reading, but had difficulty maintaining consistency day after day. As I reflect on why, I suppose that my focus was on the duty of doing what I should do rather than the delight of knowing God better. Now, that perspective is different. I read the Bible so that I might know Jesus my Lord and Savior better. Out of that relationship flows my activity for the day. Devotions in the morning gives me perspective for the day. I am learning to live for the glory of God in whatever I do. As I learn to follow Jesus, He teaches me to reflect His grace and truth to a world that needs Jesus.

The Lord brought several circumstances into my life to cause me to change and draw me to His Word. He used the prophecies and promises of the Bible to increase my faith. A study of George Mueller's life also had an impact on me. He was strong in faith. He would start each day with Bible study and prayer for the purpose of growing in intimacy with God. That has become my passion too. The third circumstance was a gift from a friend. My prayer team leader at church gave me a journal to take notes on what God impresses on me through His Word. Writing down lessons of faith helps me to retain the Scriptures and persevere in God's Word. The Bible has been influential in shaping how I live, leading me to knowledge of Jesus as Savior and Lord.

Dear God, teach me Your ways so that I might walk in Your path.

John Shirk is program director of WJTL 90.3 FM.

*Photo by Julia Mickley, grade 12
Lancaster Mennonite High School*

April

April 1

Crying Out to God

"The Lord is near to all who call on him, to all who call on him in truth. He fulfills the desires of those who fear him; he hears their cry and saves them." *Psalms 145:18–19*

When we are moved to cry out to God, it is often associated with fear, pain, or uncertainty—and we are asking God to show Himself powerful on our behalf. But this passage indicates that we are to call on Him *in truth*. And what is that truth? It is the reality that we desperately need God, we can do nothing apart from Him, and without Him we will continue to spiral toward our own destruction. Our defining moment of truth is when we admit our inadequacies and confess that we are ready to abandon ourselves completely to Him.

Pray for Lancaster County is our weekly prayer focus for the individuals, families, churches and communities of our region. Please carry this emphasis in your heart and your prayers throughout the week.

Overcoming The Walls That Divide

"It doesn't matter if you are a Greek or a Jew, or if you are circumcised or not…Yet Christ is all that matters, and he lives in all of us." *Colossians 3:11 (Contemporary English Version)*

I have always looked up to my grandfather as a great man of God who has inspired my life as a leading example of how to follow Christ and be a pastor. In the 1970s when I was only a child, my grandparents moved to New Haven, Connecticut. There this couple who were farmers from Lancaster County, partnered with God's work of bringing healing and hope to a troubled neighborhood. This was during a time of racial tension that led to violence in many neighborhoods across the nation.

It was in the midst of this racial tension, in a neighborhood far from the Swiss German roots of our family, that Grandpa walked from house to house asking people if they would like to participate in a Bible study. During a time of soul searching in our nation, with social and political upheaval, Grandpa transcended racial barriers by being himself, a Christian who loved Jesus and loved people no matter their background or experience.

I often marvel and wonder at his tenacity in the face of insurmountable odds to leave behind a witness for Jesus Christ. In the end it wasn't about methods or programs but a simple love that took life, with its ups and downs, in stride with the Holy Spirit.

Jesus Christ, our Lord and Savior who died once and for all so that all and everyone can enter into the life giving presence of the heavenly Father, destroy the barriers that divide, and create a new humanity in the body of Christ.

Rodney A. Martin is associate/youth pastor at Lititz Mennonite Church where he works with youth, young adults, outreach, and assists with preaching.

Let This Cup Pass

"…he fell with his face to the ground and prayed, 'My Father, if it is possible, may this cup be taken from me. Yet not as I will, but as you will.'" *Matthew 26:39*

When Satan approached our Lord in the desert, he tempted Jesus to forego the suffering and death that Jesus knew awaited him at the end of His ministry on earth. "You can forego all that cross stuff, and still have everything you came for. You can have the power, you can have the whole world, you can have all the people, they're all yours, without pain and suffering—just worship me, acknowledge me for who I am and it's yours."

Jesus resisted it then and he faced it again in the garden as he contemplated the terrible suffering, agony and death that awaited Him in a few short hours. And this time, he prayed gut-wrenching, blood-sweating prayer asking the Father for relief from what was about to happen, but he ended up putting Himself squarely into the Father's hands.

What is instructive as you study Jesus' life is that His pathway to glory took Him through the fiery trial of suffering and death. Jesus our example was willing to endure suffering and death in order to be in the will of the Father.

In Western culture, the concept of suffering and death is not only foreign but also repugnant. We'll do almost anything to avoid pain and suffering, yet our Lord suffered and died willingly and instructs us to do as He did.

If we desire to be part of the spotless bride of Christ, let us prepare ourselves now for the refining fire of suffering and persecution that will surely come upon the church as the end approaches.

Dear God, we thank you for Jesus our example who willingly suffered and willingly laid down His life for us. Build in us the acceptance of suffering as the pathway to glory. Help us not to avoid suffering but to embrace it as Jesus did.

Dale Weaver is senior pastor of Sandy Hill Community Church, Coatesville.

April 4

Occupy

"When the righteous are in authority, the people rejoice, but when the wicked beareth rule, the people mourn." *Proverbs 29:2 (King James Version)*

Christians have a responsibility to be involved with our world— our communities, our schools, our government. In the parable of the ten servants, found in Luke 19, we read that the master ordered them to "Occupy till I come." They were not told to hide in a cave until he returned, nor were they to just get by the best that they could until he returned. They were to occupy, to do business, to be involved in the mission at hand.

"Occupy" is defined as "to take possession of, as by invasion; to keep possession of; hold." As Christians, we have often abdicated our position of authority and leadership in our communities, educational systems and governments. We have not been the gatekeepers that God calls us to be, sitting in the gates of the city..."Her husband is respected at the city gate, where he takes his seat among the elders of the land (the rulers of the land, the people of influence in the land (Proverbs 31:23)."

What better way to see God's kingdom come to earth as it is in heaven than for God's people to step into leadership as He calls and provides opportunities for us to lead with integrity and biblical principles? "You are the salt of the earth...You are the light of the world...(Matthew 5:13-16)." We are called to be light and salt to our world. We are to occupy until the Lord returns for His church.

Father, forgive us for abdicating the positions of authority and leadership in our world that You ordained for us. Help us to rise up and reclaim our communities, schools and governments for You. Let us be faithful servants that are found by You to be actively occupying our world when You return to take your church with You.

Mary Prokopchak is a nurse and serves with her husband, Steve, on the Apostolic Council of DOVE Christian Fellowship International.

The Faith Factor

"Where there is no vision, the people perish: but he that keepeth the law, happy is he." *Proverbs 29:18*

Vision is something from God in your spirit that gives you the ability to see beyond where you are now. Vision gives you a focus or something to reach for. Everybody ends up somewhere. Some people end up somewhere on purpose—the ones with vision! Without a vision, there is a lack of direction in our lives. It feels like we have no guidance woven through our lives. To have vision is a different approach to life. It brings your world into focus.

When I was a boy on a farm working with horses and mules, being able to see the end result gave meaning to otherwise boring work I had to do. For example, as I was plowing the field, I would picture my dad planting the corn. I would visualize the corn growing, being harvested, and taken to the barn to be made into feed for the cows. The cows produced milk, which provided food for people in the community.

Vision keeps the big picture in front of you. This picture will bring motivation and energy to the daily grind of vision coming to pass. For a vision to be realized there has to be faith in the vision. I call this the "faith factor"—being persuaded your vision is from God and taking steps toward it. The fulfillment of a vision is a process or a series of actions. The quality of our lives is determined by our vision and the effort we are willing to put into fulfilling it.

Heavenly Father, open my eyes to Your vision and purpose for me.

Sam Smucker is the senior pastor of The Worship Center and serves on the executive team of the Regional Church of Lancaster County.

Listen to Him

"...This is my Son, whom I love. Listen to Him!" *Mark 9:7*

I realize I live in a world where there are many voices calling for my attention and my allegiance. The voice of politics. The voice of nationalism. The voice of materialism. The voice of philosophy. The various religious voices. And many more. I consider: how do I sort out all of these voices?

I find comfort in the words that came from the cloud at Jesus' transfiguration. "This is my Son, whom I love. Listen to Him!" When I invited Jesus into my life, I pledged my allegiance to Him. It is comforting for me to know that Jesus said, "I am the way and the truth and the life....(John 14:6)."

A constant challenge to me is whether I am listening when He tells me of the way to the Father. Am I listening when He speaks truth to me through the Word and the Spirit? Am I listening when He tells me how to live the life that is in Him? Am I listening when He calls for my allegiance to and worship of Him? Am I listening when He calls for my witness of Him to others? Am I attentive and listening?

Father, I pray for a listening ear so that I hear when You speak. Help me keep my focus on Jesus. In His name and for His glory, Amen.

H. Howard Witmer is a retired bishop and administrator in the Lancaster Conference of the Mennonite Church.

Sudden Storms

"I would hasten my escape from the windy storm and tempest."
Psalms 55:8

T
he spring season often conjures cheerful thoughts of tulips flow-
ering and trees budding. Yet, storms often accompany these
lovelies too. Recently, I felt that a relentless storm raging around
me was never-ending.

Sure, I wanted the beautiful flowers and budding trees—but not
the storms! Often that's how we want life to be, full of beautiful flowers without the storms. When a rain storm comes we usually tuck ourselves safely inside until it passes. Yet at times we're caught right in the
middle of the downpour!

Like a mature tree in a storm, my roots were deeply planted and
secure in the Lord. The trunk bent very little, but the leaves tossed to
and fro in the wind, feeling the full force of the storm. My emotions
were those leaves! As it intensified, I sensed the Lord desiring to redi-
rect my attention. He wanted me to focus on Him—not the storm. He
wanted me to become still and rest in His peace and assurance.

We may be like a tree in a storm with roots firmly planted. We
know what God has promised. We know what we should do. Yet our
emotions churn in turmoil, like the leaves on a tree. However, as we
yield our emotions to the Lord, we enable Him to control the storm
around us. We position ourselves to receive God's grace for our situation.

As we place our trust in the Lord, our tree will be like that in
Jeremiah 17:7–8, a tree that has no worries and never fails to bear fruit.
It is during the storms we recognize the depth of our faith in the Lord,
our root. We receive a renewed sense of God's love and care for us.

Thank you, Lord, that beautiful flowers follow the storm.

Lucinda Dise serves with her husband, Allen, senior pastor and elder
of Newport DOVE in Elm.

United in Heart

Pray for Lancaster County

"How good and pleasant it is when brothers live together in unity!… For there the Lord bestows his blessing, even life forevermore."
Psalms 133:1,3

Unity in Christian circles is certainly an agreed-upon principle, but it is often very illusive in reality. We speak of unity, we embrace the concept of unity, we even strive for unity—but in the end we usually agree to unity only if it fits with our own personal agendas. The unity that brings transformation from God is not an organizational unity. It is a unity built on the bedrock foundation of humble, trusting, mutually esteeming relationships that are grown over time. This is the supernatural unity that Jesus prayed about in John 17:21. The question then becomes, *Am I an agent of unity in my relationships?* Am I building relationships with others that esteem them and value them? Those are the foundational principles that build unity. It has to start with you and your relationships.

Pray for Lancaster County is our weekly prayer focus for the individuals, families, churches and communities of our region. Please carry this emphasis in your heart and your prayers throughout the week.

Circle of Blessings

"...I will bless you...and you will be a blessing." *Genesis 12:2*

Y ou're doing it all wrong!" The night before leaving for Albania, we received this comment about our travel itinerary. We had extended our layover in Switzerland to visit friends before going on to Albania. This individual, along with others, felt we should end our trip in Switzerland to be refreshed, following the heat of Albania. God reassured me with the Abrahamic blessing from Genesis 12. He told Abram that He would first bless him; then Abram will bless others.

We felt greatly blessed in Switzerland, marveling at the beautiful sights and enjoying relationships. Yes, from the rising of the sun to the going down of the same our hearts were exploding as we flew to Albania. The week of Bible camp was very intense but we could minister from the overflow in our hearts. We saw specific prayers being answered for each one of our children. We marveled at the equation: I will bless you—others will be blessed. However, as we went on to a village setting the weather was hotter, the spiritual climate dryer, and there were fewer English speakers. I reminded the children of the blessing we experienced in Switzerland. Although it didn't come as easy, we looked for God appointments and saw our children reaching out to others.

"Our flight is cancelled?" We needed to make connecting flights at 3:30 in the morning with no official in sight! There in the airport in Albania, we asked the Lord to work out the trip home, and to give us His grace. When we arrived in Frankfurt, they had overbooked economy class and bumped our family to business class for the transatlantic flight home. We were blessed—Lord, make us a blessing.

Dear Father, thank you for Your loving care. Help us to trust You with every detail and learn to go with Your flow, for our blessing and use us to bless others.

Yvonne Garber serves with her husband, pastoring at Byerland Mennonite Church.

For His Sake

"...O our God, hear the prayer of Thy servant, and his supplications, and cause Thy face to shine upon Thy sanctuary that is desolate, for the Lord's sake...O Lord, hearken and do; defer not, for Thine own sake...." *Daniel 9:17,19 (King James Version)*

In the recorded prayer of Daniel, we find him praying for the Lord's sake. Also as Jesus was teaching on prayer, He taught that we should pray for God's will and desires to come to pass. Upon examining our prayers, we may find that most of our requests are for people, ourselves or for various circumstances without really being concerned about God Himself.

Many of the prayers of men such as Daniel, Moses, Jeremiah, David and others were not focused on their concern for what would benefit them or a special need for someone else but rather they were focused on the Lord. Requesting prayer, Paul says, "...for the Lord Jesus Christ's sake (Romans 15:30)." As they made their earnest requests their hearts cried out, saying, "Lord, for Thy Name's sake!" As they prayed to Him they also prayed for Him, or you could say that as they prayed their utmost concern was for the glory of His Name!

How often have we prayed to consume things upon our own lusts? Is it possible that we would see an increase of answered prayers if our hearts would begin to burn with, "Not unto us, O Lord, not unto us, but unto Thy name give glory...(Psalms115:1)?"

Father, I love You and want You to be glorified; therefore I ask that You would conform us more and more into the image of Your Son so that He would have the preeminence in all things. For the glory of Your name, cause Your face to shine upon Your church and bless us with revelations of Your truth, Your ways and Yourself. Through this I pray that You would become more famous, and that the world would stand in awe of You and glorify Your name.

Aaron Jay Beiler pastors at Grace and Truth Ministries.

Pressing Into His Presence

"Let us acknowledge the Lord; let us press on to acknowledge Him. As surely as the sun rises, He will appear; He will come to us like the winter rains, like the spring rains that water the earth."
Hosea 6:3

Nearly thirty years ago I consumed these words from the ancient prophet Hosea. Although I was only a child, the Spirit of God planted this scripture in my mind. It revealed to me that it was the longing of God to come to His people and to appear before them so that they might live in His presence. As I grew older, I longed to have my experience of God move beyond my intellect, yet the experience of His presence always seemed just outside of my groping heart. At times my faith grew weak. Perhaps it was not to be a reality for me. But nothing else satisfied my longings. And then one day, like the gradual appearance of the dawn, I began to know His presence. The experiences were as real to me as the physical coming of the morning sun. What fullness of joy became mine (Psalms 16:11).

Today I cannot give to anyone the specifics of how and when God will come, for we cannot bring on His appearance by a simple formula. But I am convinced that it is indeed the great longing of God to appear to all people. I join my voice with that of the prophet Hosea. Press on to know Him for He is faithful and His promise to appear is truth. King David assures us that the presence of God is a worthy pursuit when he exclaims, "Better is one day in your courts than a thousand elsewhere... (Psalms 84:10)."

Dear God, thank you for the testimony of the scriptures that You desire for Your people to know Your presence. Grant me faith and perseverance to press on. Come, Lord Jesus into my life.

Last year, **Barry Stoner,** concluded several years of ministry as assistant pastor of Mellinger Mennonite Church.

Unfair Treatment

"Brothers, as an example of patience in the face of suffering, take the prophets who spoke in the name of the Lord. As you know, we consider blessed those who have persevered. You have heard of Job's perseverance and have seen what the Lord finally brought about. The Lord is full of compassion and mercy." *James 5:10–11*

To appreciate this passage, you must read James 5:1–11. In verses 1–6, James addresses the wealthy and oppressive landowners who are part of this local body of believers. Then in verses 7–11 he speaks to those who are being taken advantage of. Take note: he didn't tell those who were being mistreated to stand up for themselves or to lead a mutiny against the rich landowners. Instead he calls them to patience, an attitude of self-restraint that does not try to get even. He is clearly challenging these believers to be longsuffering and to endure the unfair treatment.

What about you? Have you been treated unfairly? Maybe you've even received this kind of treatment from fellow believers. Maybe it's not just in the past, but is something you're dealing with today. I'm sure you can justify why you should stand up for yourself or simply remove yourself from the situation or the person who is mistreating you. I'm also sure you can find others who care about you who will feel sorry for you and encourage you to demand justice, and who may even try to get justice for you. But guess what? According to James 5:7–11, God is calling you to be patient. This will not happen through self-determination, but only as you fully surrender to the power of the Holy Spirit.

Dear Heavenly Father, You are calling me to a place of patient endurance. I acknowledge that I can't do this in and of myself, so help me to die to my flesh so that by Your Spirit You can empower me to press on and bring glory to Your Name.

Jeff Burkholder is pastor of adult ministries at Congregational Bible Church in Marietta.

Opportunity or Opposition

"...there was given me a thorn in my flesh....Therefore, I will boast all the more gladly about my weaknesses, so that Christ's power may rest on me...I delight in weaknesses, in insults, in hardships, in persecutions, in difficulties. For when I am weak, then I am strong." *2 Corinthians 12:7–10*

We all face circumstances that make us feel vulnerable, perhaps even helpless. The most trying events in my life are caused by my legal blindness obtained from damage to my optic nerves at birth. Childhood and adolescence were particularly difficult in terms of "fitting in" to expected norms, but even in adulthood the social aspects of dealing with a disability are difficult to overcome. I can change my environment to make dealing with blindness more tolerable, but I cannot change stereotypical attitudes in other people.

Perhaps the single most life-changing revelation to me was when I discovered that although I cannot change other people, through God I *can* change my response to ill treatment. I am not a slave to sin, but I am a slave to righteousness (Romans 6). In my inability to respond righteously, God's strength accomplishes forgiveness and graces me with repentance to release me from bitterness and resentment. My focus becomes His-ability in my dis-ability, and it allows me to view offenses as opportunities rather than opposition. My spiritual disability (without Christ) is much more limiting than any physical impairment. As for earthly blessings, God has graced me with a wonderful wife of 25 years, children who are wholeheartedly following Christ, home ownership, employment, travel and ministry opportunities which even surpass the experience of many persons without a disabling condition. "Therefore, I will boast all the more gladly about my weaknesses...."

Lord, help me daily to accept my human limitations, and grow in my dependence on Your strength to accomplish the tasks at hand.

Ed Hersh provides counseling and healing prayer ministry, trains lay counselors, and helps leaders receive spiritual renewal.

His Shame, Our Gain

"Fixing our eyes on Jesus, the author and perfecter of our faith, who for the joy set before Him endured the cross, despising the shame, and has sat down at the right hand of the throne of God."
Hebrews 12:2

Once a young farmer dreamed of college for his child. For years the father saved for his son's education. After years of sacrifice the young man gained admittance to university. The farmer proudly sent his son on the train to the school many miles away. The father's dream had been realized!

Several years passed. The son could not come home during breaks because of the expense. Finally, the farmer could stand it no longer; he had to see his son. He journeyed several days to the school. When he arrived he clattered down the street in his old farm wagon struggling to find his son. At last his eyes glimpsed a handsome young man! The farmer could barely control himself. He traveled a bit closer then yelled out, "Son!" The young man turned and saw his father in the wagon. He was embarrassed, distraught that his friends might see the farmer, the wagon, and his own roots. He said, "You must be mistaken old man. Take that old clap trap and go home." The farmer sat in silence before he slowly turned the wagon and began the long trip home. When he arrived, he walked past his wife and sat down. Suddenly, she heard a thump. Her husband lay on the floor dead of a heart attack! A son's shame brought about a father's early death.

Shame is a powerful controller. Jesus knew the shame of the cross. But out of great love Jesus disregarded its shame and suffered on our behalf. His shame brought our gain. May we not allow shame to govern us.

Dear God, thank you for loving us by giving Your Son to take our shame upon Himself.

Steve Brubaker is the director of Residential Programs for the Water Street Rescue Mission in Lancaster city.

The False Idol of Numbers

"The Lord said to Gideon, 'With the three hundred men that lapped I will save you and give the Midianites into your hands. Let all the other men go, each to his own place.'" *Judges 7:7*

When Gideon was facing a critical battle with the Midianites, the Lord directed him to narrow his troops from 10,000 to just 300 men. Vast numbers were not important to God; He wanted obedient warriors who would follow Him. Biblical unity is a majority with God. We try to make numbers the measure of the success of our unity. We make an idol out of numbers by thinking that our success is represented by the number of people filling our sanctuaries or auditoriums.

God is not impressed with the size of the crowd we attract; He is impressed by the hearts of those who are willing to be obedient. God is more interested in engaging a few hungry, holy, and humble hearts than He is in seeing a stadium full of people whose hearts remain unbroken and unchanged. The size of the crowd is not necessarily an indicator of God's blessing. We can be more effective if we concentrate our efforts on bringing together those with hungry hearts. That will be God's majority.

Pray for Lancaster County is our weekly prayer focus for the individuals, families, churches and communities of our region. Please carry this emphasis in your heart and your prayers throughout the week.

April 16

We Win By Losing!

"...unless a kernel of wheat falls to the ground and dies, it remains only a single seed. But if it dies, it produces many seeds. The man who loves his life will lose it, while the man who hates his life in this world will keep it for eternal life. But I, when I am lifted up from the earth, will draw all men to myself." *John 12:24–25, 32 (New King James Version)*

This is how Jesus described His own death and resurrection: He uses a law of nature to explain His strategy. Seeds cannot reproduce without giving up their own existence, but in their death lies a harvest. Jesus sowed His life so that the Father could reap a harvest of many lives.

We are some of the harvest and seed of God that has sprung up out of the death of Jesus. The process of sowing and reaping, dying and new life goes on—a chain reaction started by the voluntary death of Jesus. If we hang on to our life we will lose it, but if we give it up, we will find unlimited life. Our outer man must be broken so that the new life of God inside can come alive. If we are not broken, and if we hang on to our self-life we remain useless to God.

In the kingdom we win by losing! Kingdom principles are the very opposite of what natural man would expect. We gain by losing our life. Fruitfulness arises out of death. We embrace death, receive the life of God, and then release that life to others.

Lord Jesus, thank you for sowing Your life to secure a harvest on earth which includes me! Father, forgive me for being so protective of the life You gave me. I want to participate in Your law of sowing and reaping and gladly give my life to You to use in releasing life to others. I want my selfish natural man to be broken so that Your life can flow through me to others. Let the harvest be multiplied through me!

Barry Wissler, senior pastor of Ephrata Community Church, leads HarvestNET, a resource ministry linking churches and ministries, and serves on the executive team of the Regional Church.

Jesus Believes in You

"Immediately Jesus reached out his hand and caught him. 'You of little faith' He said, 'why did you doubt?'" *Matthew 14:31*

This text comes from the story of Jesus walking on the water. In the story Jesus walks on the waters of the Sea of Galilee. The disciples see Him and they think He's a ghost. Jesus tells them that He isn't a ghost. Peter then says, "If it is You, tell me to come out to You on the water," and Jesus tells him to come. Peter gets out of the boat, takes a few steps, and then starts to focus on the winds and waves and begins to sink. He cries out for Jesus to save him and Jesus does. But Jesus wonders why Peter doubted.

The first question that comes to my mind when hearing this text is why did Peter think he could walk on the water in the first place? The second thing I wonder about is whom did Peter doubt— Jesus or himself? Jesus called Peter to be His disciple. Rabbis only called people to be their disciples if the Rabbi believed the person could be like him. Jesus called Peter because Jesus believed that Peter could be like Him. Jesus believed in Peter, even giving him the name Peter, which means Rock. That is why Peter believed he could walk on the water, because his Rabbi was walking on the water. The person that he doubted was not Jesus but himself.

We usually hear that we need to believe in Jesus. But I am telling you that Jesus also believes in you. He believes that you can be like Him. He believes that you can change the world, one person at a time. Doesn't that make you want to serve Him even more?

Jesus, thank you for believing in me, even when I don't believe in myself. Thank you for seeing me not how I am but how I can be. Amen.

Ryan Braught is the pastor of Youth Ministries and Nurture at Hempfield Church of the Brethren.

April 18

Just Do It!

"For whatever is born of God overcomes the world. And this is
the victory that has overcome the world—our faith. Who is he
who overcomes the world, but he who believes that Jesus is the
Son of God?" *1 John 5:4–5 (New King James Version)*

A life-style of overcoming—"prevailing against the world" began for me the day I received Jesus Christ as Lord of my life.
Recognizing the incredible price Jesus paid for my liberty in-
spires me to focus on those things that matter most. James 1:13–15 is a
daily reminder to me that resisting temptation is the first step to overcoming sin in my life. Not dealing with temptation can lead to undesir-
able consequences. It is no longer acceptable to excuse being short-
sighted, short-tempered, fearful or impatient. Overcoming the impulse
to be negative in my thinking and speaking requires me to have faith. I
need to trust in the living God who is able to cause us to triumph in all
things (2 Corinthians 2:14).

Tom Burnett, a passenger on the hijacked United Airlines flight on
September 11, 2001, called his wife four times from his cell phone
during the ordeal. In his last call to her he said, "...we are going to *do
something"* to subvert the terrorists' plans. His actions, along with those
of his fellow passengers and crew members, saved innumerable lives,
at the cost of theirs. Their decision of faith and courage will never be
forgotten.

Overcoming requires me to "do something" with the gifts and calling that have been given to me. Overcoming is not just the act of repentance from sin and forsaking my old way of living—but a conscious
effort to please the Lord in all that I do as a celebration of new life.

*Gracious Father, thank you for giving me the opportunity to live for
You in everything I do. Grant me the strength, courage and conviction
to do only those things that honor You and give You praise.*

Mary J. Buch is senior pastor and founder of the New Covenant Church
(Breakout Ministries) in Salunga.

A Good Day

"Rejoice in the Lord always...." *Philippians 4:4*

A re you having a good day?" The question came from the hostess at the local restaurant I frequent for breakfast. It was just a little past seven in the morning, but I responded, "Yes, I am having a good day." She smiled and said, "I always like hearing you say that you're having a good day. It helps me to have a good one."

This little verbal exchange has some history. Like many restaurant employees, she often rings up my bill and says, "Have a good day." Several months ago, I began responding, "I plan on having a good day" or "I am already having it." You need to know that I am not being trite. It is a genuine belief. If it were only so many words, she would have figured it out by now. If it were only so many words instead of a truth that I try to passionately affirm daily, it would not have impacted her as it had.

The Apostle Paul understood the power of attitude in shaping our character and our witness. That's why Paul commanded that we "rejoice in the Lord, always" and why he directed us to think on "praiseworthy things." Without setting your mind (shaping your attitude) by focusing on praiseworthy things (like the day the Lord has made that we will rejoice in), it is too easy to develop a sour attitude or a discouraging one—or worse, a repulsive one.

Would the people who encounter you daily, who hear your words, and who watch your life, see an attitude that they desire for themselves? Would they experience an attitude that helps shape their days in God-praising ways? If the answer is not a resounding "yes," then it's time to get to work practicing the instructions of these verses.

Father, each day You give me a reason to rejoice. Let that rejoicing be evident to all.

Dr. Stephen Dunn is senior pastor of the Church of God of Landisville and is denominational trainer for Becoming a Contagious Christian.

Your Mom is Dead!

"Precious in the sight of the Lord is the death of His saints."
Psalms 116:15

It wasn't supposed to turn out this way. I had grown up watching television and no matter what happened to Little Joe on *Bonanza*, he always seemed to somehow pull through. When my dad called that late Wednesday night back in 1983, he said, "Your mom is sick. She's been rushed into surgery. Pray." Well, I just knew that she would pull through.

When the phone rang around 1:30 in the morning it was my dad. "Doug, your mom is dead." He was crying and my heart was breaking. "Come soon, please. Come soon." And with that he hung up. I was stunned. My mom hadn't even been ill. It was such a shock.

I miss my mom. Heaven took on a new meaning with her death. I have (almost) always believed in Christ and the "hope of glory," but with my mom's death it all became more personal, more inviting, something to look forward to.

When the casket was being taken from the church out to the hearse, the entire congregation was standing outside. Suddenly, one person began to sing the old hymn by Fanny Crosby, "Blessed Assurance, Jesus is Mine!" As that one person began, the others soon joined, so that by the time the chorus was reached, the entire congregation had joined this wonderful old song. My dad, who was, along with the rest of the family, walking with the casket, later would say, "It sounded like a choir of angels!" And so it did.

Death is hard. I will likely never get over the death of my mother. But I have also come to know that the death of a true Christian is, while sad, also something that is incredibly "precious" in God's sight.

Lord, teach me to think Your thoughts after You: to see things as You see them and to accept the things which You have ordained. I pray in Jesus' name, Amen.

Doug Winne is the pastor of Evangelical Free Church, Lititz.

God's Rain

"Ask the Lord for rain in the springtime...." *Zechariah 10:1*

Flower gardening is my hobby. After a day at a desk and computer, I enjoy being outdoors in God's creation. As spring turns to summer, I look forward to seeing all the colorful flowers in my garden.

But in 2005, the month of June was very dry. After a cool spring, the weather suddenly turned hot. Where there should have been splashes of color, my garden had listless green leaves—but very few flowers. Every morning or evening, I'd take my watering can and water the plants that looked thirstiest. As I was doing this, I'd pray for rain. Still the days and weeks went by with no rain. Finally, near the end of the first week in July, the rain started pouring from the sky! Rain soaked into the thirsty ground. Almost overnight, my garden came to life. Within a week, there were colorful flowers everywhere. A few days of God's rain did what *weeks* of my efforts with the watering can couldn't accomplish.

God taught me an important lesson through this. My main job is to pray and ask God to work in impossible situations. In a short time, He can do what years of my human efforts could never accomplish. Yes, it's important to work and do the best that I can from day to day. But I need to take the time and make it a priority to pray, to ask God to send the rain of His Spirit. Only He can bring revival to the dry places in my life, and to the people in the dry and thirsty land around us.

O God, how I need You! Without You, all my human efforts amount to nothing. Holy Spirit, come and fill the empty places in my life today. Let Your rain bring revival to our dry and thirsty land.

Jane Nicholas is a writer and editor. She and her husband Bill are part of DOVE Christian Fellowship in Elizabethtown, the community where they live.

Personal Breakthrough Prayer

Pray for Lancaster County

"...The earnest prayer of a righteous person has great power and wonderful results. Elijah was human as we are, and yet when he prayed earnestly that no rain would fall, none fell for the next three and a half years! Then he prayed for rain, and down it poured. The grass turned green, and the crops began to grow again." *James 5:16–18 (New Living Translation)*

The requirements for personal breakthrough prayer are simple: *earnestness* and *righteousness*. According to this passage, Elijah is an example of an ordinary man with extraordinary power in prayer. When he earnestly prayed for no rain, God answered for an extended period of time. When Elijah then asked God to restore the rain, God did so in great measure—and in a way that turned drought into abundance. Because Elijah was both righteous in God's eyes and earnest in his prayers, God showed Himself powerfully through Elijah. Imagine that kind of demonstration of God's power today—through ordinary followers of Christ! The world would have to take notice that God responds to His people. Let your prayer be that God will use you, as an ordinary person, for breakthrough prayer that is powerful and gets wonderful results!

Pray for Lancaster County is our weekly prayer focus for the individuals, families, churches and communities of our region. Please carry this emphasis in your heart and your prayers throughout the week.

April 23

The Prize

"I press on toward the goal for the prize of the upward call of God in Christ Jesus." *Philippians 3:14 (New King James Version)*

Ever feel like you have had just about enough? I found myself there a few years back during a particularly difficult period when the bottom appeared to be falling out of my life. I remember driving back to work after an excruciatingly humiliating meeting where I had to deal with the aftermath of someone else's mistake. I cried (literally) out to God and told Him, "I don't want to learn anymore lessons!" What I was actually saying was, "Stop working in my life, God. I want to be left alone!" It didn't take long for me to realize the ramification of my demand. Did I really want the Lord to stop working in my life? Was I willing to step out of His refining and preparatory process, just so I didn't have to experience the growth pains? Not on your life. I knew I wanted all that the Lord had for me.

I believe I found a key to going through times of trial. I stopped feeling sorry for myself and changed the way I prayed. Rather than asking God to change or remove my circumstances so that I could get back to "business as usual," I began to pray that God would do His work in me, internally, so that when the circumstances were resolved, I would not be the same person! Life's lessons are a ready tool in the Hand of the Lord to help us reach our ultimate goal—to be like Jesus!

Heavenly Father, thank you for the challenges I am facing right now. I take my eyes off the circumstances and put them back on You. Please do Your wondrous work in my heart, making me more like You.

Mike Myers is an ordained minister and is the founder and headmaster of Dayspring Christian Academy, a Principle Approach school utilizing America's classical, biblical method of education.

                                                                    God Stories

April 24

More Grace

"...but He gives us more grace." *James 4:6*

While I was leading worship at our church several years ago, our pastor invited anyone who had a specific need to come forward to receive prayer. A number of people responded to this invitation. After the worship time concluded, I walked toward my seat. Looking beyond this, I noticed a newly married couple who still remained up front. Almost as if unconscious, I felt led to continue walking past my seat to this couple. I knelt near them and began to pray.

As I silently prayed for them, a strong sense of fervency came over me and I began to pray from the very depths of my being. I was aware of this couple's situation—the husband had shared his concern that they would never be able to have children. As I prayed, I thought the Lord confirmed to me that the husband would be a father of children. Believing that the Lord was directing me to pray specifically, I prayed for this man's healing and that he would indeed be the father of both natural and spiritual children. When I finished, I returned to my seat without the couple even knowing I had prayed for them.

About one month later, I was with this couple when the wife announced that she was pregnant! In fact, they had determined that the child was conceived a day or two after they had received prayer. Furthermore, the husband told of how he had experienced an extraordinarily deep work in his heart and body while at the altar. I recounted to them the story of how God led me to pray for them. We all marveled and rejoiced at this amazing outpouring of God's grace on each of our lives. The rejoicing in God's grace continues with the birth of each new child: they now have three!

Lord, whether giving or receiving Your grace, it's all a gift from You!

Brett R. Miller serves on the music team of New Covenant Christian Church.

The Shield of Faith

"Take up the shield of faith, with which you can extinguish all the flaming arrows of the evil one." *Ephesians 6:16*

Flaming arrows were often used in battle in ancient Rome. The arrows were rather short (something like long darts) that had a specially designed tip that was dipped in tar or pitch then set on fire. The shields the soldiers of ancient Rome used were made of two sheets of wood that were glued together and were large enough for a full grown man to hide behind. The shield was designed, not to deflect arrows, but to "catch" them. The front of the shield was covered with linen and leather. A soldier could duck down and hide himself behind his shield. The flaming arrow would strike the shield and, because of its construction, completely extinguish the flame. This is a marvelous picture of Christian faith.

Christian faith means trusting in God by following the teachings and model that Jesus Christ set for his followers. "Faith in God" means that the believer first seeks to honor God with the believer's life in obedience to Him, trusting Him to provide and protect the believer. This was how Jesus lived His life. He was completely obedient to the Father so that, even when His obedience led Him to the cross, He really did suffer and He really did die, yet God raised Him from the dead! Jesus' obedience eventually cost Him everything; He ultimately lost nothing. Even in death, Jesus gained the victory.

And so, too, for the one whose faith is in Jesus Christ today.

Lord we trust You today and choose to live a life of obedience to You.

Jim Gambini is the former pastor of the Mount Pleasant Brethren In Christ Church in Mount Joy.

A New Heart

"I will give you a new heart and put a new spirit in you. I will remove from you your heart of stone and give you a heart of flesh." *Ezekiel 36:26*

I was sure the surgery would be a long and difficult process. The infection had taken hold in my heart and the damage was serious. Could I make it through heart surgery? Was I prepared for the road ahead?

I was smack in the middle of my teenage years and the battle I faced was not actually a physical one, but a spiritual one. I had already developed my share of ideas of what it meant to live in Lancaster County. It felt conservative, rigid and sheltered here. I had a growing infection of cynicism, sarcasm and judgment about the people living right around me. I could hardly wait to graduate and experience life elsewhere.

In my early 20's, after time spent in missions and college, my husband and I prayed about where God would plant us next. The whole world was before us and we thought we were willing to go anywhere.

Then the Lord clearly guided us back "home" to Lancaster County. All of a sudden, all the symptoms of my infection resurfaced. "Lord, couldn't it be anywhere else?" I wondered. But, just two short months later, we found ourselves settling in Ephrata, Pennsylvania. I began the process of complete surrender to God's purposes, and He began the process of heart surgery in me. He faithfully replaced my old misconceptions with His perspective. He gave me a new love for our land and the people here, allowing me to feel His heartbeat and passion to see this county transformed for His glory.

Precious Jesus, thank you for graciously giving me a new heart and putting a new spirit within me. Thank you for Your incredible plans and purposes for our county. May they all come to pass!

Bonita Keener, wife and mother of four, helps lead prayer in the region and serves as an elder with her husband, Brent, at New Life Fellowship in Ephrata.

The God of All Comfort

"Praise be to the God and Father of our Lord Jesus Christ, the Father of compassion and the God of all comfort, Who comforts us in all our troubles, so that we can comfort those in any trouble with the comfort we ourselves have received from God."
2 Corinthians 1:3–4

When surgery complications resulted in fifteen days in the hospital and fifty-two days bed rest, I was overwhelmed by a flood of comfort and compassion—an experience I had never had before.

Our family physician is a good listener with a tender spirit. When he sensed my discouragement with the slowness of my recovery, he made a house call. My doctor came simply to encourage me, to assure me that I was gaining ground and that I would recover soon. On his way out to his car, he stopped on our back porch and asked, "May I pray for you?"

"Oh yes," I said, "please do." He placed his arm around my shoulder and tenderly asked the Lord to bring healing to my body and peace to my heart and mind. This became a turning point in my healing and remains a precious memory. He came to encourage yet he did more: he comforted. Comfort is a ray of light in darkness; comfort warms both body and soul. I never prayed for it. I prayed for healing. When the Heavenly Father said, "Not yet," my emotions, soul and spirit were in the "slough of despond." I didn't need encouragement at that time; I needed *comfort*. I got *comfort*!

If our prayer had been answered in the way we asked, we would have rejoiced in the victory. But I would have been denied the comfort of my heavenly Father and of His children who were gifted to "Weep with those who weep!" What a loss that would have been.

Father, thank you for sometimes delaying or withholding our demands in order to bless us with Your comfort and the comfort of the saints.

Paul Hollinger is owner/manager of WDAC-FM, "The Voice of Christian Radio," Lancaster.

We Will Reap

"...Don't get discouraged and give up, for we will reap a harvest of blessing at the appropriate time." *Galatians 6:9 (New Living Translation)*

It was Saturday night at Creation Music Festival and I had given up. We had given our best effort and there was nothing else we could do. Seated next to me at evening worship was the "unreachable boy." We had tried everything to connect with this student but nothing seemed to penetrate his personal force field. During the worship time, I felt God lead me to ask the boy to stand up. I didn't want to do it. It was Saturday night and the boy hadn't stood, clapped, smiled, or shown any sign of response all week! Why should it work now? I had a pretty good feeling that the leading was from the Holy Spirit, so I bent down to ask the boy to stand up anyway. What happened next was amazing.

When I went to ask him to stand, what came out of my mouth were the words, "Do you know what we're doing?" I couldn't believe that I said that! My brain was totally thinking other words. He responded that he didn't know what was going on. I explained that people who love Jesus want to tell him how much they love him. We were doing that by standing and singing to Him. I explained that I couldn't force him to join us, but I would be glad if he did.

A few minutes later, the boy was on his feet. I almost passed out. His church youth leaders had fountains of tears rolling down their cheeks. It got more exciting when later on that evening the young boy decided he wanted to follow Jesus Christ. This time he stood, but with a much greater purpose.

God displayed that no one is outside of His reach. People can turn to Him, even when we least expect it.

God, thank you for always being just in time!

Dave Coryell serves with youth and leadership ministries at First United Methodist Church of Ephrata.

Pray for Lancaster County

Corporate Breakthrough Prayer

"Blow the trumpet in Jerusalem! Announce a time of fasting; call the people together for a solemn meeting. Bring everyone—the elders, the children, and even the babies. Call the bridegroom from his quarters and the bride from her private room." *Joel 2:15–16 (New Living Translation)*

When God instructed the people to come together for a time of repentance and fasting, He did not choose the more mature believers or those who had time to spare. He called everyone regardless of their spiritual maturity—from the elders to the babies. And He did not instruct them to find a convenient time when the majority of the people could come together. God said to call even the bridegroom and the bride because their future together did not take precedence over the need to come before the Lord in corporate repentance.

To experience true breakthrough prayer as a corporate body of believers, we must cease trying to structure our lives around our own schedules and levels of comfort. If we are to see revival in our churches and communities, we must put aside time and convenience—and embrace desperation for God.

Pray for Lancaster County is our weekly prayer focus for the individuals, families, churches and communities of our region. Please carry this emphasis in your heart and your prayers throughout the week.

What Are You Waiting For?

"Taste and see that the Lord is good...." *Psalms 34:8*

One of the primary things the Lord is doing in the church today is calling believers to a "deeper yearning for Him," a "deeper experience of Him." It is part of the "harp and bowl" phenomena sweeping across the church in every denomination and branch.

Harp and bowl comes from a reference in Revelation 5, and is the combining of two powerful spiritual disciplines—intimate worship and intercessory prayer. When combined they seem to release a powerful move of God to accomplish His purposes on the earth.

In the verse noted above, the Hebrew word translated "taste" literally means "to discover by personal experience." God is inviting His beloved children to draw close for themselves and discover that He is good. It is not enough to take someone else's word on this. If I eat something and tell you it is good, how can you really know unless you eat some for yourself? God is calling His church to intimate worship and experience with Him out of which powerful intercession will flow and God's purposes be fulfilled.

Have you tasted for yourself the incredible goodness and power of our God? His hands are outstretched and He is inviting you in. What are you waiting for? Taste and see that the Lord is good—beginning today.

Father, stir up the desire in my heart to draw close to You and taste and see that You are good. I long to know You more intimately, experience You more fully, and serve You more effectively. In Jesus' name, Amen.

Hub Smith is pastor of Columbia Christian Fellowship in Columbia.

May

Cast Your Bread

"Cast your bread upon the waters, for you will find it after many days." *Ecclesiastes 11:1 (New King James Version)*

Over the past couple of weeks, my heart's cry went something like this: "Lord, I want to see people changed, and I want to see people truly living the Word of God. I know that You have changed me and I know You can change others!" Nevertheless, I was so sorrowful about the tragedies in people's lives—the broken families, the substance and alcohol abuse that have shattered so many lives.

Then, just the other day, while doing my daily routine, loading my truck, a gentleman approached me. "Excuse me, sir. May I ask you a question? Are you a preacher?"

"Yes, I am," I replied.

He said, "I knew it! I knew it! Sir, ten years ago I remember you when I was in prison. I came to a prison service and heard your preaching. The message you spoke changed my life! I was shipped upstate to another prison and never saw you again. But my life changed dramatically over the past ten years. I just want to say 'thank you' for sharing that word with me; it changed my life!"

We exchanged phone numbers and we are going to stay in touch. I was so encouraged to hear from him. Many times we ask ourselves, "God, are You really using me?" And all God asks us to do is to cast our bread, which is Jesus, upon the waters of the world. Jesus promised that He will produce the results and change people's hearts.

Father, I pray that You would allow our faith to be activated by the Word that You have spoken to us. Help us to believe what You have said, "I am the bread of life, he who comes to me will not hunger, and he who believes in me, will never thirst."

Marvin Lyons serves as assistant chaplain and church volunteer at the Lancaster County Prison.

The God Kind of Faith

"So Jesus answered and said to them, 'Have faith in God. For assuredly, I say to you, whoever says to this mountain, "Be removed and be cast into the sea," and does not doubt in his heart, but believes that those things he says will be done, he will have whatever he says. Therefore I say to you, whatever things you ask when you pray, believe that you receive them, and you will have them.'" *Mark 11:22–24*

Jesus was telling the disciples to have "the God kind of faith." The God kind of faith sees and believes those things that are not as though they were. The God kind of faith has a vision for something that is already done in the spirit, but is not yet manifested in the natural. Jesus is explaining to the disciples that they can have anything they ask for when they pray believing in their hearts that what they say will come to pass.

There are two things to keep in mind regarding this passage. One is to remember when we are asking in prayer, that we line up with the Word of God, and two, not to harbor any unforgiveness towards anyone. The following verse in this passage of scripture reads, "*And if you stand praying, forgive, if you have ought against any.*" So, it is important to always walk in love towards everyone. In addition, for us to keep our life's vision alive and strong, we have to keep watering it by speaking the Word of God over it—thanking God for it and seeing with our spiritual eyes those things that are not as though they were.

Father, I praise You for the Word You gave me to speak over my life. Lord, I desire to keep my vision strong and alive, so I will keep it watered by Your Word and speak those things that are not as though they were.

Sherlyn Smucker serves and ministers alongside her husband, pastor Sam Smucker, in various areas of ministry at The Worship Center in Lancaster.

Bugs and Bibles

"How sweet are your words to my taste, sweeter than honey to my mouth!" *Psalms 119:103*

In Papua New Guinea, when the first rains came after the dry season, we had lots of large bugs flying around outside at dawn and dusk. They looked like June bugs, but larger. They are called *muna* (pronounced "moon-ah"), and are considered a delicacy, especially by the national children. They would run around in the mornings batting them out of the sky and putting them in cans or pop bottles to be cooked later.

Several years ago as I was watching the antics of bug-catching, I thought about the parallels between bugs and Bibles. For us, eating bugs holds little appeal because we don't understand it and haven't experienced it. (I did get up the courage to try them one time. I discovered later that I should have removed the legs and wings before frying them. Maybe that's why I felt sick after I ate them)!

Anyway, the whole idea of eating muna bugs seems pretty foreign to us. For many Bibleless peoples, God's Word seems pretty foreign, too. It may well contain wonderful spiritual nutrition, even choice delicacies. But the people lack access to it. It's not available in the language they understand. Why should they want to "eat" it?

This is our task (our mandate)—to change the inaccessible and the strange into the available and delicious. As God's Word is translated into the heart languages of the people, as they are taught to read it and are discipled in it, true spiritual change and growth begins to take place.

Dear Father, don't let me take Your Word for granted. Help me to treasure Your Word, to eat thankfully from all that You supply. Enable us to make Your Word available to the millions of Bibleless peoples of the world.

Nelson Blank and his family are missionaries with Wycliffe Bible Translators. They served in Papua New Guinea, and now serve at the Wycliffe Northeast office in Willow Street.

A Help or a Hindrance

"In the same way, let your light shine before men, that they may see your good deeds and praise your Father in Heaven."
Matthew 5:16

One day as I was praying, I felt the Lord asking me to go and talk to my neighbor. Later that afternoon I stopped in to see Mark. When I inquired how he was doing, he said he was uneasy because of surgery he was facing. Mark was afraid that he might die during the surgery, and his doctor had told him he might die without it. When I asked if he was ready to die, Mark responded that he was not. He then proceeded to tell me that as a child he was forced to go to church. But there was a down side. His parents appeared to be good Christians on Sunday, but during the week it was hell on earth at home. Mark said he would only accept Christ if he were going to serve God 24/7. Mark was not ready to go 24/7. I prayed for Mark that day and later visited him in the hospital after he had his surgery. I kept in touch with Mark and learned a lot of his tough journey through life.

I invited Mark to a men's Resurrection Breakfast, held a few days before Easter. Mark accepted my invitation and we went together. After a great breakfast and a touching presentation by the speaker, people were invited to respond to the call of Christ on their lives. Mark stood. He decided that he was ready to accept Christ as his Lord.

At the time of this writing, Mark and a friend of his are meeting with me and my wife as we go through the book of Luke together. We are having a great time sharing together, and he asks many hard questions. Mark is learning what it means to be a Christian 24/7. May God be praised!

Father, may we so live that our lives may not be a hindrance to others finding you as their personal Savior.

Fred Garber is pastor at Bossler Mennonite Church.

Redemptive Love

"This is love: not that we loved God, but that He loved us and sent His Son as an atoning sacrifice for our sins." *1 John 4:10*

I had been a bi-vocational pastor for almost twenty-five years. The job I held was a very demanding management position, and trying to juggle home, ministry and occupational responsibilities was difficult. After a series of attempts to make a change, I found myself in the same position, tired, frustrated and burned out. And that is when God stepped in to give me the "best discipline of my life." On Sunday, July 4, 2004, while playing the most non-serious volleyball game I can remember, my Achilles tendon tore. Fortunately it was not totally severed, and I did not require surgery.

The following day, my daily devotions were in the 12th chapter of Hebrews. The 13th verse jumped out at me: "Make level paths for your feet, so that the lame may not be disabled, but rather healed." After much prayer, I came to the conclusion that God disciplined me as a warning to keep me from deeper problems. I felt directed to resign my position and allow God to show me what He wanted me to do.

After months of training a new manager, the Lord once more confirmed my direction through His Word. Today I am Director of Human Development/Company Chaplain at the same place of employment. What a joy it is to know that you are where God wants you to be. Sometimes, the love of God must be stern so we will awaken to the best that He has for us. What a blessing it is to know that God cares enough about His people to allow pain to cause us to consider our paths! And why shouldn't He? All of God's love toward us is redemptive.

And our love toward Him flows out of our redeemed relationship.

Father, thank you for Your redemptive, directive, love.

Joel N. Hershey is the senior pastor of Blue Ball Church of the Brethren.

Pray for Lancaster County

May 6

Travailing Breakthrough Prayer

> "Hannah was in deep anguish, crying bitterly as she prayed to the Lord. And she made this vow: 'O Lord Almighty, if you will look down upon my sorrow and answer my prayer and give me a son, then I will give him back to you. He will be yours for his entire lifetime....'"
>
> *1 Samuel 1:10–11 (New Living Translation)*

Hannah knew how to pour out her heart to the Lord in the midst of her great anguish and sorrow. She was so desperate for a son that she was willing to pray with an unusual depth of emotion and fervency.

In fact, Eli the priest thought she was not in her right state of mind because he could see her lips moving, but heard no sound. For Hannah, her prayers were between her and God, and she was not about to put on a polite front. She was willing to travail in prayer for the one thing that most gripped her heart.

Scripture says that the Lord remembered her prayer and gave her a son. She named him Samuel "because I asked the Lord for him." Are you willing to travail in prayer for breakthrough—not letting go until God answers you? Are we all willing to join in travailing prayer for revival because we simply do not want to live another day without the very presence of God? What is in your heart, and how far are you willing to go?

Pray for Lancaster County is our weekly prayer focus for the individuals, families, churches and communities of our region. Please carry this emphasis in your heart and your prayers throughout the week.

God Stories

Called to Peace

"...Do not be troubled, for his life is in him." *Acts 20:10*

Wand that great assurance this scripture gives us. We do not have to worry, fret or panic about anyone as long as "His Life," eternal life, is within. In this verse, Paul tells us, "Do not be troubled." Why? Because Christ is *in* this person. What knowledge, what depth, what insight, revealed to Paul. Paul is certain, as we need to be, that all you need is Jesus. As Jesus said in Luke 24:38, "Why are you troubled and why do doubts rise in your minds?" There is only one Prince of Peace, and His stillness, quietness and rest is to be manifested in us as fruit of His Spirit. As believers we've been given that deposit and our desire is for others to find this peace, peace beyond all under-standing. It doesn't mean we won't be hurt or disappointed or troubled but that we need not react that way. There is no greater peace than knowing that Our Lord and Savior has power to still us at all times.

Over and over His Word calls us to peace. The Lord is the One who holds our hand (Psalms 37:24). He is our strength in time of trouble (Psalms 37:39). He is the Father of compassion and God of all comfort, who comforts us in all our troubles (2 Corinthians 1:3–4). He is our very present help in trouble (Psalms 46:1). For He Himself *is* our peace (Ephesians 2:14).

Thank you, Lord, for Your peace. Draw us to those around us who long for this peace. Open our hearts and eyes. Give us Your words to say to those who need You. Help us to be willing vessels used for Your glory. "Let the peace of Christ rule our hearts since as members of one body we are called to peace (Colossians 3:15)." Amen.

Karen L. Caplinger serves as a children's Sunday School teacher at New Covenant Christian Church. She is blessed with an adopted son.

Into the Wilderness

"By faith Abraham, when he was tested, offered up Isaac...concluding that God was able to raise him up, even from the dead..." *Hebrews 11:17–19*

What would have happened if God had not stopped Abraham? The only way for Abraham to pass the test was to act on his decision to obey. He expected to kill his son, and expected God to raise him from the dead. How often do we think that just being willing to sacrifice our "Isaacs" is good enough? But is that the same? Is God sure to stop us?

After being a pastor for eleven years, I sensed God's clear direction that it was time to move forward into a vision I had carried. I was excited about what God was doing regionally and my involvement in it. Then, in April of 2004, God spoke again, "Are you willing to go into the wilderness for a time of preparation and lay down ministry?"

"Yes, Lord."

For the next three months God confirmed this word in many dramatic ways. In late August, I announced my resignation, and amazingly, by my last Sunday (October 31, 2004) God had brought another pastor ready to begin the following day.

Jesus reminds me that when a seed *dies* it bears much fruit. The gifts and the calling are without repentance, but we are called to be followers of Jesus, not followers of the calling. I increasingly die to the vision and calling each day. I now work in sales. I am learning to let go of *everything* and yet hold on in faith that God will bring me into whatever it is He ultimately desires and has planned for me. After all, even Jesus had to die to complete His ministry. Whatever God leads us to do we can trust in His unending love for us.

Dear heavenly Father, help us to trust Your love and be true followers of You.

Dean Witmer, a former pastor, now works for Rohrer's One Hour Heating and Air Conditioning.

Beauty

Psalms 19

Our family was waiting on the observation platform for the Old Faithful geyser when a thought crossed my mind. As I watched hundreds of hopeful tourists who had come thousands of miles to see this thing erupt, we were expecting a certain degree of timeliness. I remember thinking, "What if God decided to give Old Faithful a break for just one eruption?" He would have a lot of irate tourists on His hands. But as predicted, the geyser erupted with glorious splendor—on time (pretty much). It worked...and it was beautiful.

At the core, "beautiful" is a word we ascribe to something that is operating according to God's design. The Psalmist reminds us that the heavens, the sky and the sun all live up to their intended design. They work according to God's dream for them. Each day when the sun rises and sets, God is glorified by its beauty. And while each sunrise and sunset has its own unique signature, *that* it happens is just as glorious as *what* happens.

The writer goes on to ascribe the same quality to the Royal Law of God. He calls it perfect, trustworthy, right, illuminating, pure and sure. I don't often consider the Law something beautiful. Perhaps this is because the "law" that I have struggled to obey is often one deficient of the qualities that make God's Law all that it is. The Law of God is brilliant, because it originated in the mind of God. It is His dream and plan for how we should live in relationship with Him and with one another. And, like the sun, when it works according to the dream of the designer, it is beautiful and brings glory to its Author.

Jesus, help us to love Your dream for our lives. May we treat Your Law as the glorious work that it is. Bring it into reality in our lives and in the lives of our neighbors that Your Father may be glorified.

Dan Snyder is executive director of Lancaster Youth Network of Churches (LYNC), Lancaster.

A Clear Conscience

"…we commend ourselves to every man's conscience in the sight of God." *2 Corinthians 4:2*

"If some unbeliever invites you to a meal…eat whatever is put before you without raising questions of conscience."
1 Corinthians 10:27

How can an American terrorist blow up innocent men, women and children in Oklahoma City, with a *"clear conscience"*? Or a Palestinian mother strap a homicide bomb on her teenage daughter with a *"clear conscience"*? Or any mother abort her unwanted baby with a *"clear conscience"*? Conscience will tell every human created in God's image to *do* right. Conscience will *never* tell us what *is* right!

Do not let conscience be your guide. Only God's Word is trustworthy to tell us what *is* right. Our culture, parents, teachers and pastors teach us what *is* right. Even as Christians, our fundamentalist, denominational, charismatic and Amish cultures have different lists of what *is* right, or wrong, in our application of Romans 12:1. Be transformed, not conformed.

The word *conscience* is found 32 times, only in the New Testament. The Apostle Paul clearly teaches in the above passages, that every man—even the unbeliever—has a conscience that tells him to *do* right according to man, but not always what *is* right before our Lord and His Word. Thus, conscience is controlled by *us*; we can make it operate for good or evil, we can defile it, purge it, sear it or kill it. Conscience is not a pre-programmed computer through which God tells us what *is* right or wrong. The Bible, God's eternal Word, is truth.

Heavenly Father, thank you for creating in all mankind a conscience that tells us to do right! Give us each a clear conscience, clarified by Your Word, empowered by Your Holy Spirit. Amen.

Paul Hollinger is owner/manager of WDAC-FM, "The Voice of Christian Radio," Lancaster.

Welcome To Our Family

"God places the lonely in families...." *Psalms 68:6 (New Living Translation)*

The miles flew by quickly. After months of prayer, godly counsel, interviews, background checks and an overwhelming stack of documents, we were finally on our way. All that remained was an almost seven hundred mile trip and a good night's rest and we would see the fruit. We were to receive the two-month old boy the Lord led us to adopt.

We talked about the sights that passed by our minivan. We shared hopes and dreams for our newest family member, whom we knew only through a few photographs. We listened to "Adventures in Odyssey." And we prayed. One of our prayers for our new son was simple, but heartfelt: "Lord, help him to know he is home when he is placed in our arms."

The long-anticipated day arrived. We nervously got ready and drove to the church where we received our new son during the Sunday morning service. Before we knew it, it was over. We took turns holding the baby and posing for photographs. Changing into travel clothes, we prepared for the return trip. And then it happened. A church member came over to congratulate me as I made the first of several trips to the van. He shared hesitantly that, "though it might sound strange," he had the distinct impression that the baby knew he was home the moment he was placed in my wife's arms. Tears filled my eyes and I thanked him, reassuring him that it was not strange, but an answer to prayer.

A short time later, other members stopped to speak with me. Embarrassed, they wanted me to know that although they had witnessed several placements, this one stood out because our baby somehow knew he was home when placed in my wife's arms.

Father, thank you for placing us in Your family through Jesus Christ. Reveal to us that we are truly home in Your house.

Don Riker serves congregational, ministry, and business leaders with Teaching The Word Ministries in Leola.

Complete Dependence on the Holy Spirit

"And I will ask the Father, and he will give you another Counselor to be with you forever—the Spirit of truth…you know him, for he lives with you and will be in you." *John 14:16–18*

There seemed to be no reason for it. I was struggling through a season of discouragement and crying out to God, "Why?" Over a period of time, I heard the Holy Spirit say so clearly, "There is a bigger picture. The Father *is* at work in your life, LaVerne. Trust Me. Make prayer a priority and learn to worship Me and be thankful, especially in the home."

The Father is always at work in our lives (John 5:17), even when we don't feel close to Him. It is during those times we must depend on the Holy Spirit so He can instruct and guide us to hear what the Father is saying.

Jesus told His disciples that the Father would give them "another Helper" (Holy Spirit), that He may be with them forever (John 14:16). The word *another* in Greek is *allos* which means *one besides; another of the same kind*. The Holy Spirit will do in us what Jesus would do if He were physically present with us! Do we recognize the power within us as we yield to the Holy Spirit?

The Holy Spirit is truly our Helper. He desires to comfort, strengthen, advise, convict, exhort, intercede and encourage. Will we yield to Him moment by moment? Let's wake up each morning with, "Good morning, Holy Spirit, what is the Father doing in my life today?"

Thank you, Holy Spirit, that You come alongside us and help us to hear the Father's voice. We depend completely upon You to live victorious and fruitful lives!

LaVerne Kreider serves with her husband Larry giving oversight to DOVE Christian Fellowship International. She also serves on the leadership team of a micro-church near Lititz.

Persistent Breakthrough Prayer

Pray
for
Lancaster
County

"And will not God bring about justice for his chosen ones, who cry out to him day and night? Will he keep putting them off? I tell you, he will see that they get justice, and quickly. However, when the Son of Man comes, will he find faith on the earth?"
Luke 18:7–8

The widow in Luke 18 is well-known for repeatedly coming before the judge in an appeal for justice. The judge finally relented because she wore him out with her persistence.

The judge may not have had the widow's best interest in mind in his final decision, but Jesus still uses her as an example of effective, persistent prayer. Jesus points out that even more so our righteous God will answer the prayers of His chosen followers—those who cry out to Him day and night. Certainly crying out for revival is exactly the form of justice that God would like to bring upon our churches and communities. May He find us faithful!

Pray for Lancaster County is our weekly prayer focus for the individuals, families, churches and communities of our region. Please carry this emphasis in your heart and your prayers throughout the week.

May 14

Mother Kept Praying

"For the eyes of the Lord are on the righteous and his ears are attentive to their prayers." *1 Peter 3:12*

As I was growing up, I would often walk past my parents' bedroom door in the evening and see one or both of them on their knees praying. That sight made quite an impact on me. They didn't pray out loud, so I didn't know exactly what they were talking to the Lord about. But I was reasonably certain that a common topic was... me!

There were numerous times when I went through "wild spells," and I'm sure it looked like I was headed for a life of rebellion and sin. But somehow I always ended up repenting at our church altar and getting back on track. Only years later did I put two and two together and realize that God had honored my parents' faithful prayers during those rough times and kept me from going off the deep end.

One time, after re-committing my life to the Lord, I told my mother that I was sorry for all the grief I had put her through. She responded, "Oh, that's okay. You know, you thought you were getting away with a lot of stuff behind our backs, but your father and I always knew when things weren't right between you and the Lord. We just kept praying."

What a great legacy she left: *she just kept praying.* And I believe those prayers are still being answered in my life and even in the lives of my children and grandchildren!

Lord, thank you for blessing me with a praying mother. That's what I want to be, too. Please, Jesus, will You help me to stop worrying and instead—just to keep praying?

Sharon Charles enjoys assisting her husband John at Abundant Living Ministries, a Christian marriage and family counseling center, Lititz.

In Everything Give Thanks

"Give thanks in all circumstances, for this is God's will for you in Christ Jesus." *1 Thessalonians 5:18*

My wife and I were looking forward to purchasing our first home. We found a nice lot, met with a builder and looked over the plans. We only needed our loan to come through. We applied for a government loan for first-time home buyers, knowing they would only approve a limited amount of applications. We committed the whole thing to the Lord and asked Him to open or close the door according to His will. But we felt sure God would have our application approved. We made plans to go out and celebrate over dinner as soon as our loan was accepted. But to our great disappointment we received word that we didn't get our loan.

I then felt God challenging me about my attitude. Had I not asked Him to close the door if it was not His will? Why then was I only thankful for God's will when it was a "yes" but not a "no"? Were they not both equally an answer to prayer? Was I only thankful when I received what I wanted? Could I not trust God's wisdom in closing the door and be grateful? So my wife and I decided to give thanks for the closed door as we went out to celebrate God's answer to our prayer over a wonderful dinner.

Looking back, I can now see the wisdom and protection of God closing the door. I am still learning to give thanks in all circumstances.

Help me to be thankful not only for the "Yes" answers but also the "No" answers to my prayers. I put my trust in You as the all wise and loving God who is in control of my life. I will give thanks in the midst of my circumstances today.

Lester Zimmerman is senior pastor of Petra Christian Fellowship, overseer of the Hopewell Network of Churches, and serves on the council of the Regional Church of Lancaster County.

Knocking Down Strongholds

"We use God's mighty weapons, not those made by men, to knock down the devil's strongholds." *2 Corinthians 10:4 (Paraphrased)*

The Bible shows us from the earliest days of history that war had a religious significance. That trumpets were blown and cries went up. God went forth with the armies, dwelling in the midst of the camp. The spoils belonged to God. As we see in 2 Corinthians, Paul is also telling us that we need to use the might of God to knock down the devil's strongholds.

As a former Army soldier, I served in Germany for two years guarding the East and West German borders. Those crossing over from the East to the West were so thankful to be free. We currently find the world again trying to establish freedom for another country. I am hoping that we as Christians realize that war is wrong and peaceful methods must be used first. If we as a nation have to use military force, we had better ask ourselves whether we are going in order to fight the devil's stronghold. Could it be that our purpose is to bring spoils to ourselves?

As I talk to other soldiers over the years, they realize dying is the hardest thing we can ask a man to do. But they also knew that if they were asked to, God would be with them. Bless those daily who have died for our freedom. I now invite you to pray with me.

Dear God, I call on You to show us peace through Your love, not through war. But if we do need to go into battle against the devil, give our leaders and the leaders of other nations what You will for us, and not our own desires. Amen.

Russell L. Pettyjohn served as a Lititz borough councilman for 12 years and is now serving in his 12th year as Mayor of Lititz Borough.

Obedience to His Calling

"The one who calls you is faithful and He will do it."
1 Thessalonians 5:24

When God called me to consider campus ministry as a senior in Bible school, I thought God was speaking to the wrong person. I had never considered campus ministry, nor did I have the desire to do so. Yet I wanted to walk by faith, so I did not reject the calling totally, but rather put it back in God's hands and asked Him to bring it about in His timing, not by my pursuits.

This verse from I Thessalonians became very real during this time as I realized that God's calling is also the opportunity to experience God's character, God's divine leading, and indeed God actually doing it.

Currently I am completing my 13th year as a campus minister at Millersville University. The Lord has done a marvelous thing and I have seen and experienced the promise of this verse. Hundreds of young adults have been touched with the Good News of Jesus Christ through the campus ministry. My heart's desire has completely changed from the time of the calling. Where there was once no desire to be in campus ministry, there is now a strong passion for what the Lord has called me to do.

I am so grateful that the Lord went above and beyond the desires of my heart and called me to something that was on His heart. When God calls you, He is also the One who will equip you for that calling and the One who takes care of the end results as well. You can trust God when you walk in obedience to His calling.

Dear God, keep me true to the calling You have placed upon my life. Thanks, God!

Duane Metzler serves as campus minister to Millersville University and pastor of University Christian Fellowship.

God is In Control

"Frantically they woke him up, shouting, 'Teacher, don't you even care that we are going to drown?'" *Mark 4:38 (New Living Translation)*

When finishing Bible College, my world came to a screeching halt. My sister was brutally murdered by her husband. Our family was in shock. How could this have happened? It felt like God fell asleep when we needed Him most. We wondered, "Where were You, God, when Janice was being attacked?"

During this time of raw grief I read Mark 4. The disciples were frantic. The storm threatened their tiny boat. It felt like they were going to drown. They saw Jesus asleep at the back of the boat! Confused and a bit ticked off, they shook the sleeping Savior. "Don't You care that we are going to drown?" they asked.

The Roman Christians asked a similar question while Nero was emperor. He killed Christians for sport, using them as human torches to light the night skies for his parties. It was to those like these that Mark wrote, "Master, don't You care that we are perishing?"

The answer is the same for the disciples in the boat, the persecuted Christians and me! "Of course I care, enough to give you peace in the middle of your storm. Trust me. All things are under My control!"

I do not know what painful ordeal you might be facing, but I do know this: nothing is out of God's control. We may face a brutal storm, we may even suffer and die; but God is in control and God is good. Trust and faith placed in Him is never a mistake!

Dear Lord, You are in control of the winds and waves of our lives. Even when it seems like You are sleeping, we place our faith and trust in You. We do not always understand Your ways and the wisdom of Your plan. Forgive us when we fail to trust You, and increase our faith each day.

J. Daniel Houck is the pastor of the Table Community Church of Lancaster.

The Parable of the Cake

"O taste and see that the Lord is good: blessed is the man that trusteth in him." *Psalms 34:8 (King James Version)*

If your experience is like mine, you may have heard people say they are simply dissatisfied with the spiritual food they receive at their place of worship. With this thought in mind, the Lord directed me to write the following parable.

One day as Jesus was walking with His disciples, the crowds gathered around Him. A small child was eating a cupcake and offered one to Jesus.

Taking the cake, Jesus held it up for all to behold, and He began to teach them.

"The Kingdom of Heaven is likened unto a man eating a piece of cake, who with clean hands and whetted appetite anticipates the delectable forthcoming experience. Upon consuming a portion, he savors the moment and then calls the cake maker to offer his praise and to beg for the recipe. Upon receiving his request, he goes forth to his friends and cries aloud, 'Come and enjoy the most delicious food one can eat, for I hold in my hand the secret to the best cake that can be found.'

"For truly, I am the Cake of Life. He that eats of my desserts shall never hunger for any other. For out of his heart shall flow the icing of sweetness and the richness of contentment that will climax with the eternal partaking of the wedding cake that God is preparing for all of my bride, at our wedding in Heaven."

Do you desire to receive "more cake" when you go to church? Take a more active roll in preparing yourself for this event. Leave the milk bottle at home and take the fork and knife instead. He that is prepared to eat at God's table will never be disappointed!

Lord, help us to taste and see that You are good every time as we gather to worship You!

Joel N. Hershey is the senior pastor of Blue Ball Church of the Brethren.

My Limited Expectations

"The wind blows wherever it pleases.
You hear its sound, but you cannot tell
where it comes from or where it is going.
So it is with everyone born of the Spirit."
John 3:8

God's work will always be unique. Count on it! The Bible is full of examples of unusual and unimaginable ways that God showed Himself powerful and faithful.

From the very beginning, God's people have been challenged with the unexpectedness of God. Of course, there are the ways of God that are forever true and unchangeable, but as Winkie Pratney says, "When an infinite person expresses Himself finitely, it always comes out differently."

The challenge for us is to suppress our tendency to want to program God to act according to our expectations. He does not make Himself accountable to man's notion of how He should act. Our expectations of the infinite are very, very finite and God will not limit Himself to our expectations of Him. We cannot expect God to show up in the same way He did last week or last year. He cannot be stage managed.

We must learn to take delight in the unexpectedness of God. If we do not yield our limited expectations over to His infinite nature, we may be looking the wrong way and miss His unexpected appearance.

Pray for Lancaster County is our weekly prayer focus for the individuals, families, churches and communities of our region. Please carry this emphasis in your heart and your prayers throughout the week.

Crowned With Lovingkindness

"Bless the Lord, O my soul; and all that is within me, bless His Holy name! Who crowns you with lovingkindness and tender mercies, who satisfies your mouth with good things."
Psalms 103:1, 4–5 (New King James Version)

I had been avoiding going for a dental checkup for years. My teeth had some serious damage from grinding them during sleep and I knew the repairs were likely to be expensive. Finally, I made an appointment and went to see a dentist. My worst fears were confirmed when the dentist told me I would need four crowns, along with some other repairs, for a whopping total of $5,800! Since our family had limited dental coverage, this would hit the wallet pretty hard. My first reaction was to fret and try to finagle a workable, man-centered solution.

Later that week, I read Psalms 103:1, 4–5 in a devotional calendar. The verse explained how God "crowns us with lovingkindness and satisfies our *mouth* with good things." As I read the verse, the Holy Spirit spoke to my heart and showed me that this verse was a *rhema* word (or an illumination of the Word for personal application) concerning my dental dilemma. My faith began to rise for a "God solution." Faith won out over worry and I was led to seek a second opinion from a particular local dentist.

After an examination, this dentist laid out a plan to take care of the dental work in a series of stages over a few years—*all within our insurance limits*. It was the fulfillment of God's promise to me. Every time I remember this testimony, my faith rises to see God's Word fulfilled!

O God, thank you that You speak to us through Your Word and through Your Holy Spirit to give us insights that are personal and intimate. Cause our faith to rise for the fulfillment of Your promises to us.

Sarah Erk is a wife and mother of three children, and serves with her husband, David, on the deaconate team at New Covenant Christian Church in Washington Boro.

Wholehearted Mentoring

"And Caleb said, 'I will give my daughter Acsah in marriage to the man who attacks and captures Kiriath Sepher.' Othniel son of Kenaz, Caleb's brother, took it; so Caleb gave his daughter Acsah to him in marriage." *Joshua 15:16–17*

Following his well-known spy mission, Caleb appears to slip into political obscurity. After wholeheartedly serving out his military obligation during the invasion of the Promised Land, Caleb, now in his eighties, asks that he be granted his inheritance. He consciously selects land inhabited by giants. This wasn't patriarchal hubris; there was purpose in his choice. Lacking a son himself, Caleb takes his fatherless nephew, Othniel, along with him into the mountains of Hebron. When they reach the first giant stronghold, Caleb leads the attack and subdues the oversized inhabitants.

At the next stop, he does something strange. This lifelong man of action sits out the attack, instead offering his daughter as a reward to the man who will successfully lead the assault. It's not in the Bible, but I like to believe that as he made that speech, Caleb cast a challenging glance in the direction of his nephew. Othniel, instructed and inspired by Uncle Caleb's example, wins the victory. The years pass by and the old guard have now died off. Israel backslides and falls into the hands of their enemies. God needs a strong leader to deliver His people from their oppression. Whom does He choose as the first judge over Israel? God chose Othniel, the giant fighter, mentored for that very moment, by Caleb.

Lord, remind those of us who are called "senior citizens" that now is not the time to rest on our laurels. Give us the strength and grace to show our spiritual sons and daughters, by example, how to be victorious warriors for You. Amen

Jay Doering is a member of the pastoral team of the Parker Ford Church of the Brethren near Pottstown.

God Stories

We're All Weak

"But God chose the foolish things of the world to shame the wise; God chose the weak things of the world to shame the strong. He chose the lowly things of this world and the despised things, and the things that are not, to nullify the things that are, so that no one may boast before Him." *1 Corinthians 1:27–29*

I looked around my church one Sunday morning, and this is what I saw: single mothers struggling to make ends meet, divorced women trying desperately to keep up the mortgage, men and women with substance abuse problems, people who have been in jail, people with emotional and mental illnesses, disabled people, grandparents raising their grandchildren to save them from abuse, blended families, and troubled kids. Then there were those of us who thought we were strong and wise until God showed us how weak and foolish we were. Our little congregation is, to be honest, a mess. Sometimes I find myself envious of the ministries that can be supported when the congregation is bigger and more well off than ours.

But our ragtag gathering is a living illustration of what Paul was telling the Corinthians. Where, outside the church and twelve-step groups, do we find people crossing socioeconomic lines to gather voluntarily for fellowship? As Brennan Manning says in *The Ragamuffin Gospel*, underneath our veneers of polish and control, we are all ragamuffins, wretched and poor before God. We just need to recognize it.

"My grace is sufficient for you, for My power is made perfect in weakness," God tells Paul in 2 Corinthians 12:9. Celebrate the weakness in your church. In it, God shows us His strength.

God of power and grace, pour out Your strength on us, the weak and poor, that we might display Your might to the world. Help us to recognize our helplessness without You. May we be one in Jesus Christ. Amen.

Helen Colwell Adams is a reporter for the *Sunday News* and lay leader at Pearl Street United Methodist Church, Lancaster.

Everything New

"He who was seated on the throne said, 'Behold I am making everything new....'" *Revelation 21:5*

One day at the age of twelve, sitting beside an old water pump, God spoke to my heart, asking, "What are you going to do with your life?" My heart, hardened by religion, answered back, "I can make it on my own."

Eleven years later, on the Wednesday night of revival week, my heart knew I could no longer make it on my own. My mother's prayers for me all those years bore fruit, convincing me I needed the Lord. The title of the message that night was, "Are You a Christian?" explaining the difference between religion and a relationship with God through Jesus Christ. Like a sponge soaks up water, my heart soaked up the Word of God. I responded to the invitation, knelt at an altar, and yielded my entire being to the Lord Jesus. All of this had to be a God-thing because I was my own man. No one pushed me around.

As I left the church later, the sky, the stars, the moon seemed brighter than I had ever seen them before, proving that all things had become new. Since that evening in 1968, my life has never ceased to be new. Every morning the mercies of God are new: I have never been the same again!

Dear Lord, You are so awesome. I can never reach the end or the bottom of You! Always, newness of life belongs to me in You. I rejoice in that today. Amen.

Lester Eberly serves on staff at DOVE Christian Fellowship Westgate as Small Group Administrator.

Clothed by God

"I delight greatly in the Lord; my soul rejoices in my God. For he has clothed me with garments of salvation and arrayed me in a robe of righteousness...." *Isaiah 61:10*

The morning started badly. I had stayed up too late trying to complete some urgent items from my to-do list. So I slept a little late and woke up to face a full day. Of course, my first appointment (the dentist) filled me with eager anticipation—NOT. I was racing the clock and losing. I took a fast shower, dried my hair, brushed my teeth and ran to the car, bemoaning the fact that I was skipping breakfast. As I started out of the driveway, I found a banana and ate it on the way.

I arrived on time and felt relief until I looked down and noticed that I had some banana smeared on my t-shirt. Then as I began to clean that off, I saw...I had put my pants on inside out. ARRGGH!

Walking into the office I feigned nonchalance as the receptionist said, "Hi Karen, how are you?" I replied, "I'll tell you in a minute," and dashed into the restroom. After quickly changing my pants and cleaning my shirt, I returned to the desk with a relaxed (looking) smile on my face and explained what had happened. I was glad that I could provide a humorous moment for someone's day.

Although I was frustrated by my disarray, it was an easy thing to slip into the restroom and get myself straightened up. But sometimes I let my spiritual life get into disarray. I have things smudged or inside out and it seems impossible to fix. The truth is I cannot fix myself. But God can and God will.

Lord, I am grateful for Your salvation. All of my efforts may lead to disarray, but You array me in a robe of righteousness.

Karen Boyd is a small group leader at ACTS and serves on the board of the Pennsylvania Homeschoolers Accreditation Agency.

May 26

A New Perspective

"For our light affliction, which is but for a moment, is working
for us a far more exceeding and eternal weight of glory."
2 Corinthians 4:17 (New King James Version)

Some years ago when a persistent affliction became unbearable
and discouragement threatened to overtake me, God gave me
His perspective on the above verse. Phrase by phrase, God re-
oriented my thinking. *"For our light affliction."* I could agree with the
affliction part, but light? There was nothing light about this heavy burden I was carrying! *"Which is but for a moment."* Momentary? How
about long-term, nagging, unending! *"Is working for us."* The affliction is actually working on my behalf? Instead of working against me,
it's working for me—producing something worthwhile? Okay Lord,
now You have my attention. So what's it producing? *"A far more exceeding and eternal weight of glory."* Hmm...so Lord, You're saying
that this heavy, nagging, unending affliction is feather-light and fleeting compared to eternity, and is producing in me glory that will last
forever? Now *that's* something I can get excited about!

Armed with this new perspective, I jotted the verse on a 3x5 index
card, headed outside to a vacant school yard, and began marching around
and declaring the scripture out loud. I wanted Satan to hear that I was
no longer letting this affliction have the upper hand. "The affliction is
lightweight and fleeting," March, march, march. "It's actually working
to produce incredible glory within me. March, march, march. "It's a
heavyweight glory and it's gonna last forever. March, march, march.
With each pounding step the enemy lost his grip on me, discouragement lifted, and triumphant joy flooded my heart.

*Father, when afflictions weigh me down and show no sign of easing,
remind me of Your perspective—that they're light and fleeting compared to eternity, and that they're producing for me a far greater glory.*

Lisa Hosler serves as president of Susquehanna Valley Pregnancy
Services and is a member of the council of the Regional Church of
Lancaster County.

Letting Go of Human Notions

Pray for Lancaster County

"Then Job replied to the Lord: 'I know that you can do anything, and no one can stop you. You ask, "Who is this that questions my wisdom with such ignorance?" It is I. And I was talking about things I did not understand, things far too wonderful for me...I had heard about you before, but now I have seen you with my own eyes. I take back everything I said, and I sit in dust and ashes to show my repentance.'" *Job 42:1–3, 5–6 (New Living Translation)*

At the end of his experience of tragedy and desolation, Job was confronted with the reality that he did not know God as well as he thought he did. One of the greatest and most liberating truths is the fact that God is bigger than we can imagine! It is liberating because we can freely let go of our preconceived notions of how God should or should not act in any given situation.

Once you let go of your expectations of how God "ought to act," you are free to watch in amazement at how He does everything so perfectly. As we pray, may we do so with great liberty—that God is free to work in my life, my family, my church, and in my city as He desires. Letting go of our limited human notions is part of the romance of knowing our God. He is so lovingly unpredictable! Let go and be ready for whatever He may choose to do.

Pray for Lancaster County is our weekly prayer focus for the individuals, families, churches and communities of our region. Please carry this emphasis in your heart and your prayers throughout the week.

Real or Counterfeit?

"...These people honor me with their lips, but their hearts are far from me." *Mark 7:6*

My family attended church every Sunday during my childhood. When I was eleven years old, we went to a special evangelistic meeting and since I really didn't want to go to hell, I gave my life to God, as much as I understood. I made a decision to receive Christ as my Savior.

Seven years later, a friend confronted me: "If you were to die tonight, are you sure that you would go to heaven?" I honestly didn't know the answer, so I said, "Nobody knows that."

The young lady didn't hesitate with her answer. She said, "Well, I know."

I had come face to face with the truth. I didn't know Jesus as my Lord. I had continued to live my life my own way, without submitting to His Lordship in every area of my life.

Later that night, when I opened my Bible at home, everything seemed to be written directly to me. I read where Jesus said, "You hypocrites!" and I knew I was a hypocrite too. I came to the realization I was living like a counterfeit Christian. I appeared outwardly righteous, but inwardly I was not experiencing the life of Christ. That night I said, "Jesus, I give You my life. If You can use this rotten, mixed-up life, I'll serve You the rest of my life."

God miraculously changed me the moment I reached out in faith to Him. My attitudes and desires changed. Even my thinking began to change. I was clearly transformed because Jesus Christ had become my Lord. I now knew I was a new creation in Christ, and I am eternally grateful to Jesus.

Thank you Lord for delivering me from the web of hypocrisy and shining your light on my heart.

Larry Kreider is the international director of DOVE Christian Fellowship International and serves on the executive team of the Regional Church of Lancaster County.

God Will Take Care of You

"Your heavenly Father knows that you need all these things."
Matthew 6:32

In the spring of 1999, after 10 years as an illustrator with a local design company, I found myself out of work. No more big pay check. No more paid vacation. No more 401K. No more health insurance for me, my wife and kids. No dental. No vision. No nothin'!

I pounded the pavement with my portfolio. I let my fingers do the walking through the Yellow Pages. I mailed my resume all over the county. I searched job sites online. I prayed. I interviewed. And no full-time work materialized.

Meanwhile I grabbed whatever came my way to provide for the household. I taught cartooning at a local charter school. I worked in a bookstore for $7.00 an hour. I took a position as a receptionist in a large office building. I continued to interview, pitch resumes, knock on doors. But no full time work.

During this time, God's provision came to us in many amazing ways. A crew of Amish-Mennonite brothers roofed my house for the cost of the shingles ($400 instead of $4,000). The City of Lancaster did $16,000 worth of rehab work on my home (even putting in new toilets)—for free! The Office of Vocational Rehabilitation bought me two new hearing aids ($4,000 worth). A group of local churches provided Christmas presents for every member of my family.

Today, I still don't have a full-time job position. But God has provided freelance work and several part-time ministry roles which not only utilize my gifts but provide for my household in abundance. Last year, we gave 15% of our income to our local church and the work of the kingdom. Seek Him first: He'll take care of the rest.

Dear God, may I know all You have is mine as I need it. Thank you!

Mark Ammerman is an author, artist and communications director of the Regional Church of Lancaster County. He serves on the leadership staff of In The Light Ministries in Lancaster City.

Blind

"…he judged me faithful, appointing me to his service, though formerly I was a blasphemer…But I received mercy…and the grace of our Lord overflowed for me with the faith and love that are in Christ Jesus." *1 Timothy 1:12–14 (English Standard Version)*

For the first two years of our marriage, we lived in a sophisticated, planned city in another state. Since we had not really made friends there, we thought we would join a church when we moved so we could be more involved in the community where we lived. I thought I would join the choir. I was a 21-year-old college student when my husband and I walked into the closest church. It was Mennonite. There was no choir. We sat in the back and when the preacher said, "Let us pray," every one turned around and looked at us before they knelt at their bench.

We had never experienced a preacher actually explaining the Bible, so we thought we should learn more about this world-changing book. However, I did not plan to believe in God. As we continued to attend, sometimes folks would ask me, "Did you go to church regularly before?" I thought, "Sure, I was there almost every Easter and Christmas Eve. That's regular." I started carrying a Bible that had been given to me many years before. I was embarrassed when someone remarked on my "new" Bible. The edges were still shiny gold.

A few months later, I was in the basement of the music building of my college, practicing a popular song from the radio, *Amazing Grace*. As I sang the words, "I once was blind, but now I see," I felt an indescribable awareness that God was real. My blind eyes saw. On that day I decided to follow Jesus.

Lord, I thank you for making Yourself known to me. I ask You to reveal Yourself to those who are still blind.

Karen Boyd is a small group leader at ACTS and serves on the board of the Pennsylvania Homeschoolers Accreditation Agency.

Joy in His Presence

"You will show me the path of life; in Your presence is fullness of joy; at Your right hand are pleasures forevermore." *Psalms 16:11*

When I was twelve years of age, I attended a two-week Christian camp for boys in Ontario, Canada. The ministry of the camp had a profound impact upon my life. As a result of that ministry I yielded my life to the lordship of Jesus Christ.

Two years later I had the privilege of attending that camp again. Only this time, being a little older and somewhat preoccupied with mischief, I caused numerous problems with the various pranks in which I was involved. The leaders of the camp could not believe that I was the same boy who had attended two years before. They presumed that I was getting nothing out of the ministry and they were considering sending me home. Thankfully they did not send me home even though they presumed that I was learning nothing.

Actually I did receive something. Each day they had studied Psalms 16:11. That text impacted my life so that I later chose it as my life verse.

That verse assured me that God would indeed direct my path through life. However, the text also promised that "in His presence is fullness of joy." That is, not only in His presence in heaven but in living in His presence here and now.

Finally, that text assured me that at His right hand there are pleasures forevermore. So I thank God for this text that so impacted my life even though at that time at camp I did not appear to be listening to all that was being taught.

Gracious Lord, I thank you that You so wonderfully direct our steps and bestow upon us the blessing of Your presence. Thank You also for the glorious certainty of enjoying Your presence forever. In Your precious Name, Amen.

Rev. Dr. Eric G. Crichton is pastor emeritus of Calvary Church, Lancaster.

June

Through the Waters

"When you pass through the waters, I will be with you." *Isaiah 43:2*

As a student teacher at Millersville State, I was driving to my off-campus residence one night. The rain was steady and the night very dark. Lights from oncoming traffic momentarily blocked my vision so I slowed down. Suddenly, a pedestrian stepped out into my traffic lane to avoid a puddle of water. Jamming on the brakes did not avert the thump, the flailing body on the windshield, nor the broken body on the watery pavement. In that moment the word *horrible* reverberated through my entire being. Kneeling by the crumpled body, I cried out a primal scream, "Help!" Neighbors did. The ambulance crew and policeman performed their services. The policeman showed me one unbroken item from the dark overcoat of the man walking "with the traffic"—a partially consumed bottle of whiskey.

God worked through many people to show me He was with me. The pastor from whom I rented a room listened empathetically. My father was steady and reassuring over the telephone. The next morning my supervising teacher made a place for me to explain the headlines and my feelings to our students, and the principal offered to listen when I needed to talk. Neighbors called the police with helpful information. A fellow student and a faculty member voluntarily called the police to speak as character witnesses for me. A father whose family was my "home away from home" accompanied me to the viewing while the deceased's family were understanding and forgiving.

When I felt fragile, the prayers of many strengthened me. A few days later I was exonerated of responsibility for the accident. God was with me through the support of many others.

Father, thank you for the way You show You are with us in tragedy and trial. Move through me to help others in difficult situations.

Keith Yoder is founder of Teaching The Word Ministries, and serves on the Regional Council of the Regional Church of Lancaster County.

Art by Amy Mishler, grade 6, Roherstown Elementary School
Jannah Martin, grade 2, Clay Elementary School

June 2

Green Things Are Growing

"...We will in all things grow up into Him who is the Head, that is, Christ." *Ephesians 4:15*

Sure, I'll do it." I happily agreed to share at a Prayer Summit where 50 leaders of pro-life ministries from across the nation would gather for three days to seek the Lord through worship and prayer. I thought I was agreeing to share what God's taught me about leading a ministry from a posture of worship and prayer. I'd taught on it before, so my comfort level was high.

As it turned out, upon arriving at the Prayer Summit, I learned that I would also be part of a four-person facilitation team whose job was to tune into the Lord throughout the Summit to sense how He wanted the three days to flow.

Yikes. This was now outside my comfort zone and beyond my experience. To top it off, I viewed the three other team members as spiritual giants with big ears that readily heard the Lord's voice.

The weekend went well, thanks to the Lord's leadership and how easily the four of us worked together. But it was not without its moments of awkwardness and painful stretching for me.

Afterwards, I lamented to my support group friends, "I felt so green!"

One wise friend responded to me simply, "Green things are growing."

And I thought to myself, "She's absolutely right. I'd rather be green and growing than brown and stagnant." I'm so glad I stepped into that new area of spiritual leadership, and I've remembered my friend's admonition when other challenging assignments have come my way.

Lord, I'll say "yes" to any assignment You have for me, whether I'm experienced or new to it. The important thing isn't my expertise, but my obedience. I can count on You to show up and do the work through me.

Lisa Hosler serves as president of Susquehanna Valley Pregnancy Services and is a member of the council of the Regional Church of Lancaster County.

God Stories

Persevering Leadership

Pray for Lancaster County

"'...Naked I came from my mother's womb, and naked I will depart. The Lord gave and the Lord has taken away; may the name of the Lord be praised.' In all this, Job did not sin by charging God with wrongdoing." *Job 1:21–22*

Job was a man of integrity, great wealth, and prestige. He feared God and was blameless before Him. Yet Job suffered devastation beyond normal human endurance. He lost absolutely everything, but he hung on to the one thing he could—his relationship with his God. In the midst of grief and overwhelming discouragement, he still persevered by praising the name of the Lord.

In the end, as a reward for his enduring perseverance, God restored to him twice as much as he had before. Let's walk the path regardless of the cost, knowing that God's heart is for those who will not give up in the face of opposition.

Pray for Lancaster County is our weekly prayer focus for the individuals, families, churches and communities of our region. Please carry this emphasis in your heart and your prayers throughout the week.

Hope Realized

"Then I saw a great white throne and Him who was seated upon it." *Revelation 20:11*

A nxiety stirred within me as I walked to the door. Even the most Godly servants detest receiving the news he had received—acute leukemia. But Dick was alert, pleasant, and ready for a pastoral visit. His demeanor quickly settled my anxiousness.

Dick shared with me his trip to Philadelphia for a second opinion. The doctor had gone over his records thoroughly, and then said to him, "Dick, I agree with everything your doctors have done and with their diagnosis. You do have acute leukemia and it will take your life. It is time now for you to decide what your next step will be."

Dick said, "I know what my next step will be: my next step will be into the presence of the Lord." As he said them, the words invigorated his spirit, and as he relayed them to me he glistened with the holy radiance of one who has been in the presence of the Lord.

He told his story to everyone. It was his eternal hope realized through God-given assurance. A few weeks later he awoke smothering. He called for help, but things were changing rapidly. Suddenly, Dick looked knowingly into the right corner of the room, then slowly his eyes moved from the right corner to the left. He smiled broadly, closed his eyes and died.

At the funeral, I asked, "Wouldn't you like to know what Dick saw? Did God send an angel to receive his own, or did Jesus, himself, come to take Dick home to heaven?"

The truth is we will never know what Dick saw, but we can know as surely as Dick knew that we will see the Lord. After all, it is His promise to each and every believer.

Dear Lord, let me live today as if it were my last day. May I be ready at every moment to enter Your glorious presence.

B. W. Hambrick has served as senior pastor of Ephrata Church of the Nazarene for nineteen years.

Trusting His Plan

"...plans to prosper you not to harm you...." *Jeremiah 29:11*

This happened to me about thirty years ago but continues to impact my life and the lives of others even today. At the age of forty-two, I had a broken marriage, and there was a separation. Three years later my husband acquired a divorce. In the first years of the separation I was faced with many decisions. How would I support an eight year-old son and myself? Where would we live? Through many ways the Lord used people in my family to make it possible for me to buy the property. My son and I lived there through his growing up years.

About twenty years later I heard God say, "Enjoy this property setting because you won't be living here much longer." In the next two years I had a stirring inside to move to Lancaster city. The church I attended, as well as participation in Volunteers In Probation and Parole at the Lancaster County prison, took me to the city many times a week. I decided to take a step and contacted a realtor.

I had no money to buy a house without selling the one where I was living. Keith, my son, had married by now, and he and Jodie had a son and no money to buy a house either. A very helpful friend of mine arranged for a loan for me from some private individuals. Keith and Jodie rented the property I owned. In this way I could afford to pay a mortgage.

I had lived in the country all my life. How would I like city living?

Well, even for some weeks before I moved I felt like I was going home whenever I drove to Lancaster. I really enjoy city life. This house has been a blessing to me. It has also been used by the Lord to be a place where three individuals have been able to get a start into the next phase of their lives.

Lord, all I can say is "thank you." You are faithful!

Kathleen Hollinger is a mother, grandmother, great-grandmother. She serves as a prayer ministry leader for ACTS Covenant Fellowship.

Rivers In The Desert

"Do not call to mind the former things, or ponder things of the past. Behold, I will do something new, now it will spring forth; will you not be aware of it? I will even make a roadway in the wilderness, rivers in the desert." *Isaiah 43:18–19 (New American Standard Bible)*

It was a most amazing sight. My guide took me to a high point overlooking a large river that cut right through the desert. With my back to the river, all I could see was sun-baked, barren land dotted with scrub brushes. But as I turned toward the river everything became green and lush. There was a clear line where the desert stopped and fresh vegetation began.

I was immediately reminded of the scripture where Isaiah prophesied about rivers in the desert. There, right before my eyes, was an example of God's message to His people. (Do not be discouraged by the hardships you have encountered. I am going to do something new, something fresh. Where there has been barrenness, I am going to bring forth life and fruitfulness.)

Perhaps you feel like you have been going through a spiritual wilderness. Or maybe you are discouraged by the condition of the world around you. Well, the good news is that God still desires to work in and through His people today! Ask Him to refresh you and use you to touch the lives of those around you.

Dear God, thank you for the promises in Your Word, promises to give us a future and a hope. Thank you for the way You are constantly at work in our lives, leading and guiding us even through times of hardship. Please touch me afresh and anew with Your presence today. Make me an instrument of Your transforming power to those around me. Flow through me as a river in the desert to bring Your life to a lost and dying world.

Mark Van Scyoc serves as an elder and mission director at DOVE Christian Fellowship Westgate, in Ephrata.

His Plan For Us

"For we are God's masterpiece. He has created us anew in Christ Jesus, so that we can do the good things he planned for us long ago." *Ephesians 2:10 (New Living Translation)*

Recently I had the opportunity to be involved in setting up a non-profit foundation. In the process I decided to research other foundations and was inspired by one named The W.K. Kellogg Foundation. The founder W.K. Kellogg is best known as the inventor of corn flakes and founder of the cereal giant. In the early 1900s while other founders of big industry were building summer cottages with 40 car garages, he felt his money was better used in helping people help themselves. In 1934 he set up a foundation that to this day donates millions a year to helping people in need all over the world.

This is a man who "had it all," but chose to use his wealth to help others. He wanted to do good and did so by channeling money to those in need. So what does God want us to do? The Bible tells us in Ephesians 2:10 that He wants us to do good. If fact, we are His masterpiece and he created us anew in Jesus so we can do good things. He even planned good things for us to do long ago.

Even though God calls us to do many different things in life, each of us is motivated differently. For me, I love to give. It gives me energy and excitement. For some, it's serving, or teaching—or it could be many other things. We may not have the resources in the large way that Mr. Kellogg did, but God wants us to bless people by doing good the way He called us.

Lord, show me today what good You would have me to do to help build Your kingdom.

Jerry Weaver is executive vice president and co-owner of Quality Custom Cabinetry, Inc.

The Gift of Forgiveness

"Do not judge, or you too will be judged." *Matthew 7:1*

I was 54 years old and should not have had to be dealing with this inner pain. My wife Sandy and I found ourselves talking and praying but somehow making no apparent headway. I was sure that it must be Sandy's stuff that was continually coming up between us that was causing all this turmoil. She kept saying we should get some help, and with reluctance and a hard heart I finally said, "Okay, I'll go along to a counselor!" Somehow, from the first visit with our counselor and for many weeks to come, the focus was on me! Time after time it became evident I had a lot of anger pushed deep down inside me, and it was stored up against my dad. Finally, I was able to let it go. I remember praying and asking Jesus, if it was at all possible to let my dad know that I forgave him and no longer was holding him responsible for all that I had blamed him for. My dad had passed away and so I had no way of telling him myself.

That very week I received an e-mail from my son who was on deployment in the Persian Golf. In a nutshell, he said, "Dear Dad, I have been doing a lot of thinking and soul searching while we are doing circles around this pond, and I want to tell you I have been angry with you over some stuff. I have been thinking about it and I want you to know that I forgive you and no longer will hold any of that stuff against you." Now, that's how I remember it. My son may have said it a bit differently, but the truth that God spoke into my heart has changed my life. I believe forgiving my father somehow opened a way for my son to forgive me.

Father God, thank you for showing me this truth, it has set me and my son free!

John Weaver does building maintenance for a local nursing home, and serves as a prayer counselor for Breath of Life.

June 9

You Have Not Because You Ask Not

"If any of you lacks wisdom, he should ask God...." *James 1:5*

A few years back I was blessed to serve on staff at a large church. One of my early opportunities was as the head of maintenance. God has blessed me with a fair amount of common sense, but there are a lot of areas in which I am technically challenged. I remember one Friday afternoon a call came in that the air conditioning in the kitchen had quit, and it was to be used pretty heavily that weekend. My helper, who could have easily solved the problem, was off on a long weekend, so there was no one to whom I could pass the buck. My first thought was to call a company to come repair it, but the Holy Spirit said, "You can do it."

So up to the roof I went, and it wasn't long before I was soaking wet. Your guess: nerves or heat? As I took the unit apart I prayed, "Lord you promised to help us do what you've called us to do. A lot of people will suffer or be blessed in the outcome of this task. Please give me the wisdom I lack." After about 10 minutes of poking, picking and praying, my hand came to rest on a condenser and the Holy Spirit said, "That's it." I took it out, went to the supply house, bought a new one and replaced it.

After I turned the power back on, I went to the thermostat and thanked God for the wisdom of His Word. I threw the switch, the air got cooler and people got blessed, but God got the glory. That incident and several others gave me the faith and courage to believe God in spite of my circumstances. Today I pastor a church, not because I want to, but because God said to. "With God all things are possible!"

Dear Lord, thank you for giving us the wisdom to make a difference.

Leo Neff pastors Lighthouse Community Church in Elizabethtown.

United Leadership

Pray for Lancaster County

"As soon as they were freed, Peter and John found the other believers and told them what the leading priests and elders had said. Then all the believers were united as they lifted their voices in prayer.... After this prayer, the building where they were meeting shook, and they were all filled with the Holy Spirit. And they preached God's message with boldness." *Acts 4:23–24; 31 (New Living Translation)*

P eter, John, and the believers were faced with strong opposition and persecution against any further spread of the gospel. They had been threatened that they were no longer to speak of Jesus. But instead of retreating in fear, they came together and prayed in unity and appealed to God for greater courage and boldness. God answered their unified prayer in such a powerful way that it shook the building.

There was no question that God was commissioning them to go forth under His power and blessing. If transformation is to overtake entire communities, a unified voice among leadership will shake the foundations of society!

Pray for Lancaster County is our weekly prayer focus for the individuals, families, churches and communities of our region. Please carry this emphasis in your heart and your prayers throughout the week.

Does Sin Pay? Never!

"He who conceals his sins does not prosper, but whoever confesses and renounces them finds mercy." *Proverbs 28:13*

Years ago while serving as a pastor in another state, I faced a "God-sized" challenge. Our beloved treasurer was discovered to be taking money from the church. An audit revealed that over the period of a year the amount stolen was over $10,000. As a new pastor, I called my veteran pastor father to ask him what I should do. His fatherly advice was, "I don't know since I've never faced that situation before."

Together with the elders we sought wisdom and guidance from God. The man was confronted with his sin. He acknowledged his wrong and revealed his devious plan of concealing it. His family was devastated and embarrassed; his health was damaged, his reputation was ruined, and he certainly did not prosper.

But God's grace intervened because he renounced his sin, confessed it publicly to the congregation, and repaid every penny over a period of years. Mercy was shown to him by a loving and forgiving heavenly Father. His family was restored, his health returned, his congregation was forgiving, and God was glorified.

God taught me through a very painful time the devastating ravages of sin and His abundant grace when it is confessed and renounced. Does sin pay? Never!

Father, search me today and reveal any hypocrisy, fraudulence, and sin so that I might confess and renounce them and live in the light of Your abundant mercy. Amen!

David D. Allen is associate pastor of Calvary Church, Lancaster.

June 12

Amazing Love

"But while he was still a long way off, his father saw him and was filled with compassion for him; he ran to his son, threw his arms around him and kissed him." *Luke 15:20*

On January 2, 2004, my life was changed forever. On that day my son, Kaiden Patrick Braught, was born. On that day I became a father for the first time. I can't begin to tell you all the things that have changed since that day. My wife and I went from being DINKS (Double Income, No Kids) to parents with about one and a quarter salaries. We don't go out as much. We also have seen the hand of God when it comes to finances. But I can tell you that one of the greatest things that came from becoming a father is seeing scripture in a whole new light. I began to see the story of the prodigal son in a different way. I used to see it only from the perspective of the prodigal son. But now I also see it from the perspective of the father.

I have begun to see God's love for me by looking at the love that I have for my son. I am amazed that God would allow His one and only Son to become human, knowing that His creation would beat, abuse, mock and kill Him. There is just no way that I would give up my son for anyone. It blows my mind to realize just how much God the Father loves each and every one of us, whether we are following Him or even when we have gone our own way, like the prodigal son. How amazing to know that God continues to look for us, and when we return to Him, He is filled with love, embracing and forgiving us.

Father, I can't begin to thank You enough for the amazing love that You have for me.

Ryan Braught is the pastor of Youth Ministries and Nurture at Hempfield Church of the Brethren.

Shine On!

"You are the salt of the earth...you are the light of the world. A city on a hill cannot be hidden...Let your light shine before men, that they may see your good deeds and praise your Father in heaven." *Matthew 5:13–16*

We are God's ambassadors here on this earth. He desires that the people we rub shoulders with would experience His love through us. I have been challenged by these verses on two different occasions. Each time it was at large Christian gatherings. One time was at a Christian concert and the other was a regional worship time. Hundreds of people were worshiping God with great passion and enthusiasm. As I watched those crowds of people worshiping, I could not help but wonder how our communities would be different if every person took that same passion and enthusiasm for the Lord outside the four walls of those auditoriums. The church has the good news that our world is looking for. Each of us carries the responsibility for sharing it with others. We must take it outside the walls of our churches to those who do not come to us. We must be lights that burn brightly in our workplaces, neighborhoods, and schools.

Dear Lord, help me to be a city on a hill that cannot be hidden. Give me the courage to passionately share You with others so that they will experience You when they meet me. Help me to affect my sphere of influence with Your love. Amen.

Kevin Horning is senior pastor of New Life Fellowship in Ephrata.

Flag Day

"The Lord your God will take His curses and turn them against
your enemies—against those who hate you and persecute you.
The Lord your God will prosper everything you do and give you
many children and much cattle and wonderful crops; for the Lord
will again rejoice over you as He did over your fathers."
Deuteronomy 30:7,9

While serving on a missions team, we were with a group of
Brazilian youth. I asked them if they had a feeling of pride
when they saw their Brazilian flag. Their answer was a resounding "Yes!" I encouraged them in their answer and reminded them
that it is a good thing to have a sense of pride for their flag and country.

I have often thought back to this time and have come to realize it is
good to have an element of respect and honor for your flag. We have
been told that we are citizens of heaven, not of this world, and we
understand this is true. But Paul boasted of his citizenship of Rome.
We are also citizens of our own countries.

As we see our flag, let's appreciate the brave young people who
have fought for our freedom as they followed their country's colors
onto the battlefield. Let's pray for our nation to see righteousness and
godly character fill the land.

*Father, touch our families, our churches and our government to cause
our generation and future generations to follow You.*

LaMarr Sensenig with his wife, Naomi, serve as spiritual parents and
intercessors.

God Stories

Desperate for God

"Whether you turn to the right or to the left, your ears will hear a voice behind you saying, 'This is the way, walk in it.'" *Isaiah 30:21*

I have always prided myself in taking control of my life, believing that hard work will reap a great reward. Having a plan and methodically executing that plan always seemed like the sensible and proper approach to almost every situation in life, especially in operating a business. However, if we wish to follow the leading of the Holy Spirit, we must relinquish control to God. I recently read the book *Fresh Wind, Fresh Fire* by Jim Cymbala, noting the following quote, "I discovered an astonishing truth: God is attracted to weakness. He can't resist those who humbly and honestly admit how desperately they need Him."

Recently I delivered the Sunday message at my church. I felt inadequate and desperate for a word from the Lord. However, the word that the Lord gave me was a controversial one. At one point, I dismissed the entire subject as too difficult for me to deliver. But because it was God's word, I would deliver it no matter how inadequate I felt. I knew I had heard that "voice behind me" telling me "this is the way, walk in it." As I desperately called out to God to grant the words to say, God moved and many responded to the word of the Lord, receiving breakthroughs and experiencing God in a new way.

As we follow the leading of the Holy Spirit, God often puts us in situations that we can't possibly handle, and when we reach the end of ourselves, we will hear that voice behind us telling us to turn to the right or the left.

God, grant me the faith and courage to follow Your path for my life, and to not rely on my own strength and understanding. Amen.

Deryl Hurst is the broker and an owner of Realty 1 and serves as an elder at DOVE Christian Fellowship Westgate, in Ephrata.

Could Revival Start in Prison?

"For the earth will be filled with the knowledge of the glory of the Lord, as the waters cover the sea." *Habakkuk 2:14*

As I move in various circles of churches and Christian leaders, I often hear references to and anticipation of a coming revival. I have heard many mission stories from China, Peru and Ethiopia: stories of persons coming to faith because of volunteers giving time in Florida to help those with storm damage; reports of renewed cooperation of church leaders in our area as they seek God; pastors in several towns praying together weekly and seeing amazing results. It is exciting to realize that God is at work in many different parts of the world. The Habakkuk promise seems to be coming true.

Then one day, as I was inside Lancaster County Prison doing some reviews with our chaplain staff, I heard more stories: an inmate that experienced physical healing, a prison Bible study class which is receiving answers to their prayers, Alpha course teachers bringing prayer requests from the "outside" for the inmates to pray about, and a chaplain leading a correctional officer to the Lord.

My heart was stirred. Could revival start in prison? I believe it has already. Will God do a cleansing and renewing work among very needy persons who are incarcerated? I know He is doing that right now. Praise God, His glory is spreading, inside and outside the walls, just as the waters cover the sea.

Dear God, may Your name and glory keep spreading to all parts of our needy world. Bless our brothers and sisters who are in prison today. May Your renewal be at work in their lives. And may each of us, no matter where we live and serve, be faithful in sharing Your love to those around us.

Nelson W. Martin is director of support for Prison Ministries and overseer of the Lititz District of Mennonite churches that are part of Lancaster Mennonite Conference.

Humble Leadership

Pray for Lancaster County

"Now Stephen, a man full of God's grace and power, did great wonders and miraculous signs among the people. Opposition arose, however, from members of the Synagogue of the Freedmen…These men began to argue with Stephen, but they could not stand up against his wisdom or the Spirit by whom he spoke." *Acts 6:8–10*

Stephen was not picked for one of the upfront, prestigious leadership jobs. He was chosen to help with the daily distribution of the food—something that was distracting the other apostles from the preaching and teaching of the Word of God. But yet in Stephen's humility to serve where there was a need, God used him as a powerful display of His glory.

When an argument in the synagogue arose, God so filled Stephen with His Spirit that no one could stand up against him. In fact, scripture says later that everyone in the council ended up just staring at Stephen because his face became as bright as an angel's. People no longer saw Stephen; they saw the very presence of God in him! This is truly humble servant leadership that glorifies God alone.

Pray for Lancaster County is our weekly prayer focus for the individuals, families, churches and communities of our region. Please carry this emphasis in your heart and your prayers throughout the week.

A Father's Care

"He tends His flock like a Shepherd: He gathers the lambs in His arms and carries them close to His heart...." *Isaiah 40:11*

I have a special memory when I think about Father's Day. I was seventh in a family of eleven, so there was not a lot of time for personal attention given to each one. However, I don't remember ever feeling like I was one of many and I didn't count. It made for lots of give and take for all of us.

I especially liked sitting on our couch behind the space heater in the evening. It was so nice and warm there, and soon I would be asleep. When I would wake up in the morning, I would be in my bed, and most times didn't remember how I had gotten there! Papa had carried me to bed while I was sleeping, which became a regular occurrence, though I never heard him complain about it. There were times I would waken to feel him tenderly lifting me in his big arms, carry me and lay me down in my bed. It surrounded me with peace and with such a sense of well-being that I was soon sleeping soundly again.

I wonder if I have learned to let God do for me what Papa did. God would like to "carry me to bed" while resting in His care and provision instead of seeing me think so much or work so hard to figure things out! He would like me to rest, to be at peace and trust in Him while He does the work.

Heavenly Father, I would like to thank You on this Father's Day for giving Your very best for me. Though Your love reaches to all Your creation, yet that love is real for each one of us. You are my Good Shepherd. Gather me in Your arms and carry me close to Your heart again today, in Jesus' name, Amen.

Naomi Sensenig with her husband, LaMarr, serve as spiritual parents and intercessors.

The Father's Validation

"Jesus answered, 'I am the way and the truth and the life. No one comes to the Father except through me...' Philip said, 'Lord, show us the Father and that will be enough for us.'" *John 14:6–8*

Growing up without being validated by my biological father created an unyielding desire to receive affirmation from some masculine figure. My grandfather provided an oasis for the first seven years of my life; however, that ended when my mother moved to Chicago, Illinois. The separation from my grandfather caused my young world to be filled with unanswerable questions.

During my adolescent years I would do anything just to be acknowledged. The pursuit of significance led me to join the military hoping to find validation. However, due to the lack of self-esteem I was drawn into a negative life-style of blatant sin. After being discharged from the military, I was submerged in substance abuse. Returning home and trying to find significance only led to a deep sense of hopelessness and shame derived by my addictive life-style.

I began to think perhaps I was born to be a drug addict. At this time in my life, a young man shared the story of God the Father's love expressed in Jesus Christ. Shortly after being exposed to the gospel, I surrendered my life to Jesus Christ, and a few weeks later I experienced an in-filling of the Holy Spirit. During this process of transformation, all that I did not receive from my earthly father was given to me by my heavenly Father. I have significance because I know who I am and why I exist. Words cannot express the joy that is in my life. John 14, verses 6 and 8, are key scriptures in understanding the way to the Father's validation.

Spirit of God, pour out the love of the Father in the lives of those individuals that like myself needed to be validated.

Rev. Emanuel J. Oliver is urban ministry director of Light of Hope Community Service Organization.

From Wrestling to Overcoming

"Your name will no longer be Jacob, but Israel, because you have struggled with God and with men and have overcome."
Genesis 32:28

Following a decade of steady growth, the congregation where I served my first pastorate descended into brutal conflict. Internal self-doubts and external attack became familiar and unwelcome companions. Those months were a dark night of the soul. Private prayers were desperate cries of anguish, anger and appeals. Head and heart raged. Psalms, read aloud in my prayer closet, became expressions I never before dared deposit at God's throne.

Then God broke through dramatically, but not with personal justifications for which I yearned. Would I embrace breaking as a potential tool in His hands shaping me into greater usefulness? Would I, by faith, declare the resurrection an adequate foundation upon which to stand, demanding no further evidence of His grace? Would I shift my focus from wrestling with man to wrestling with Him? Like Jacob, would I not let go until He granted the blessing of a new name?

I wish I could say I answered "Yes" easily. That would be ego building, but not reality. And the biblical story is one of honest reality. What I can say is that God's grace faithfully takes the mustard seeds of "Yes" that we declare—and grows them! Grows them into realities that deepen joy and infuse us with expanded kingdom impact!

These truths are indeed good news. For who of us never wrestle through dark nights of the soul? And who of us don't recognize in the struggle that deliverance into a new day is our only hope?

Gracious God, when life is hard, keep my hands in Your hands as I wrestle with faith, until I let You dance me into a new day of freedom.

Bob Petersheim is pastor and director of the LEAD Ministries arm of Teaching the Word Ministries. He is called to LEAD (Lead, Empower, And Disciple) leaders into kingdom freedom.

Surprise Supply

"And my God will meet all your needs according to his glorious riches in Christ Jesus." *Philippians 4:19*

I remember it just like it was yesterday, even though it was over six years ago. Parents of students at my high school were leading a retreat called "The Path of Purity," during which they would teach biblical life-style principles of purity.

When I heard about it, I wanted to go. I am not exactly sure what drew me (well, maybe I do), but it was on my heart. However, the retreat cost $100. That was $100 neither my parents nor I had to fund the retreat, so I released the desire. Apparently God didn't want me to go.

I was wrong. The very last day that the money was being accepted, someone from the school office called me in and handed me a note saying that God had directed them to pay my way to the retreat. There was no name at the bottom. I cannot describe my surprise and gratitude. God had made a way where there seemed to be no way.

Not only was I now able to go on the retreat, but I was also strengthened in my belief of God moving on our behalf. I had told very few people of my desire to go and didn't even pray about it very fervently. I do not know to this day who provided the money. (Well, maybe I do—the heavenly Father who knows what I need and when I need it.) Nothing is too hard for Him.

Jesus, thank you for Your provision in miraculous ways. So many things are out of our hands, yet You know them intimately. You know each moment of the day before we wake up. Help us rely on Your foresight and power. We rest in Your direction upon our lives. Amen.

Mandi Wissler is a graduate of Lancaster Bible College, currently seeking God's next steps—possibly in performing at a local theater and living a life-style of befriending, mentoring and discipling young women.

Miracle Babies

"...their sorrow was turned into joy and their mourning into a day of celebration." *Esther 9:22*

W
e had spent three years trying to have children—going through treatment for both of us—to no avail. The doctor told us, "It will be nearly impossible for you to get pregnant spontaneously" (without invitro fertilization). At that point, we put it in the Lord's hands and stopped all treatment. We knew that our God is a God of wonders and miracles and that He could very easily give us children.

At that point, we started praying about adoption. We felt a really strong peace about it, and in just a matter of a week, we were told of a newborn baby girl in an orphanage in another city in Brazil. We went to see her when she was 2 days old and immediately started the adoption process.

A month later, in September of 2004, at a crusade in our city of Fortaleza, we went to help translate. We had a strong feeling that we should ask for prayer for ourselves in regards to the infertility that we were facing. On the last night of the crusade, just as everyone was being rushed out of the building, we pulled one of the pastors aside and asked him to pray for us. He prayed, and that very next month I got pregnant!

We continued the adoption process and finally were able to bring Giselle home on April 4, 2005. Larissa was born on July 18, making our two daughters just 11 months apart. One year ago we were facing infertility, but God has turned our sorrow into joy, and increased our family rapidly! Both our daughters are miracle babies.

Jesus, You always hear our cries. Thank you for hearing and answering prayer.

Chris and Chad Miller are DCFI missionaries in Fortaleza, Brazil. They are members of DOVE Christian Fellowship Westgate, in Ephrata.

Free From Fear

"I cried out to the Lord in my suffering, and He heard me. He set me free from all my fears." *Psalms 34:6 (New Living Translation)*

My husband Dave and I were eagerly anticipating our July 2005 summer vacation to a remote part of Northern California. We were each other's favorite person to spend time with, and a week before we flew to California, Dave smiled and said, "We grow closer when we're on vacation, right?" I responded, "Yup, because we love being together!"

For four days in California we wandered deserted beaches, explored coves, watched playful sea lions and dolphins, and gazed up at towering redwoods. We napped, grilled on our deck, and played rummy. We each said that it was our best vacation ever.

On the fifth day we took a deep sea fishing trip. Dave quickly caught salmon and a huge lingcod, but we returned to the dock early because of his severe seasickness. We had no idea that less than two hours later Dave would see Jesus face to face and I would face my worst fear. At the age of 43, Dave suffered a heart attack and died.

I am walking through the most horrible situation I could imagine—being without my husband and best friend. Yet Jesus is so near. And I've realized that when you live through the thing you feared most, you have nothing else to be afraid of. You become fearless, except for a holy reverential fear of a beautiful, loving, sovereign God who is worthy of all trust and praise.

Father, thank you that I don't have to fear what might happen today or tomorrow. Make my heart fear and worship You only, and help me understand that everything You do is worthy of my trust (Psalms 33:4).

Kati French is a mother and grandmother, and serves as executive director at Susquehanna Valley Pregnancy Services.

Will God Really Hear and Answer?

"...if my people, who are called by my name, will humble themselves and pray and seek my face and turn from their wicked ways, then will I hear from heaven and will forgive their sin and will heal their land."
2 Chronicles 7:14

There are obstacles that can keep us from walking confidently on the path of revival. One of the obstacles is our theological misperception about who God is and how He works. Some believe that transforming revival is a mysterious process only known in the sovereignty of God. In this belief system, there is nothing we can humanly do to affect the hand of God. This fails to account for the very heart of 2 Chronicles 7:14. The Lord clearly states that there is a part for us to play in the process. *If my people will...then will I....* If we meet the requirements, God will be faithful to fulfill His part—to forgive and heal. God *wants* to heal our land. Are you willing to fulfill your role in revival and transformation?

Pray for Lancaster County is our weekly prayer focus for the individuals, families, churches and communities of our region. Please carry this emphasis in your heart and your prayers throughout the week.

June 25

Encourage One Another Today

"But encourage one another daily, as long as it is called Today, so that none of you may be hardened by sin's deceitfulness."
Hebrews 3:13

This summer we went to Albania on a short-term missions trip. The father of a particular family the missionary team in Goricaj had related to had died unexpectedly at age 47. He left behind his wife and two children, who were faced with the daily task of farming their few acres and operating their small store and club. We intended to visit their home, but were unsure how this could work out or even if it would be appropriate for us to visit.

Yvonne and I planned a prayer walk through the village. While walking and praying we sensed a spirit of heaviness over the village. Along the way, we noticed a well-traveled path that led to a grave with no stone but which was colorfully decorated. We were shocked to realize that God had led us to the grave of the man who had died 50 days ago. We spent time praying for the visit we would hopefully have with his wife.

The next day the Lord opened up a way for us to visit this dear widow who was obviously still in mourning. The missionary that accompanied us served as our translator. The Holy Spirit became the encourager as our hearts were knit together through our identifying with her loss. I sensed the Lord telling her that when she was ready to operate the store and club again that He would want it to be a lifegiving place. We prayed that the Lord would become her husband and that she would receive the goodness and mercy of the Lord all the days of her life.

Dear Father, I pray that this Today would mark the beginning of many Todays for the body of Christ to encourage one another. In the name of Jesus, Amen.

Joe Garber is pastor of Byerland Mennonite Church, Willow Street, and Western Lancaster County Prayer Group.

June 26

He Speaks to Us Beyond Words

"The heavens tell of the glory of God. The skies display His marvelous craftsmanship. Day after day they continue to speak; night after night they make Him known. They speak without a sound or a word; their voice is silent in the skies; yet their message has gone out to all the earth, and their words to all the worlds." *Psalms 19:1–4 (New Living Translation)*

I thoroughly enjoy the full moon, so much so that I keep a lunar cycle schedule in my date book. Each month I eagerly await its arrival. When it appears, I use it as an opportunity to gaze upon it as well as take notice of how much light it sheds upon my surroundings. Often times if we are together, Duane and I will stop what we are doing, embrace and take several moments to look at a full moon. Each time we do, it rekindles our amazement of God's power, wonder and beauty: He is reflected there. Who else could create such an incredibly phenomenal and awe-inspiring masterpiece?

When mankind considers the complexity and vastness of the heavens, the result is a "knowing" deep within that there is a sovereign God who is making Himself and His ways known in real and intimate ways. Purposeful gazing, meditation and reflection upon the moon consequently result in praise and adoration of God.

Lord, thank you for the tangible ways in which You are making Yourself known. Reminders of You and Your love are everywhere present—if only we would take the time to stop, look and listen in silence.

Reyna Britton, RN, is the director of accreditation and quality standards for Lancaster General Hospital and is the wife of Duane Britton, senior pastor of DOVE Christian Fellowship Westgate Celebration.

All Things

"I can do all things through Christ who strengthens me."
Philippians 4:13 (New King James Version)

I am reminded of God's faithfulness when I quote this familiar verse. Recently, our family was planning to go on a mission trip to Brazil for two weeks. I must admit that I suffer from the "what if" syndrome. Thinking about traveling in a foreign country got the syndrome kicked up in full gear. What if I get sick? What if I can't sleep at night? Will my kids be okay? How will I be able to travel for 37 hours? I followed the leading of the Holy Spirit and my adventurous husband, and I agreed to go on the trip. After all, going on a mission trip is something that every committed Christian "should" experience in their lifetime, right?

Well, we went to Brazil and I had a marvelous, enriching and enlightening experience. We met precious people with whom we continue to correspond. Did I get sick, have trouble sleeping or struggle with the traveling? Yes. But God's grace covered every area and He gave me the strength and courage to continue even when I wasn't feeling on top of my game. The Lord was building my faith while He was boosting my strength. So now when I think of missions it isn't something I think I "should" be involved in, but something I desire to be involved in because I know that I can do all things through Him who strengthens me.

Lord, thank you for grace and strength that You give us each day. We don't know what each day holds, but we know that You will be right there with us giving us everything we need to accomplish what You are asking us to do.

Mim Hurst is a full-time mom and a part-time volunteer at various organizations, including women's ministry and counseling/mentoring.

God Opened the Door

"...Apart from me you can do nothing." *John 15:5*

I used to think that if I knew the will of God I would be able to do it. I was vice chairman of the Department of Psychiatry at Pennsylvania State University College of Medicine where I had worked for over 20 years. I was within sight of retiring with full benefits. Then I heard the voice of God, "I want you to leave your full time employment at Penn State." He confirmed the word in many ways.

I rejoiced that I had heard the word of God. But I was not able to leave. Every time I approached my chairman (who was my father in the profession of psychiatry) he would propose a new arrangement which seemed reasonable but which in the end kept me at my job. I did not want to displease my chairman; he had blessed me since my youth and I had led him to the Lord.

Time passed. I became desperate. I called together a group of brothers and pleaded, "Brothers, please pray for me. I am unable to do what I know God has called me to do. I am as powerless as the alcoholic to set myself free." The brothers laid hands on me and prayed for deliverance.

Two days later, I spoke with my chairman, saying, "I must leave. If you do not allow me to go it will be like having Jonah in the boat; it will be bad for you and for me." He was quiet for a long time and then said, "I'll let you go. But first let me retire and then you can resign." I rejoiced. This was God's doing!

Oh Lord, I need Your direction and I need Your strength and grace to do what You direct. Without You I can do nothing.

Enos Martin, bishop in New Testament Fellowship of Mennonite/ Anabaptist Churches, also provides psychiatric care in several local prisons.

June 29

Glorious Freedom

"...the glorious freedom of the children of God." *Romans 8:21*

The events of several years ago taught me afresh that God really knows who we are and earnestly desires that we walk in the freedom He purchased for us.

Thursday: A friend with whom I was meeting said he felt led to pray for me that the "walls" that were holding me in prison would be demolished. When he finished praying something began happening to me. Indeed, inside it felt like the walls were gone and I was free.

Friday: Circumstances occurred which tested the new freedom I was entering.

Saturday: I asked God to show me His favor by allowing me to find a very specific gift for my mom—a certain antique dish for which I had been searching for about 3 years. As I prayed, I felt led to go to a certain antique shop about 35 miles away. I drove to the store, walked in, walked directly to one section and found the exact dish!

Sunday: I met with a friend before church. He said he had been impressed by the Lord to tell me that I had been in bondage, like one in shackles. At this, he took my hands, wrapped a chain around them and secured the chain with a lock. He told me the chains symbolically represented the bondage I was in and the Lord wanted me released. He then took out a key and told me that it is the power of the cross that sets us free from the things that bind us.

During church, I gave a testimony of what had been happening in my life. When I finished, the guest speaker for the day stood up and said that while praying in the morning, he sensed that God had given him a verse for someone that day. "...I will free your prisoners...." (Zechariah 9:11). "That someone is you!" he said.

Lord, may we each know and reflect Your glorious freedom.

Brett R. Miller serves on the music team of New Covenant Christian Church.

My Every Need

"...Yet I have not seen the righteous forsaken nor his descendants begging bread." *Psalms 37:25*

In December 1991, my bank account had a balance of $9.47 of which $5.00 was for gas to get me to work that week. As I was preparing my son for bed, he shared with me his thoughts of all the toys he was hoping to receive for Christmas. I gently explained why we were going to have a dry Christmas that year. There was a moment of silence and then he said, "Mom, you don't have to get me anything for Christmas: you are my Christmas gift." We prayed, and I tucked him in bed. I cried myself to sleep that night.

The next morning at work I received a call from a dear friend. She asked if I was putting up a tree. I told her I was not planning on it. She went on to explain that her friends had purchased two trees and did not have anyone to give one to. She asked if I would take one of the trees "free of charge." I gladly accepted the offer and quickly made arrangements to have the tree picked up and delivered to my house.

The gentleman whom I asked to pick up the tree offered to purchase the ornaments and assist with decorating. His only request was that I would have my son in bed before the arrival of the tree. Knowing how much this meant to my son, he wanted him to be surprised to see the decorated tree in the morning. I agreed. The next morning my son woke up to a beautifully decorated tree. He ran to my room yelling, "Mommy, where did the tree come from"? I told him Jesus provided the tree. Not long after this blessing we were blessed with a Norfolk Island pine tree with large bills attached to it. Our Christmas that year went from dry to showers of blessings.

Dear God, thank you for supplying all my needs according to Your glory.

Noemi Willis is a member of New Covenant Christian Church.

*Photo by Kristin Palazzo, grade 9
Lancaster Mennonite High School*

July

Pray for Lancaster County

Give God No Rest!

"O Jerusalem, I have posted watchmen on your walls; they will pray to the Lord day and night for the fulfillment of his promises. Take no rest, all you who pray. Give the Lord no rest until he makes Jerusalem the object of praise throughout the earth." *Isaiah 62:6–7 (New Living Translation)*

God is most certainly sovereign in all His ways, yet with amazing mystery He invites us to call upon Him for the fulfillment of His promises. Our tendency is to try to figure out God's ways through our filter of rational thinking.

But why would we think we can even begin to understand the ways of an infinite God? Instead, we should simply take God at His Word. If He tells us to cry out to Him and give Him no rest until He answers, then let's do it!

Jesus taught the same principle in Luke 18 with the parable about persistence. The widow was persistent in crying out for justice, and the judge eventually relented and granted her heart cry. Although we may not understand how this principle intersects with the sovereignty of God, may that not hinder us from acting on His clear invitation to call upon Him to fulfill His promises. Do not give God rest until He establishes His presence in your community!

Pray for Lancaster County is our weekly prayer focus for the individuals, families, churches and communities of our region. Please carry this emphasis in your heart and your prayers throughout the week.

Into Deep Waters

"Save me, O God! For the waters have come up to my neck. I sink in deep mire, where there is no standing; I have come into deep waters, where the floods overflow me." *Psalms 69:1–2 (New King James Version)*

It was a lazy afternoon in the tenth summer of my life. Little did I realize that my future days rested on the happenings of the next few hours. We were vacationing at the beach and everything pertaining to beach living was included in our schedules. Sunshine was prevalent and the week was going great.

The adults were clamming about 50 feet from where I played close to shore. As time wore on, I desired to be where the clammers were. Desire turned to decision and I was on my way to clam.

Suddenly the ocean floor dropped away from my feet. I could not swim, so I went to the bottom three times. By the third time, I felt a calm come over me, even though I knew I could not reach the surface again. "Would I die at an early age?" I thought. "Things are very quiet down here."

Then Someone within me said, "Raise both your hands above your head." Believe me, I did!

Soon I was breathing delicious, delightful air. The man who rescued me remarked that because I raised my hands, he located me faster. God spoke those words to my spirit. I am eternally grateful to Him and my rescuer.

Lord God, not only have You saved me from the physical ocean, but you saved me from an ocean of sin and degradation. I'm grateful! Continue to lead and guide me in Your ways this day. Amen.

Sharon Eberly serves with her husband, Lester, at DOVE Christian Fellowship Westgate Celebration in Ephrata.

Sufficient Grace

"Since I know it is all for Christ's good, I am quite happy about 'the thorn,' and about insults and hardships, persecutions and difficulties; for when I am weak, then I am strong; the less I have, the more I depend on him." *2 Corinthians 12:10*

W hen I became the Fire Chief in May of 1998, I was treading through uncharted waters. Subsequently, I experienced many difficult situations, people and problems, along with the heavy responsibilities of providing fire protection for the city. Working in a political environment with a labor union was challenging. I often felt limited and not able to provide the best possible fire protection. I needed to hand over to God my feelings of being unsuccessful.

After September 11, 2001, I met the Lancaster City Police Chaplain, Lewis Nixon. When I told him that the fire bureau did not have a fire chaplain, he said, "Yes, you do." As a result of the tragic events occurring during 9/11, God brought Fire Chaplain Lewis Nixon into the fire bureau and into my life. God used him to reveal areas of weaknesses that I need to release and to encourage me to have a deeper relationship with the Master. As a result, I die to self on a daily basis and continue to seek His will for me.

No matter what situation you're in or limitations you may have, if you turn to God with all of your heart and allow Him to work through you, the Lord will be glorified. All we need to do is be faithful and pray.

Dear Lord, thank you for the many blessings that You have given to me. Please help me to remember that Your grace is sufficient for me and in my weakness Your power is made perfect. May I accept who I am, not dwelling on my inabilities and limitations, but embracing Jesus with all my heart and knowing that You are in complete control. Amen.

Jeffrey I. Pierce is the Lancaster City Fire Chief.

Liberty For All

"...Proclaim liberty throughout the land to all its inhabitants."
Leviticus 25:10

Recently, I was involved in a prayer event at the U.S. Supreme Court. This was a time of repentance and declaration for issues relating to the founding of our nation. I was accompanied by two First Nations couples (Iroquois leaders) and several African-American pastors. The Mohawk representative told the story of how the Iroquois chieftains had come to Philadelphia in 1775 in order to bless the newborn nation of America. One year later, the Declaration of Independence was written and spoke of divine providence while declaring that all men were created equal. The Liberty Bell, which was rung as a confirmation of this Declaration, is inscribed with Leviticus 25:10.

About a decade later, the Constitution was framed. No specific mention of "divine providence" was included nor were the Native or African Americans included in the liberties there outlined. The resulting outcome of a Civil war and continued oppression of First Nations people has been a blemish on our nation and in particular on the church.

As I pondered these conditions as well as the recent dialog concerning poverty and racial inequities that were made during Hurricane Katrina (note President Bush's speech on racism and poverty after the disaster), I asked myself if the liberty intended by our forefathers and by Jesus in Isaiah 61 is really flowing from the body of Christ (the church) into our nation. Pastor Willy, the Mohawk leader, responded to me when asked what it would look like if restitution for past wrongs were made from the church to First Nations peoples. He said, it would be our two peoples walking together into the harvest, each contributing its gifts and honoring the other's.

Lord, help us to begin again and consider our independence day in Christ and seek how You may link us as brothers: Native, African, Latino, Asian and European Americans in the harvest.

Robert Doe, M.D., is the Lancaster County Prison Physician.

Never Say Never

"So everywhere we go, we tell everyone about Christ. We warn them and teach them with all wisdom God has given us, for we want to present them to God, perfect in their relationship to Christ. I work very hard at this, as I depend on Christ's mighty power that works within me." *Colossians 1:28–29 (New Living Translation)*

I would never have remotely considered myself an evangelist or even a missionary. Never. I came to know the Lord out of a crisis. As a married woman, I was raped in my own home by a burglar. By the time I answered an altar call, I was a desperate woman. I was in therapy, on medication and suicidal. I had tried every way to recover, so why not try Jesus? I never dreamed where that short walk would take me.

Within months I was off medication, out of therapy and working in a Christian school. I thought this was funny because I said I would never work with kids. Later I came to Pennsylvania and my first paying job was for the Lancaster Pregnancy Center as its director. I knew how to teach, but I was afraid of public speaking. I soon got over that. I became the ministry's date rape speaker and started counseling abuse and rape victims.

One day after 9/11, a man called me and asked if I would go to Central America and speak in schools about abuse along with an evangelistic team. Including that initial trip, I have been on five trips and spoken to thousands. Whether I am in a foreign country, in a local school or in my counseling office, I want to reflect Christ, and if I am allowed, I will speak of Him wherever I go.

Father in heaven, may I never say "never" to You. Saying "yes" has been such an adventure, and I pray that this adventure has touched the lives of students and teachers for Your name's sake.

Connie Shea is director of counseling and education for Susquehanna Valley Pregnancy Services.

He Keeps My Tears

"You have kept count of my tossings; put my tears in Your bottle. Are they not in Your record?" *Psalms 56:8 (New Revised Standard Version)*

Five years ago, our family was in the midst of a move to attend seminary in Virginia. One Sunday morning we sang "Step by Step." As I sang the lyrics, "And step by step You'll lead me, and I will follow You all of my days," I began to cry. *God, this is too hard.* This song was followed by "I give You my heart...Lord, have Your way in me." I couldn't sing for the tears. *God, this move is way outside of my comfort zone.*

I had never in my wildest imagination even thought of taking classes at a seminary. But God had it in His imagination. He took my tears and put them in His bottle and gave me a picture of a path that was shrouded in fog, where the end was not visible. God promised that as I walked, the way would become clear.

I shed many more tears over the next years of transition as I faced one challenge after another, culminating in a career change. I learned that I could trust God to carry me through a difficult task and that taught me to trust God through the next tasks that I faced. "I love the Lord, for He heard my voice. He heard my cry for mercy. Because He turned his ear to me I will call on Him as long as I live (Psalms 116:1–2)." God put my tears in His bottle as He is faithful to His promises and deeply loves and cares for us.

Dear God, I thank you not only for Your listening ear, but for coming close enough to catch our tears and put them in Your bottle. God, today I am feeling grief for (give voice to your tears). Thank you for love and Your faithfulness. In Jesus' name, Amen.

Judy Zook is an associate pastor at New Holland Mennonite Church.

Christian Community

"So then you are no longer strangers and aliens, but you are
fellow citizens with the saints, and are of God's household."
Ephesians 2:19 (New American Standard)

My friend, Joetta, tells the story of the time she went to a new
church. A man came up to her and said, "Hey, how are you
doing?"

She replied honestly, "Terrible," to which he responded, "Good.
Glad you're here."

Why are we not hearing each other's hearts? Christians should not
feel like strangers or foreigners in the church. We should feel like we
are connected because we are fellow citizens of God's church. Howard
Hendrix, the author of *Exit Interview*, said 53,000 people leave the back
door of a church every week. One reason they leave is because the
church does not provide Christian community.

This generation is looking for genuine Christianity. They can easily spot what's genuine and what isn't. They're looking for deep relationships and a connectedness. The body of Christ must offer that place
where people can learn to accept one another and see God at work in
each other's lives.

How did Jesus say the world would know we were His disciples?
Jesus said the world would know we were His disciples by the quality
of life evidenced in the community of the redeemed. The world, including the church, is full of hurting people, who need a listening ear
and loving touch.

*Lord, we want to open our hearts to people today. Help us to reach out
in genuine agape love to those around us. In Jesus' name, Amen.*

LaVerne Kreider serves with her husband Larry giving oversight to
DOVE Christian Fellowship International and also serves on the
leadership team of a micro-church near Lititz.

Teach Me Your Ways

"...You have said, 'I know you by name and you have found favor with me.' If you are pleased with me, teach me your ways so I may know you and continue to find favor with you...."
Exodus 33:12–13

Moses had the incredible opportunity to spend time in the presence of God, speaking to Him as a friend, face-to-face and with great favor. Yet Moses wanted more; he wanted to be taught the very ways of God.

We need to be free from confusion and misunderstanding by asking the Lord to teach us His ways—just as Moses asked. This means we must learn to follow His footsteps and recognize where He is walking. The word used here has the idea of a path well trodden, or a manner of conducting oneself.

As a people of God in vital, living relationship with Him, we must have this same prayer: *Lord, teach us Your manner of conduct. Show us the road You travel; let us see Your footsteps along the way.* There can be no theological misperception in saying that God is faithful to His Word. So when God speaks of restoration and healing of our land, He will be true to His Word if we fulfill our role in seeking His ways and asking for His favor.

Pray for Lancaster County is our weekly prayer focus for the individuals, families, churches and communities of our region. Please carry this emphasis in your heart and your prayers throughout the week.

I Gave at the Office

"...work, doing something useful...that [you] may have something to share with those in need." *Ephesians 4:28*

The slogan, "I already gave at the office," is a humorous attempt people use to excuse themselves from giving to charity; however, the workplace is a perfect environment in which to give on a regular and consistent basis. As a Christian employer, I have discovered that most employees really do want to reach out to help those in need. With this in mind, our company put some strategies in place to get our focus, values and priorities aligned so that we can reach out beyond ourselves and be stakeholders in impacting the community.

In any given year, our company is typically underwriting leadership development in underdeveloped countries, providing scholarships and sponsorships to underprivileged kids locally and across the globe, underwriting education centers and initiatives, and supporting charities within our local community.

We currently have a program that allows our team not only to raise money, but also to do hands-on work for others. Each year we have one local and two global charities that are supported through this endeavor. Money is raised through "jeans days" and "coffee days" once a month. Employees pay $10 to wear jeans to the office, or $1 for each cup of coffee they drink. We provide a snack box where snacks are sold and the profits used to benefit a specific charity. We also have a "salary match" in which employees may donate a portion of their salaries, which is matched by our company. Our hands-on activities include redecorating a room in a local shelter and supplying needed items.

Employers and employees alike are called by God for ministry in all aspects of our daily lives. We work not merely to have a means of support, but also that we may use our resources as a way of giving back (both locally and globally) and, in return, be doubly blessed.

Lord, help us to put our faith in action in the workplace as we help not only ourselves but others as well.

Daryl Heller is co-founder and CEO of Premier Companies, LLC.

Perfect Love Casts Out Fear

"...Perfect love casts out fear...." *1 John 4:18 (New King James Version)*

I had hit one of those "dry spells" in my spiritual walk—prayerlessness, autopilot ministry, and academic approach to His Word. I asked God to show me why, so I could put this episode behind me. He faithfully revealed that:

Fear is my issue. I am afraid—ultimately of Him(!) because of the pain He allows. **Love** is His remedy. I need to consistently position myself to *experience* His love—to "be still" in order to "be filled."

Draw near is His invitation, yet my current tendency is to *shrink back.* **The journey** is His priority, not merely arrival at the "right" *destination*—it is the process of getting there that is His handiwork.

Trust is *His* question. "Will you still trust Me in this?" is His repeated query. **Pain** is *my* question. Lurking in my heart these past stalemated months has been, "What will He require next, and will it hurt very much?" **Pride** is my enemy. Each of my defeats begins with the word "self": self-indulgence, self-protection, self-sufficiency, self-righteousness, self-pity.

Spiritual friends are His assignment. He alone is my *Source*, but they are His intended *resource*. He has identified three "older women" He is calling me to ask to have input into my life. **Enemy voices** have been my undoing, questioning His goodness, love, wisdom—resulting in my fearful estrangement from Him. The trap this time has been their *subtlety.* I had learned to recognize the Enemy's *boisterous* blamings, but this time they have been *whisperings*, disguised as my own thoughts.

Struggle and resistance have been my pattern. Pain has often caused me to *resist* His work in me, but I don't want to be found struggling while the will of my Lord is being done.

Father God, grant me a deep trust in Your omnipotent goodness and enable me to fully experience Your love!

Peggy Huber is director of Women's Ministries at Calvary Church in Lancaster.

Endurance Through Hope

"We continually remember before our God and Father your work produced by faith, your labor prompted by love, and your endurance inspired by hope in our Lord Jesus Christ."
1 Thessalonians 1:3

It was a hot and humid morning when a group of bicycle riders met at Marietta to ride the borders of Lancaster County. They had practiced hard in the previous month for an endurance ride that was titled the "Nightmare Ride." They had a goal of returning to the starting point after 177 miles around Lancaster County. As the riders enjoyed the sunrise and had thoughts of finishing, the heat and humidity were taking their toll. The hope of finishing the ride became more and more real to them as the cramping continued and the sense of giving up grew stronger. Their bodies were starting to reach the point of fatigue, but they had set their minds to endure and to finish the ride. After about twelve hours of riding, some started to cross the finish line.

The young Thessalonica church needed to be encouraged in their faith with the thought that "we want to cross the finish line," and they found their hope in a real and living God. We can learn from their endurance and strong faith during a time when they would have been persecuted for their belief in Jesus Christ.

There may be times that we feel like giving up, but we can endure, and as the riders on the "Nightmare Ride" were excited when they crossed the finish line, so we can be excited when we endure and overcome the feelings of giving up, to cross the finish line of our lives. Our goals inspired by Jesus Christ will exceed any goal set for earthly gain.

Dear Lord, we want to endure the struggles we have in life for the joys You are setting before us. Give us the strength that we need today to endure. Let Your Spirit guide us today. Amen.

Dave Musselman is pastor of worship at Village Chapel, New Holland.

Faith 101

"...the righteousness of God is revealed from faith to faith...the just shall live by faith." *Romans 1:17*

Shortly after a personal encounter with the Holy Spirit (eight years ago) my wife and I were traveling to a restaurant thirty minutes away. We had a worship recording playing when I was overcome by the presence of God and tears began streaming down my cheeks. I had never experienced Him in this way before and could barely remember the drive once we arrived.

At the restaurant I realized that I had a clear one-sentence message from the Holy Spirit in me that I couldn't recall hearing. The dinner conversation was sparse that night as I tried to process what had transpired. On the way home I told my wife that the Lord had told me, "I am going to heal Liz [not her real name] and you will have a part in it." Liz had been diagnosed with an invasive cancer that was entangling her abdominal organs. My wife said, "Oh, when we get home you'll have to call and tell her." I thought to myself, "she's going to think I'm hearing things," because these events were relatively unheard of in our church.

Nevertheless I made the call. Liz answered saying that she had requested prayer with the pastor and elders the following morning. Liz implored me to join them. I said I would check with the pastor because personal prayer ministry didn't usually involve non-elders. Following the Sunday morning service we laid hands on Liz, and God gave me an unusual assurance that the healing was absolutely completed. When Liz went on to have the operation, the surgeons found the cancer was contained in a bread-loaf sized membrane—not entangling *anything*. It was a quick removal and she has been cancer-free since. Hallelujah!

Lord God, thank you for being true to Your Word and rewarding my obedient faith with faith.

John Hughes is worship leader and elder at Gates of Praise House Church Network.

He Supplies our Needs

"...For your Father knows the things you have need of before you ask Him." *Matthew 6:8*

The Lord sent us home to Iowa for Christmas visits amidst wind, snow and ice. We had a clear understanding of who to visit and when. As we prepared to go north from one location to another, the weather forecast gave blizzard warnings and sub-zero temperatures. But it was an assignment of the Father's heart. There was need to love, laugh and take a meal to a friend who couldn't get out anymore.

As we drove toward our destination, large snowflakes began to fall. There were deep ditches on either side of the narrow access road. Driving slowly, but surely, on unplowed streets, we parked on the street in front of our friend's house. We spent a couple of hours there, enjoying sweet fellowship, noting the steady fall of snow. Slowly, carefully, we navigated the streets back to the access road. We had entered a world of white. Everything looked level. Inching forward cautiously, we seemed to be on solid surface, and we could just make out the main roadway ahead.

Suddenly the rear wheel on the passenger side dropped. I stopped immediately. My girlfriend opened her door and jumped out declaring, "I'll take a look at it!" My "No!" was too late. She found herself in snow above her waist. Instantly, out of nowhere a large pickup truck appeared. The driver took a quick look and hooked his chain to the back bumper. Suddenly identical brothers appeared, walking home from work. Quickly they joined as "spotters" for the truck driver and the car was rapidly and gently moved to solid ground. In seconds they all disappeared. Yet, ahead I could still see the tracks the truck had made as it came in! We looked at one another and said, "Before we asked..."

Father, thank you that the demonstration of Your word is evident! You knew what/who we had needed and sent us help. Thank you Lord. Amen.

Diana Oliphant serves abroad with Global Missions of The Worship Center, Lancaster.

A Matter of Perspective

"As the heavens are higher than the earth, so are my ways higher than your ways and my thoughts than your thoughts." *Isaiah 55:9*

We were visiting my grandparents' home in Puerto Rico. On this particular day we took a day trip to El Yunque, a tropical rainforest. As we walked into a clearing, we noticed an old pavilion that could offer a welcome relief from the heat. As we got closer, we saw hundreds of lizards playing in the shady sanctuary.

My dad, mom, brother and sister scrambled after the lizards, trying to catch them. I captured one and placed it on my dad's shoulder. Swoosh! Suddenly, the little lizard took a flying leap off my dad's shoulder and landed directly on the center of my face! His little feet clawed into my eyes and nose as he struggled to gain a foothold. I screamed frantically and jumped up and down. He only clung on more tightly. Through the lizard legs, I noticed my family. Why were they not coming to my rescue? My mom was making frantic movements. Was she coming to help me? No, she was grabbing the video camera and trying to record the action! The rest of my family was laughing. In fact, they were laughing until they were crying. Well, I was crying, too, and I gave one last scream, and the lizard broke free.

Although traumatized at the time, now that I look back on it, it is quite hilarious. It is just a matter of perspective. It's easy to lose perspective when you're too close to anything.

Today's scripture shows that our natural way of viewing things is never the same as God's. How can we really know God's thoughts? We can know His thoughts by knowing His Word as revealed through His Spirit. His perspective makes all the difference in the world!

Jesus, reveal Yourself to me (1 Corinthians 2:14–16) and help me to trust Your perspective in all of life's situations.

Amanda Ruiz is a senior at Warwick High School and a leader of the Bible Club.

The Problem with Programs

"'For my thoughts are not your thoughts, neither are your ways my ways,' declares the Lord. 'As the heavens are higher than the earth, so are my ways higher than your ways and my thoughts than your thoughts.'" Isaiah 55:8–9

One of the greatest obstacles to God bringing transformation to our communities is...*ourselves*! When God does not quite meet our timetable, we are ready to jump in with our own ideas. We are experts at coming up with programs, and then giving God the credit when perhaps He was not part of the planning. If we are honest, pride is at the very heart of any program mentality. Our program orientation is really a way of acting out our belief that we have the answers and we can do anything if we just put our minds to it. We chart our own course, and then ask God to bless our plans. We must "unlearn" the pattern of the world and learn to wait upon God to reveal His higher ways and plans.

Pray for Lancaster County is our weekly prayer focus for the individuals, families, churches and communities of our region. Please carry this emphasis in your heart and your prayers throughout the week.

Iron Sharpens Iron

"As iron sharpens iron, so one man sharpens another."
Proverbs 27:17

Agood friend is like a mirror, encouraging us when we look great but also showing us our faults and rough edges. The closer we get, the more we see. In the morning I look rather rough. After a shower and a shave I look presentable in our bathroom mirror. But if I get really close or look at a magnifying mirror, I notice my face is still rough with pores and some stubbles that didn't get shaved off.

My closest friend is my wife. She has helped me recognize a number of rough edges in my personality. One good example is when my brother offered me a box of candy he had gone to some trouble to bring back from Hawaii. It was a variety I did not like so I suggested he give it to someone else. Afterward my wife explained that I was actually rejecting a gift from my brother. Instead I should have recognized his generosity, accepted it and shared the candy with others who would have appreciated it.

Left to our own view of ourselves and that of casual friends, it is easy to believe that we have everything together. We can be deceived about our level of maturity in our spiritual walk. We all need the fellowship of close Christian friends and a church group to show us where we should change and to encourage us as we continue to grow into the likeness of Christ (Hebrews 10:25). Regarding our role as iron that sharpens other iron, we also need to encourage others (Hebrews 10:24). Do not be quick to judge (James 4:11–12), but offer constructive criticism and support (Galatians 6:1–2).

Lord, let us be eager to grow, accepting the criticism of others and learning from it. Also, help us to encourage and correct others with helpful words and a proper attitude.

Brad Sauder is employed as a computer programmer at Signature Custom Cabinetry and is a small group leader at DOVE Christian Fellowship Westgate Celebration in Ephrata.

Anchored in Christ

"We have this hope as an anchor for the soul, firm and secure...."
Hebrews 6:19

It was on a family vacation to the seashore that we decided to do some fishing in the bay. My dad rented a little boat for our use. Feeling seaworthy and eager to fill our coolers with flounder, we set out for a day of fishing.

Upon arrival at our chosen destination, we dropped our anchor and with enthusiasm began casting our lines. It wasn't long until we realized the tide was going out to sea and it was slowly dragging us in that direction as well. Our anchor was slowing us somewhat, but was neither heavy nor secure enough to stop us from going along with the tidal pull. It was a very unsettling feeling, drifting along at the mercy of the ocean's tide. How we wished our anchor would snag on something strong and secure! This was intensified by a few moments of panic as we had some difficulty starting the engine.

As a Christian husband, father, and pastor, my anchor has been tested in times of loss and death, heartaches and discouragement, disillusionment, frustrations and temptation. This world's tides continue to change, pull and allure me. It is only by the rich grace of Jesus Christ that my anchor has been stabilized. The winds blow, the tides change, the swells intensify, the waves crest...yet my anchor holds firm and secure. It is not the size of my faith that keeps me secure...rather it is on *Whom* my faith is anchored.

The words of Edward Mote's hymn ring true in my soul: "in every high and stormy gale, my anchor holds within the veil—when all around my soul gives way, He then is all my Hope and stay—on Christ the solid Rock I stand, all other ground is sinking sand."

Dear Jesus, thank you for being the anchor of my soul. Please continue to be the captain of my vessel. Amen.

Wesley D. Siegrist is the pastor of Erb Mennonite Church, Lititz.

July 18

Thanks, Dad!

"...while he was still a long way off, his father saw him and felt compassion for him, and ran and embraced him and kissed him."
Luke 15:20

What is love? It's nice to hear it spoken, better to see it in action. Dostoevsky said, "To love a person means to see them as God intended them to be." Jesus spoke of a father that loved his son and proved it in "the prodigal son" parable.

I have a similar story about a loving dad. It begins on a Friday evening at a big football game. I was quarterbacking my high school team in a battle for first place. My shot at becoming the beloved star of my community was in my grasp as I raced 60 yards toward the goal line. However, I zigged (I should have zagged), was tackled, and failed to score. We lost by one, and I lost my shot at hero status.

My failure to succeed encouraged some "fans" to attack my character, vandalize my home and even threaten my life. The windows of my home were covered with nasty names, and the insults dug deep into my heart. Humiliated, I tearfully entered my home. Inside I found my dad, asleep, in his easy chair. My humiliation turned to rage. *Why didn't he protect me? Where was he when I needed his help?*

With the morning sun came an awesome realization—there was no more graffiti, only windows washed clean. I ran to dad who said, "I didn't want you to have to see those names again; that's not who you are; you're my son and I'm proud of you."

I wasn't shielded from the hurt caused by those who thought they could change my name; but my father gave me a better gift that morning. His actions demonstrated his love for me and pointed me to God who had taken my sins and wiped them clean through Jesus Christ, erasing forever the guilt and shame I deserve.

Thank you heavenly Father for a loving dad. Help me to be quick to receive others and unashamedly cover them with love.

Tim Brouse is the youth pastor at Hosanna Christian Fellowship, Lititz, and a volunteer girls' volleyball coach at Warwick High School.

Are We Salting the Culture?

"Then the king said to me, 'What would you request?' So I prayed to the God of heaven. I said to the king, 'If it please the king, and if your servant has found favor before you, send me to Judah, to the city of my fathers' tombs, that I may rebuild it.'"
Nehemiah 2:4–5

Pollsters and Christian leaders in America agree that in spite of unprecedented activity, resources and influence, the evangelical church in America is neither growing numerically nor is it radically distinct from society. Think of it: evangelicals are in positions of political power, Christian authors are on best sellers lists, mega churches flourish, and Christian music, schools and media are everywhere. Yet some observe that the culture is not becoming more Christian!

It is hard to hear their assessment of Christians being little different from others and exerting only token transforming influence in society. Why have we not been "salt and light" in our communities? Has fear of compromise kept us in our Christian ghetto?

Nehemiah provides an example of how we might "be in the world but not of it." He was in secular employment, a cupbearer to the king. He was very much aware of what God was calling him to do, to rebuild the wall. When he heard of the condition of his people, Nehemiah was sad in the king's presence. This emotional transparency was preceded by months of prayer and thought. Nehemiah told the king of his dilemma, and the king responded with great kindness. The king provided paperwork, a security detail, resources for the building of the wall, and assurance of continued employment when he was finished. Imagine that! God's purposes were accomplished with secular resources. Can we believe that God will use us significantly when we relate with the world?

Dear God, help me to follow You and serve others without fear or pretense.

Steve Brubaker is the director of Residential Programs for the Water Street Rescue Mission in Lancaster city.

Light and Momentary

"Therefore we do not lose heart. Though outwardly we are wasting away, yet inwardly we are being renewed day by day. For our light and momentary troubles are achieving for us an eternal glory that far outweighs them all. So we fix our eyes not on what is seen, but on what is unseen. For what is seen is temporary, but what is unseen is eternal." *2 Corinthians 4:16–18*

Light and momentary troubles..." Do *your* troubles feel light and momentary? I don't know about you, but in the midst of my hard times, they feel *anything* but *light* and *momentary!* Each day, we have a choice to make. Will we fix our eyes on what we see or on what we don't see? I challenge and encourage you today to keep your focus on the One who is inwardly renewing you day by day. You are *in process*. The struggles God is allowing provide an opportunity for you to be stretched and to grow in your understanding and likeness of Him. "So take a new grip with your tired hands and stand firm on your shaky legs. Mark out a straight path for your feet... (Hebrews 12:12–13a, New Living Translation)."

God, help me to fix my eyes on You today, trusting in Your process and knowing that I can't see the big picture like You can. You are faithful!

Ann Weldy is the administrative secretary at DOVE Christian Fellowship Westgate, in Ephrata, and serves as a worship leader at DOVE Elizabethtown.

The Power of God in Action

"I am not ashamed of the gospel, because it is the power of God for the salvation of everyone who believes: first for the Jew, then for the Gentile." *Romans 1:16*

I am from Medellin, Colombia, South America. In 1968, I came to this country looking for the opportunity to fulfill the American dream. I was looking for money, but working as a babysitter for an American family did not fulfill my expectations. So I chose to do something illegal to make the money I wanted. I started to sell drugs in Queens, New York. Our best customer was an undercover cop, and my boyfriend and I were arrested on July 14, 1983. The judge offered me 15 years to life, and I was sent to Riker's Island without bail. I entered Riker's Island without faith, without hope, without a future.

One evening at chapel, a lady from Puerto Rico was preaching about the One who is able to pick up the pieces of our lives and make us new women. She said, "His name is Jesus."

I said, "He is the One I have been looking for." That night I gave my life to Jesus.

In the place where I thought no one would love me, Jesus loved me. The place I thought was my end, became the place of my new beginning. Jesus delivered me from fear, rejection, abuse, and shame. I went back to my cell with Jesus in my heart and a Bible in my hand. I promised the Lord that I would preach to the drug lords when I came out of prison. To my surprise, five weeks later my bail was set at $7,500 and my mother bailed me out.

Lord Jesus, I thank you for forgiving all my sins, for washing them away, and for having the love and power to save even the drug dealers.

Marta Estrada is the director of New Life for Girls of Lancaster, a Christian discipleship program that helps women with drug, alcohol and prostitution problems.

Kingdom or Ministry Building?

Pray for Lancaster County

"But everyone who hears these words of mine and does not put them into practice is like a foolish man who built his house on sand. The rain came down, the streams rose, and the winds blew and beat against that house, and it fell with a great crash."
Matthew 7:26–27

A ministry built on man's ideas—even if they are great—will always be in danger of eventually collapsing around the limits of man's vision. But a ministry built on God's vision and grounded in His kingdom principles will withstand any forces that come against it.

Our reliance on programs reveals our tendency to build great ministries around our own ideas. Then we enthusiastically strategize to help others implement our great ideas. Some have observed that if Joshua had given leadership today to the miracle of Jericho's crumbling walls, he would be pressured to come out with a three-day seminar, notebook, and teaching tapes. But God did not repeat the strategy of Jericho. Each day was new and fresh as Joshua sought to hear God's vision and direction.

It is so easy to move subtly from building the kingdom of God in His way, to building our ministry according to worldly ways of finance, programming, and development. We must be relentless in our desire to truly hear from the Father for genuine, God-authored, society-changing transformation.

Pray for Lancaster County is our weekly prayer focus for the individuals, families, churches and communities of our region. Please carry this emphasis in your heart and your prayers throughout the week.

How My Garden Grows

"Let us not become weary in doing good, for at the proper time we will reap a harvest if we do not give up. Therefore, as we have opportunity, let us do good to all people, especially of those who belong to the family of believers." *Galatians 6:9–10*

My husband and I choose to plant our garden together so we don't double plant or dig up each other's work. We can't see the lettuce, spinach and peas for several weeks. Working together helps us have the best start possible on our way to a great harvest.

It takes faith to plant a garden. I know some seeds will produce many vegetables while others won't. We plant in hope of a good harvest (Romans 15:13).

Both my husband and I spend a lot of time weeding in springtime while we wait for the crop. We watch for bugs and rabbits and do what we can to help the plants become healthy. We need wisdom along the way. Maybe advice from a fellow gardener or magazine article may help our crop get through problems that come along the way.

But most important to our good harvest is the Lord. Only He makes the seeds come to life. He brings the sunshine and the rain. He sends the bees to pollinate the flowers to produce the vegetables and fruit. We help in the process, but we know God is our source for a great harvest.

Consider what your crop is: a new business, children, a peaceful home. It involves many of the same principles: communication and cooperation, faith and love, hard work and perseverance, wisdom and sound advice from experienced friends, patience and flexibility. But most of all, your help comes from God.

Dear Lord, as we enjoy the fresh fruit and vegetables this season, may we all remember to cultivate our spiritual lives to have the fruit of the Spirit in abundance. Amen.

Electa Mohler, an avid gardener, is co-president of the sewing circle at Ephrata Mennonite Church.

The Second Touch

"Once more Jesus put his hands on the man's eyes. Then his eyes were opened, his sight was restored, and he saw everything clearly. Jesus sent him home saying, 'Don't go into the village.'"
Mark 8:25–26

I was preaching a series of messages from the book of Mark and because a healing was recorded in chapter seven, I was tempted to only skim over the healing of the blind man at Bethsaida. As I was studying the question, "Why did Jesus take this man outside the village to heal him and tell him not to go into the village after he was healed?" the Lord opened my eyes to the cross reference of Matthew 11:20–21.

Bethsaida was one of the cities where Jesus performed many miracles but the people didn't repent. At that moment the Spirit of God spoke to me. Is this the reason that we don't see many miracles in Lancaster County and in our churches? We hear the message and see the power of God but our lives continue on as before with little thought of repentance. The questions came to me, "When was the last time that I repented after a message? When was the last time our churches came to repentance?" The next Sunday service was very rewarding as people came to the altar in repentance and there received a new freedom in Christ.

Dear God, help me to apply the message You are speaking to my heart. Show me the areas wherein I need to repent so that I can experience Your fullness.

Glenn A. Hoover is pastor at Carpenter Community Church.

Spirit Fellowship

"May the grace of the Lord Jesus Christ, and the love of God, and the fellowship of the Holy Spirit be with you all."
2 Corinthians 13:14

I remember the day that my heart was awakened to a whole new realm of understanding concerning the fellowship of the Holy Spirit. I had experienced His saving and infilling power in my life but the idea of personal communion with the Holy Spirit was foreign to me.

The word "fellowship" in this passage carries the idea of sharing closely together: communion, participation, intimacy, friendship and comradeship.

My theology spoke of Him as the third person of the Trinity but I knew Him more as a mystical force in my life. I never developed my personal relationship with Him in order to enter the "fellowship" that the Apostle Paul refers to in his writings.

As I studied the scripture, my heart was drawn to honor the Holy Spirit as a person in my daily walk. Since He is my helper, counselor, teacher and comforter I now ask Him to help me each day, and I am aware of His presence with me in new ways. He speaks and communes with me as a friend. I have found the fellowship of the Spirit to be precious indeed. Go ahead and begin to share your heart with Him. After all He has taken up residence in you and is ready to fellowship with you.

Father God, thank you for sending Your son to die for my sins, for being my Father, and giving Your life for me. Thank you for being my intercessor this very moment before the Father. Holy Spirit, thank you for Your daily help and guidance in my life. I want to know You better and walk in fellowship and intimacy with You. In Jesus' name, Amen.

Lester Zimmerman is senior pastor of Petra Christian Fellowship, overseer of the Hopewell Network of Churches and serves on the council of the Regional Church of Lancaster County.

July 26

Lovingly Rebuilt

"The Lord appeared to us in the past, saying: 'I have loved you with an everlasting love; I have drawn you with loving-kindness. I will build you up again and you will be rebuilt, O Virgin Israel....'" *Jeremiah 31:3–4*

This word from the Lord found in Jeremiah 31 is, to me, one of the most encouraging promises in the scriptures. Several years ago the Lord helped me get a first hand picture of His fatherly love. The incident occurred through ministering to Scott (name changed), a new believer who was recovering from a serious drug addiction problem. Scott was a resident at a transition house outside the city of Lancaster where he was slowly learning the nature of a victorious Christian life. One Monday evening as I was driving through Lancaster city, I happened to pass by Scott as he was purchasing a small packet of marijuana at a street corner. I realized that this was not coincidental since I rarely drive through the city, had never before witnessed a live drug transaction, and happened at that very second to be passing by at this vulnerable moment in his life. As he recognized me, I detected his desire to run, but instead he accepted my invitation to join me in the car. As he took his seat, I said, "Scott, God is showing you how much He really, really loves you and desires for you to succeed in a victorious walk."

Both he and I will never be the same as we better understood how much our loving Father is strategically and intimately working for our good.

O Father, I pray that You will help me to comprehend more completely Your love. Please set me free from my fears and enable me to trust You while you build in me the person I am called to be.

Lloyd Hoover is a bishop/overseer for Lancaster Mennonite Conference, executive director for The Potter's House (a prison aftercare ministry), and leader of Reconciliation Ministries.

Listen, Heed, and Put on the Armor

"When you pass through the waters, I will be with you...."
Isaiah 43:2

I thought I was going to die. Cold waves of foaming water were all around me in an instant as my body was turned upside down and sent rocketing down through roaring rapids. Gasping for air and lurching to miss rocks I only had time to think of how I could survive this ordeal. *Just moments before all had been at peace as my friends and I meandered down the lazy river on our raft.* All it took was one nasty hydraulic, around what seemed to be a normal bend in the river. And the raft we had all trusted ungraciously delivered us—no, *launched* us into the "abyss." I remember thanking God that I had listened to the directions given by the rafting instructor: "Wear your life-jacket and secure it tightly around you." I remember repeatedly thrusting my head just above the water momentarily for gasps of air in what seemed an eternity of floundering in the rapids. *But without those clear instructions and a dependable life-jacket there would have been no hope.*

It wasn't long after this event that the Holy Spirit reminded me of the important spiritual principles that He had purposed to show me through this frightening experience. **First, always listen and heed the word of God.** Since life often takes us around frightening twists and turns, it is important that we forsake our own reasoning, and trust in the revealed truths of our Instructor. **Second, put on the armor of God** because the devil is waiting around the bend to cast us into a sea of confusion and difficulty. By wearing God's armor we will be able to resist the devil and fight with the weapons God supplies. *Listen, Heed, Put on the Armor*—is God's lesson for today!

Father, create in us willing hearts to hear and obey everything You say. Dress us in Your armor so we can thrive in Your power!

Scott Lanser is pastor of New Hope Church in East Hempfield. He also serves on the staff of the Associates for Biblical Research.

Childlike Faith

"Some children were brought to Jesus so he could lay his hands on them and pray for them. The disciples told them not to bother him. But Jesus said, 'Let the children come to me. Don't stop them! For the kingdom of heaven belongs to such as these.' And he put his hands on their heads and blessed them before he left."
Matthew 19:13–15 (New Living Translation)

I am a new mother of a six-month old son. One day he was crying in his crib after a short nap. As soon as I picked him up, he stopped crying and cuddled against my shoulder. It didn't take him long to become content again. All he needed that afternoon was a gentle hug from someone who loves him dearly. Children are receptive to the love we give them.

Jesus teaches some important lessons in His gospels about little children. He doesn't say that heaven is for children only, but that we need to approach God with an attitude of childlike faith in Him. This doesn't mean we can be immature or childish, but we are supposed to have a trusting heart like a child.

Children don't know everything about us, but they trust us when we show that we care. Jesus tells us in His Word that He loves us. In 1 John 3:1, the Bible says, "See how very much our heavenly Father loves us, for he allows us to be called his children, and we really are!" We certainly don't know all the mysteries of God, but we have to believe and trust what we do know about Him. As we study His Word, pray and follow Christ, we will grow up like mature sons and daughters of the king. The gospel is simple to understand. Let's believe it and have a childlike faith in Jesus!

Thank you, Lord, for the simplicity of the gospel. Help us to have faith like a child to believe all that it tells us. Help us also to mature in our faith as we follow You each day.

Jewel Horst is an activity leader at Mennonite Home Communities.

Enterprising the Gospel

"When Simon saw that the Spirit was given at the laying on of the apostles' hands, he offered them money and said, 'Give me also this ability so that everyone on whom I lay my hands may receive the Holy Spirit.' Peter answered: 'May your money perish with you, because you thought you could buy the gift of God with money!'" *Acts 8:18–20*

Simon saw an opportunity to benefit from a good thing, and he was willing to exchange money for the power of the Holy Spirit. Although that may seem outrageous, there are times that we also are tempted to merchandise the free gift of God.

If we rely more and more on programs to accomplish our goals, we run the risk of making the gospel an enterprise for us to run. We attach profitability to our ministries, and suddenly we are charging people to use "our prayers" or hear "our insights" into scriptural truths. We explain it as the fruit of our labors, but when does it become merchandising of those things that God gives freely?

As Jack Hayford states: "Preoccupation with those things sneaks up on us. It comes so seductively, and without constant guard against it, then we become entrapped in our own achievements." We must honestly and ruthlessly examine our motives and our actions.

Pray for Lancaster County is our weekly prayer focus for the individuals, families, churches and communities of our region. Please carry this emphasis in your heart and your prayers throughout the week.

Seeking + Working = Prosperity

"In everything that he undertook in the service of God's temple and in obedience to the law and the commands, he sought his God and worked wholeheartedly. And so he prospered."
2 Chronicles 31:21

As a young person desiring to serve God, I would many times direct huge quantities of effort toward a particular project I was undertaking, assuming that God would bless my blood, sweat and tears. Though I saw some success from my 80 hour per week efforts, I later found that God would rather that I not work so hard, but leave some of the work for Him.

In fact, I was challenged to relax and find out more what He was already doing and get on board with Him. I guess you would call this approach co-laboring with Christ. I learned quite a bit about letting Him take the initiative. However, occasionally I would err on the side of not pulling my weight, and failure would occur due to my slacking.

Hezekiah seemed to have a balanced approach to all that he did for the Lord. In Chronicles, we find that in everything he did, he sought the Lord and worked wholeheartedly...and the result was that he prospered. The truth is that we need to seek God *and* work hard. The result will then be blessed and prospered by the Lord.

God, I desire to be fruitful with my time, energy and talents. I want to leave a lasting legacy for Your kingdom on the earth. I realize that You want to work with me and You want me to work with You. Help me to develop this partnership so that together we can see Your Kingdom come on the earth. I want to seek You for Your will and favor, but at the same time be faithful to work wholeheartedly to see Your will come to pass. Amen.

Brian Sauder serves on the apostolic council of DOVE Christian Fellowship International, directs DCFI's Church Planting and Leadership School and is on the Manheim Central School District Board of Directors.

Enjoy the Ride!

"...I will not in any way fail you nor give you up nor leave you without support. [I will] not, in any degree leave you helpless nor forsake nor let [you] down (relax My hold on you)! [Assuredly not!]" *Hebrews 13:5 (Amplified Bible)*

One Sunday we had our married children over for dinner. While still seated at the table, I took our youngest grandson at the time (Payton) on my lap. We were having a little one-on-one fun time between the two of us, when all of a sudden, the legs of the chair (an auction bargain) gave way, and Grandma and Payton ended up on the floor, still in a seated position!

Payton was screaming in fear, but once I saw no one was hurt, I started laughing hysterically, thinking how funny we must look to everyone around the table. I tried to comfort Payton as the rest of the family joined in the laughter!

Payton now laughs, too, when he remembers, because he knows that he was safe in Grandma's arms. I often think how I am like Payton, screaming with fear inside because I am taking an unexpected ride in my life: something is happening that I don't understand. And yet, all the time, my heavenly Daddy is holding me, reassuring me that I am safe in His arms. I just need to trust Him.

In hindsight, I can usually laugh, too, as I remember that wild ride with Jesus, and it builds my faith for the next unexpected ride! Jesus whispers, "Don't be afraid, I hold the stars, moon and all the planets in place. I can hold and keep you too, so enjoy the ride!"

Father, as I face anything today that I was not expecting, or something I don't understand, and I am afraid, help me to get my eyes to focus on You and know I am always safe in Your arms.

Jeanette Weaver and her husband Don serve as deacons and small group leaders at DOVE Christian Fellowship Westgate in Ephrata.

Photo by Apryl Becker, grade 11
Lancaster Mennonite High School

August

To Listen and Obey

"Let everyone bless God and sing his praises; for he holds our lives in his hands, and he holds our feet to the path."
Psalms 66:8–9 (The Living Bible)

It began in April as just an idea that popped into my head. It soon became a strong conviction. *I needed to stop working for the summer.* We own our own business and by June 11, my replacements were trained.

On June 13, Children's Social Services contacted me. They were removing my eleven-year-old granddaughter from her father's house. Would I be willing to take care of her?

I have twenty-two grandchildren, and I see them regularly except for this child. She lived with my daughter's ex-husband and I rarely saw her. It was clear that God had set everything into motion. I was free for the summer and could take care of her.

She came into our home dazed. Our life was very different from hers. As weeks passed, we learned that many rural experiences were brand new to this city child. It was fun to watch her reactions. Ocean waves were great; bugs were to be avoided at all cost; riding bicycle was freedom; tomatoes grow on big vines?

The most intriguing thing to her was that we were all Christians. She wanted to know what that meant. She loved devotions and church and Bible school. She asked question after question. I was unsure about what she understood, so I answered her inquiries but did not push. She was the one who surprised me. She accepted Jesus into her heart on July 31 at Sunday School and announced it to everyone gladly.

So I had the summer off. The reality was, I worked harder than my job would have required, but how very precious was God's reward!

Jesus, thank you for speaking into my life. Help me as I listen for Your voice. I want to hear You and obey You.

Andrea Bomberger attends Newport DOVE. She is editor of her church newsletter and wife of Henry, president of Bomberger's Store, Lititz.

August 2

Persevere, and Finish Well

"You need to persevere so that when you have done the will of God, you will receive what he has promised." *Hebrews 10:36*

In his book *Lead On*, John Hagee tells the story of three young ministers of the gospel who were bursting onto the ministry scene in the late 1940s. Two of the three had already achieved notable influence. Chuck Templeton and Bron Clifford were preaching dynamos. One university president, after hearing Templeton preach to a crowd of several thousand, called him the most talented and gifted young preacher in the United States. Bron Clifford was also believed to be someone who would greatly impact the church world. Both Templeton and Clifford started out strong. But by 1950, Templeton left the ministry in pursuit of a career as a radio and television commentator. He eventually decided that he no longer believed in orthodox Christianity. Clifford's story is nothing short of tragic. By 1954, he had left his wife and two children. Alcohol was the vice that destroyed his life. Only nine years after being the most sought-after preacher in the United States, Clifford was found dead in a sleazy motel room.

You may be wondering who the third evangelist was. His name is Billy Graham. While Templeton and Clifford were enjoying their success, Graham was establishing boundaries within his personal life and ministry that would ensure his longevity.

Paul was shipwrecked, in prison and beaten (2 Corinthians 6), but he refused to quit. In the garden of Gethsemane, the devil wanted Jesus to give up. Praise God He did not quit! Let's purpose in our hearts to persevere and leave a godly legacy.

Lord, we know it is by Your grace that we will experience the fruit of perseverance, which is the legacy of an obedient life and of not quitting. Help us, Lord, to persevere and to finish well!

Larry Kreider serves on the executive team of the Regional Church of Lancaster County and as the International Director of DOVE Christian Fellowship International.

What We Can Take to Heaven

"But life is worth nothing unless I use it for doing the work assigned me by the Lord Jesus—the work of telling others the good news about God's mighty kindness and love." *Acts 20:24*

The phone call came late one evening. Mother informed me that my Daddy was very ill and that we should make a trip to their home in Williamsport early the next day to see him. When we arrived at their home, Daddy had drifted off into unconsciousness, and Mother said she believed it was only a matter of time until the Lord would call him home. I had heard that our sense of hearing is one of the last things to leave our bodies, so I spoke to him about many things we had done over the years and what he had meant to me. As I contemplated what else to say, I decided it probably would be a good idea to check his pulse. As soon as I found it, I felt one good solid heart beat and then…it stopped. I looked up at Mother and said, "Daddy just went home to be with the Lord!" At that moment I was overwhelmed at the miracle that the Lord had just allowed me to experience. The only heartbeat that I ever felt from Daddy was his last one. It reminded me of my last days with him. He realized that his days were coming to an end. I'll never forget when he said, "You know, the only thing that I'm taking with me to heaven is people whose lives I have influenced for the Lord." It is not material possessions that are going to matter at the end of life, but it is the lives we have touched and brought to our wonderful Lord Jesus Christ.

Dear heavenly Father, thank you for allowing Glenn and me to reach many people with Your good news of salvation. Help us to always remember that each person that You put in our path is an opportunity to touch them for Your glory.

Shirley Eshelman, along with her husband Glenn, are the founders of Sight & Sound Ministries in Strasburg.

God's Strength in Weakness

"You are those who justify yourselves before men, but God knows your hearts. For what is highly esteemed among men is an abomination in the sight of God." *Luke 16:15*

"...he knows the secrets of the heart." *Psalms 44:21*

We have all met people who talk about their many accomplishments, their big house, flashy car or expensive clothes and vacations. Messages on TV, the media and the culture, judge a person's importance by their beauty, intelligence, strength, popularity or wealth.

God looks directly at a person's heart as a gauge to see whom He will trust with His assignments. He often chooses the least talented, weakest and most insignificant persons to perform the greatest tasks. Stuttering Moses was chosen to lead about 2 million Jews out of Egypt. Gideon, a poor farmer and the least of his clan, was used to drive out vast armies. And in more recent years Billy Graham, once an obscure farm boy, became the greatest modern evangelist ever known.

When you have a weakness or lack of ability in a certain area, God has the opportunity to show Himself strong through you. If you are afraid or too shy to stand up before a crowd to share something, God will give you such opportunities. If you lack money, He asks you to give what you can in order for Him to bless you with more. If we sow what we do have, God will multiply it and turn our weakness into a strength.

Jesus, You know my areas of weakness, my inabilities and fears. Please, help me to overcome these obstacles in my life as I trade my weakness for Your strength. Amen.

Eric Davenport is the owner of Davenport Design & Advertising and attends a local marketplace ministry Bible study through Faith Connections at Work, which is devoted to raising up workplace evangelists.

We Won't Go Without You!

"Then Moses said to him, 'If your Presence does not go with us, do not send us up from here. How will anyone know that you are pleased with me and with your people unless you go with us? What else will distinguish me and your people from all the other people on the face of the earth?'" *Exodus 33:15–16*

Going alone without God was not an option for Moses! Moses knew God's power, had witnessed His glory, and was convinced that God's presence was absolutely essential.

As time goes on, it is easy for us to slowly and gradually be lulled to a place where the "machinery of ministry" can pretty much run itself. But God is calling us, as His people, back to a place of determined faith in the power of His presence. In that simple faith, there is a dependency that draws us into deeper intimacy with Him; it is the intimacy that draws His presence.

We must cry out to the Lord, as Moses did, and declare, "We are not taking another step without Your presence." Even Jesus acknowledged that He did nothing on His own, and instead did only what He saw the Father doing (John 5:19). God is calling us back to intimate reliance on Him alone. Listen to His call back to a simple walk of intimacy.

Pray for Lancaster County is our weekly prayer focus for the individuals, families, churches and communities of our region. Please carry this emphasis in your heart and your prayers throughout the week.

The Word of Life

"As the rain and the snow come down from heaven, and do not return to it without watering the earth and making it bud and flourish, so that it yields seed for the sower and bread for the eater, so is my word that goes out from my mouth; It will not return to me empty, but will accomplish what I desire and achieve the purpose for which I sent it." *Isaiah 55:10–11*

On a hot day last August, my husband drove the digging iron repeatedly into our creek bank, making holes for me to drop-in daffodil bulbs—about a hundred of them! I had a vision of our bank resplendent in bloom the next spring, and we were sowing bulbs, believing it would be accomplished. We waited and believed, and this spring the creek bank was loaded with eye-popping, yellow daffodils. The bulbs fulfilled their promise and did what they were created to do.

God's Word is filled with promise and potential and life. Beth Moore states, "God's Word is alive and active in me." As I pray God's Word over my family, friends and myself, and as I speak it aloud, it accomplishes the purpose for which it was sent! Then I watch and wait for the beauty that will come forth as lives are changed by the Word of God. What joy to sow seeds of life!

Father, awaken my spirit to the life and promise in Your Word. Prompt me to sow Your Word generously today over my "world." Give me faith to believe and eyes to see it accomplish the purpose for which it was sent.

Melanie Horning is a pastor's wife who serves on the leadership team at New Life Fellowship, Ephrata.

More, Not Less

"Give, and it will be given to you; good measure, pressed down, shaken together, running over, will be put into your lap. For the measure you give will be the measure you get back." *Luke 6:38 (Revised Standard Version)*

Recently, I read about a man who made a sizeable gift to a school in the southwest. The director of development called him to thank him and then asked about his motivation for giving. The man said he wanted to give away a million dollars before he died. He said he was getting close to that goal.

I was struck by the idea of having such a lifetime goal. That man reminded me of the elderly man who said, as he gave more away, *"I want to bounce my last check."*

Jesus taught that generosity creates more generosity. The Message puts it this way: *"Give away your life; you'll find life given back, but not merely given back—given back with bonus and blessing."*

There's no guarantee that a generous person will become wealthier. Instead, there is a call from God to *hold on* less and to *let go* more.

If you have not yet discovered tithing, you need to *hold on* less and *let go* more.

If you have tithed all your life, tithing is too easy, and you need to *hold on* less and *let go* more.

God's promise is about blessings—and those come in much bigger measures than a larger Statement of Net Worth. God's blessings come in multiple ways, but they're always connected to your heart—that spirit of generosity that gives freely and generously.

Lord, there's so much that influences us to hold on. It's a battle to be faithful with money. Help us give away more rather than less. We trust You to cover our past with grace. Help us trust You to cover our future with grace. In the name of Jesus who gave it all, Amen.

Kent Kroehler is senior pastor at First United Methodist Church in Lancaster.

Chased By Love

"You prepare a table before me in the presence of my enemies. You anoint my head with oil; my cup overflows. Surely goodness and love will follow me all the days of my life." *Psalms 23:5–6*

I heard Joyce Meyer preach about God's goodness and love and how it follows after us. She walked in front of someone on the stage and then chased after the individual. Her point was that God's goodness and love will chase you down.

This year I have been declaring the Word of God in my life. I want to believe the Word over my feelings and circumstances, and all areas of my life—relational, physical and financial. When I see God's goodness, it makes me fall in love with Him more and more. I ask Him to make my gratitude stimulate obedience to Him.

During the summer of 2005, my husband had a goal of buying a new gas tank. We saved all our extra money and bought a 500-gallon tank. Our next goal was impressed on us by an advertisement from our fuel oil company—to buy all our fuel oil at pre-pay cost. We have never done this before. So we saved all the extras and paid $2,000 for our yearly fuel.

Finally, our older car was due for inspection and we were concerned with different noises we were hearing. We thought it would be better to invest in a 4-cylinder gas saver. All of these decisions were made and completed two weeks before the price of gas skyrocketed.

Our cup overflows; His goodness and love is chasing after us to impress on us how to live so that we will be prosperous and successful in every area of our lives.

Lord, help us to believe Your Word, to declare it in our lives and to watch for the fruition of it. For indeed, You do prepare a table for us. Your lovingkindness continually brings us to change.

Ann Mellott is a Sunday School teacher and disciple of Christ.

The Source of Contentment

"...be content with what you have...." *Hebrews 13:5*

I f it happened one time, it was bound to happen again; once the cows reached across the fence to get a taste of the fresh corn growing on the other side, there was no stopping them. Countless times during the summer months, "The cows are in the corn!" would send our family scrambling to chase the cows from the cornfield and herd them back inside the pasture.

In my 42 years as a pastor, I often ran into the "grass is greener on the other side" syndrome. Why is it that we become dissatisfied with our own situation and think others have it better? The Bible tells us, "Set your affection on things above, not on things on the earth (Colossians 3:2)." Our contentment is not found in our circumstances, but rather in our relationship with Jesus.

Today, let's allow our contentment to be rooted in our total dependence on Jesus Christ and obedience to His will.

Dear heavenly Father, help us to have the peace of God in each and every situation today, good or bad, because You are sufficient for our needs.

Parke Heller is ninety years old, a retired farmer and pastor emeritus of Hammer Creek Mennonite Church.

234   *God Stories*

Sufficient Crumbs

"And she said, 'Yes, Lord, yet even the little dogs eat the crumbs which fall from their master's table.'" *Matthew 15:27 (New King James Version)*

Long did I ponder this, for in a wounded portion of my heart I mused, "If Jesus spoke such a word to me, I'd go off whimpering like a puppy!" But then He said to her, "O woman, great is your faith. Let it be as you desire."

I asked for His explanation as to why He would speak this to her, and also what she had within that kept her there unwavering.

The Lord gave a clear answer: "She knew that a crumb from My table was enough, and that crumb was sufficient to meet her need!"

No longer do I focus on the "lack" or insufficiency, regardless of the situation. Grace flows, and I am becoming thankful for everything. In turn, He proves Himself faithful, time and time again.

There were places in my life where I was grumbling and complaining because the answer or portion received seemed small. When He began to open my eyes, the light of revelation illumined situations and circumstances. Places and times that often appear as insurmountable mountains now become opportunities to rejoice and stand in unwavering faith. Grace is abundant, for I now know and understand that a crumb from the Master's table is totally sufficient to meet every need.

Lord, I thank you that the portion of Your answered prayer is always just what we need. Thank you for teaching us not to compare our situations to others, but to implicitly trust Your wisdom and plan for us. Continue to open the eyes of our hearts, revealing opportunities for thanksgiving and joy as You daily work small miracles in our lives. In Jesus' name, Amen.

Diana Oliphant serves abroad with Global Missions of The Worship Center, Lancaster.

Growing the Right Kind of Fruit

"But the fruit of the Spirit is love, joy, peace, patience, kindness, goodness, faithfulness, gentleness and self control. Against such things there is no law." *Galatians 5:22–23*

I first planted strawberries for a 4-H project as a teenager and enjoyed growing them for many years. But then wandering chickens and ducks ate the berries. I wouldn't have minded sharing if they would have eaten bugs first and had the berries for dessert. Soon our raspberries were producing more fruit than our strawberry patch. I found that raspberries didn't require stooping and as much weeding, so we made the switch. Red raspberries became our early summer fruit. The nice thing about them is that they produce a second crop in the fall. And we didn't have to fight what was happening in our neighborhood to harvest our produce. Raspberries have been a winning solution.

In the Bible verses above, Paul lists nine different fruits. What situations did you find yourself in today? Which fruit did you need more of? The Holy Spirit will help us grow those fruits as we keep the soil of our hearts soft. The communities in which we live need us as Christians to be growing all of the different kinds of the fruit of the Spirit.

Dear Lord, thank you for family and neighbors that work together to make a happy community. Help us to make the world a better place as we work to produce the fruit of the Spirit in our own neighborhood. Amen.

Electa Mohler, an avid gardener, is co-president of the sewing circle at Ephrata Mennonite Church.

Turning From Indifference

Pray for Lancaster County

"...Be diligent and turn from your indifference. Look! Here I stand at the door and knock. If you hear me calling and open the door, I will come in, and we will share a meal as friends." *Revelation 3:19–20 (New Living Translation)*

Jesus gives us an invitation to hear Him, open the door, and invite in His very presence. The picture of sharing a meal with Jesus as a friend is compelling and certainly something we would desire. But the requirement is that we turn from our indifference.

In fact, just a few verses before this (vs. 16), Jesus gives a graphic warning to the church about being lukewarm and apathetic—that He will spit out those with a half-hearted love. If we remain indifferent and apathetic in our desire for the Lord, we will miss His invitation to experience His full-blown manifest presence.

Pray for Lancaster County is our weekly prayer focus for the individuals, families, churches and communities of our region. Please carry this emphasis in your heart and your prayers throughout the week.

August 13

Set Your Alarm for Midnight

"The end of all things is near. Therefore be clear-minded and self-controlled so that you can pray. Above all, love each other deeply, because love covers over a multitude of sins. Offer hospitality to one another without grumbling. Each one should use whatever gift he has received to serve others, faithfully administering God's grace in its various forms." *1 Peter 4:7–10*

I'm quite intrigued by the life of the Ephrata Cloister residents in the early 1700s. A group called the *Solitary* began holding two-hour midnight meetings. Believing that Christ would return between the hours of midnight and 2:00 a.m., they arose each midnight for worship, repentance and contemplation. It's safe to say that most of us do not carry on this tradition. I would have a lot of difficulty getting used to such a schedule, but I admire their reasoning about being ready for Christ's return.

I believe the verses above show some other ways that we can be ready for Christ's return. Pray. Love each other. Be hospitable. Serve others. Which do you find easiest to do? Which do you find most difficult? I love hosting people in my home. I find a lot of joy in making people feel comfortable. We host many international guests, and we offer our phone for them to call home. It's a simple way we can show Christ's love.

What are your activities today? Are they activities that Christ would like to see? Take time today to show love, offer hospitality, or to serve someone.

Lord, I know Your return will be glorious. I pray that as I remain in this world, You will help me to love others, offer hospitality without grumbling and to use the gifts that You have given me to serve others. Thank you for the joy that I find in doing these things and thank you for being the example of perfect love.

Lyndell Thiessen is a member of DOVE Christian Fellowship Westgate in Ephrata. She is serving as a missionary with her husband, Bruce, in Fortaleza, Brazil.

August 14

Fear Factor

"He will have no fear of bad news; his heart is steadfast, trusting in the Lord." *Psalms 112:7*

On August 27, 1987, we were blessed with twin sons. When I gave Justin and Jared their first feeding, Justin appeared to have difficulty digesting the milk. The next morning the doctor informed me that Justin had developed Necrotizing Enterocolitis and would be transferred to Hershey Medical Center. I wrestled with God, reminding Him of the many prayers we had prayed asking for healthy babies. Around midnight I experienced God's peace and sensed Him telling me that everything would be okay. I fell asleep only to be awakened two hours later by a nurse saying the doctor was on the phone and needed my permission to immediately perform emergency surgery. I hung up the phone feeling confused and betrayed by what I had understood God speaking to me just a few hours earlier. They surgically removed Justin's entire large intestine because it had ruptured and the dead tissue needed to be removed. Again I gave God my confusion and fears. I sensed God telling me to wait two years before I evaluated His promise that everything would be okay.

We continued to receive bad news, saying Justin's kidneys had shut down, he had a deadly infection, and the doctors only gave him a 10% chance of living. Outside of a miracle his life would soon be over. God instructed my husband to take a stand against the enemy who was trying to destroy Justin's life. Nelson stood in the gap in intercession. Family and friends stood with us in prayer. God heard our prayers. At two years old, Justin was healthy and he was okay, just as God had promised. We learned to not fear evil tidings but to trust in the Lord, our helper and healer.

Dear Lord, help us to not fear bad news, but to trust in You so that our heart will remain steadfast in You. Thank you that we can trust You to be our helper in difficult times and our healer when we are hurting.

Sue Martin and her husband Nelson serve as elders at ELANCO DOVE Christian Fellowship.

August 15

Faith and Cheap Water

"Though the fig tree does not bud and there are no grapes on the vines, though the olive crop fails and the fields produce no food, though there are no sheep in the pen and no cattle in the stalls, yet I will rejoice in the Lord, I will be joyful in God my Savior."
Habakkuk 3:17–18

During the hot summer of 1988, construction was under way for our new house. Consecutive dry weeks had allowed work to accelerate and the contractor was ready to drill a well. A common practice in Lancaster County was to hire the services of a water "smeller," someone who could use a watch, twig, or pliers to "divine" a good spot for water.

My wife, Carol, and I decided that we would not use divination to locate our well, but would instead depend on God. We stood at the dusty construction site and prayed, then placed a stake in the ground. The next day the driller arrived and we watched with anticipation. Our neighbor had used a water diviner to hit a gushing well at a short sixty feet. We expected God to do better!

The driller hit a small ooze of water at fifty feet and continued. One hundred. Two hundred. Three hundred. At four hundred feet he hit a weak stream of water. What could we say? Where was God? We trusted in Him instead of using sorcery, but we ended up with a very expensive well!

Then God spoke gently and unforgettably into our spirits. "Is your relationship with me about which god can give you cheap water? Was your trust about saving money? Or, did you want to abandon divination even if it cost you?" Suddenly faith took a deeper, more robust meaning. Our faith was about worship, not mere outcome. It was about more than getting cheap water; it was about doing the right thing.

Dear God, help me to follow You, not for merely making my life easier, but because You are worthy of trust and sacrifice. Amen.

Dave Witmer is a church planter and musician, and serves with HopeNet Fellowship of Churches.

Called By the Spirit

"For all who are being led by the Spirit of God, these are the sons of God." *Romans 8:14*

David has lived across the street, two houses down from our family, for over nine years. But I had only spoken with him once and waved numerous times. His wife is painfully disabled. Their youngest daughter, Katy, began moving around the neighborhood more freely as she got older, becoming friends with some of my daughters. Our Rebecca sensed the Lord telling her to invite Katy to go along to worship, and during our weekly testimony time, she asked for prayer for Katy and her family. She invited her, and Katy's parents agreed.

A "strident atheist," to use his words, David wondered what kind of church his daughter was attending, and whether it was healthy for her. While repairing a car one Saturday, I saw him go to our front door to ask the time of our service. Too greasy to greet a guest, I simply said a prayer. I found out later that, without a word from us, David was struck that day with three truths: that God is his Creator, that God has a plan for him, and that the Bible is His Word. The Holy Spirit assured him that there was a higher purpose for the suffering that had been such a part of his life.

David came to worship the next day, began an impassioned faith walk, and was soon baptized. I marvel at how my brother now lives across the street; not because a brother moved in, but because the Lord made David my brother. He later said that if we had knocked on his door, he would have closed it. Even when we witness or knock on an open door, it is the Lord who changes hearts! We prayed; the Holy Spirit moved!

Move, Holy Spirit, as You call Your children. Amen!

Steve Cote has been pastor of Zion Church of Millersville since 1975 and is chaplain of the Millersville Fire Company.

August 17

Take The Journey

"...The Scriptures say it is a beautiful sight to see even the feet of someone coming to preach the good news." *Romans 10:15 (Contemporary English Version)*

Ten years ago I went on a one-year mission trip to mainland China, where I taught conversational English. As English wasn't my favorite subject and, being somewhat shy, I questioned God's wisdom in calling me to such a task. But, knowing in the depth of my heart that this was where the Lord was leading, I embarked with my teammates on an unforgettable journey. There were many awesome opportunities to share Jesus Christ and interact with students and friends that we made along the way.

One of the things that sticks out to me was the trip we took across southern China. With next to no ability to converse in Chinese, we set out to see the beauty and darkness of this ancient country. In every city I checked out the Buddhist temples and watched as crowds worshiped. We talked with people in our limited Chinese and saw behind their eyes hundreds of stories about the good and bad of life. When surrounded by the silence in crowds of millions, I saw the truth of humanity's search for hope and life in a dying world that increasingly abandons them.

Some people were fervent in their worship of the gods, others about their belief in themselves and the existence of nothing after death. But the truth and reality of God's existence (a God who loves us no matter where or who we are) spoke volumes to me. Each one is created in the image of God, had their sins paid for at the cross, and can have life because of the Resurrection. But, who will take the journey to tell them?

Holy Spirit, help us to see what You're doing in this world. Then send us, heavenly Father, to meet the people You love. Help us share Jesus in our life and actions and, if necessary, in our words.

Rodney A. Martin is associate/youth pastor at Lititz Mennonite Church, where he works with youth, young adults, outreach and preaching.

Burdens are for Sharing

"Bear one another's burdens, and so fulfill the law of Christ."
Galatians 6:2 (New King James Version)

When our youngest son was born, he remained in the neonatal intensive care unit for a harrowing nine days. I had one thought in mind—to get my son out with a clean bill of health. On the fourth day, as I entered the unit, the Holy Spirit said to me, "You know, you are missing it." I thought I was missing an aspect of praying that would relieve me of the pain I was going through. The Lord had something else in mind as I heard His gentle voice, "You're so concerned about your own needs that you're missing the hurting people around you that you can minister My love to."

From then on, I entered the unit with a new focus—to reach out to those around me who also had critical family health issues. I was not the only one with problems! When the time came for our son to be discharged, it was bittersweet. I was so glad to take him home, but I also knew that my window of opportunity in the lives of the people I had come to know was drawing to a close. I prayed that I had left an impact of the love of the Lord Jesus upon their lives.

A surefire way to get your mind off your troubles is to stop focusing on yourself and focus instead on someone else's needs. "Bearing another's burdens," means carrying the load with them, standing shoulder-to-shoulder, receiving that load and sustaining that person during his time of hardship. That may take the form of prayer and words of encouragement that help lift him up.

If you see someone today that is menaced by some burden or threat, be alert to quickly help. Don't let them be crushed or destroyed. Will you help lighten the load or lift the burden of another today?

Lord Jesus, help us today to look for ways to lighten someone's load so we can help him along and point him to You.

Ron Myer serves on DOVE Christian Fellowship International's Apostolic Council.

Expecting the Supernatural

"So Peter left the cell, following the angel. But all the time he thought it was a vision. He didn't realize it was really happening...So they passed through and started walking down the street, and then the angel suddenly left him. Peter finally realized what had happened. 'It's really true!' he said to himself...." Acts 12:9–11 (New Living Translation)

I magine Peter's experience of seeing a bright light, and then suddenly having an angel standing beside him, ready to lead him out of prison. Even though Peter's chains inexplicably fell off, and the angel had to instruct Peter to put on his clothes and sandals, it was not registering with Peter that he was standing in the midst of a miracle. And when he finally grasped the supernatural move of God, he still had to explain it to his disbelieving friends.

They also had trouble understanding that they were looking at the very answer to their fervent prayers! If God is to move in answer to our prayers, it will be supernatural and beyond our human expectations. The only way for our society to be transformed on every level is through the divine and miraculous intervention of God's hand, and not through anything we can do on our own. Let's start expecting the supernatural, and not limit the hand of God with our unbelief.

Pray for Lancaster County is our weekly prayer focus for the individuals, families, churches and communities of our region. Please carry this emphasis in your heart and your prayers throughout the week.

August 20

Unbelief Stifles Mustard Seed Growth

"...The disciples came to Jesus privately and said, 'Why could we not cast him [the demon] out?' Jesus said to them, 'Because of your unbelief; for assuredly, I say to you, if you have faith as a mustard seed, you will say to this mountain, "Move from here to there," and it will move; and nothing will be impossible for you.'"
Matthew 17:19–20 (New King James Version)

Have you ever claimed the faith to achieve some fantastic feat for Jesus, like having the faith for healing, or the faith to defeat a personal demon in your life? And have you, like me and like the disciples, experienced the frustration of failure to achieve the desired result?

Jesus' reply to the disciples is instructive for us also. I think that we are often afflicted with visions of grandeur regarding what we want to achieve for the kingdom. Jesus, however, says that in order to experience great faith power, we need to first sow mustard seeds of faith.

When we sow small faith action seeds for our daily needs and watch God meet those needs, God grows our faith. As God grows our small faith seeds through answered prayer, our faith germinates, becomes firmly rooted. Before we know it, we are trusting our heavenly Father for larger and larger faith actions because the results are based on a faith that has now become firmly rooted in the soil of trust.

O Lord, increase our faith. Forgive our unbelief. Teach us to trust You to meet our small needs that we have faith for. Lord, we claim Your power to respond to our mustard seeds. And, Lord, as we trust You each day for more and more of our needs, continue to build our faith so that the large fantastic feat for Jesus is not so fantastic, but rather just another instance of watching our mustard seeds grow.

Dale Weaver is senior pastor of Sandy Hill Community Church, Coatesville.

The Call to Prayer

"Rejoicing in hope, patient in tribulation, continuing steadfastly in prayer." *Romans 12:12 (New King James Version)*

We were crossing the state of Nebraska when we saw the truck. The wind was strong and gusting with great force. The trailer portion of the truck was careening and tipping at the same time. We knew immediately it was a call to prayer for the safety of the driver and the vehicle. A few times it seemed as if he would not be able to regain control. It was a massive trailer that advertised a variety of spas. We decided he had little or no cargo. At every rest stop we passed, we hoped he would turn in. We knew he had to be exhausted in the battle with the wind.

One hundred and eleven miles later, the release from intercession came. The winds had subsided considerably and snow was blowing across the dry roadbed. We relaxed and put on some worship music. At the next rest stop, we pulled in. There was the truck parked with his lights on. We parked behind him and walked up to the cab. We could not see anyone, but knocked on the door. Suddenly a head appeared. His eyes were red and we could tell he had been crying. He rolled down the window suspiciously. "Are you all right? We have been behind you for three hours, praying," we said. He opened the door and jumped down.

He said, "I told God, 'You are going to have to help me in this one.' I have never prayed so hard in my life. A couple of times I thought that angels must have kept the rig from going over." We fellowshipped and gave thanks with him for a short time. Then the road to home called us onward.

Lord, I thank you for the support system You have put in place. Remind me when my times are dark or desperate, You have someone praying. I thank you God for hearts to hear when You need someone. Open my ears to hear Your request. Call me, Lord, when someone has need.

Diana Oliphant serves abroad with Global Missions of The Worship Center, Lancaster.

The Last Balloon

"Jesus said, 'Let the little children come to me, and do not hinder them, for the kingdom of heaven belongs to such as these.'"
Matthew 19:14

After seventeen hours of difficult weather and heavy seas, we arrived in Cuba on a sailboat. The customs officials decided to take everything we had except our personal belongings. Their reasoning made no sense at all, but nonetheless, we were left with very little to bless the church.

I planned to make balloon sculptures for the children, but had only one half a bag (fifty balloons) after customs was through with us. When we got to the Sunday School class, I counted forty kids, so I told them I would make each of them a balloon.

The inevitable happened, and kids came from everywhere. The children were exceptionally polite and patient, but the anticipation on their faces and the eagerness to receive their own special balloon was incredible. By now there were well over one hundred kids, and the number was growing!

I continued for hours, each time reaching into my bag and pulling out what seemed to be my last balloon. I ran both my pump batteries dead and continued making balloons with my hand pump. As the last child came to me, I pulled out my last balloon. I had made a few hundred balloon sculptures from one half a bag of balloons!

When we were leaving Cuba, a customs official asked if I were the guy that made the balloons. I said I was, and she asked, "Could you please make me a flower?" I reached in my bag and there were two balloons, just enough to make a flower. She laid all her important paperwork on the dock and went to tuck her flower away in the office. Returning, she cast off our lines and with a beaming smile on her face shouted, "Come back again soon!"

Father, we know that You are the Lord of the increase. Help us believe.

Clair Stauffer, author, inventor and businessman, is the director and founder of Refreshing Leaders Ministry.

The Prayer of Faith

"And their prayer, if offered in faith, will heal him, for the Lord will make him well...." *James 5:15 (The Living Bible)*

Sometimes when I am discouraged and feeling weak in faith, God reminds me of something that happened to me when I was a child. This is a story that has had great impact on shaping my faith and on who I am today.

When I was around three years old I began to lose my ability to hear. My parents first noticed that I didn't respond to them when they asked me a question or called my name. At first, they thought that I was deliberately ignoring them for one reason or another. Or maybe that I was so lost in my imaginary play world that I was oblivious to what was going on around me. Unfortunately things began to get worse. It wasn't long before my family realized that I was beginning to read lips to be able to understand what was being said to me. At this point it became clear that something was definitely wrong and that I needed to be taken to a doctor.

The tests at the doctor showed that I indeed was losing my hearing. They weren't sure what the cause was, and couldn't promise my parents that my condition would improve. It seemed likely that as time went by, I would gradually lose my ability to hear to the point that I would become totally deaf.

Thankfully my parents are people of prayer and have deep faith in God. Not long after the first doctor visit, I was anointed with oil as my family laid their hands on me and prayed a simple prayer of faith that God would totally heal me and restore me to complete health. It is an incredible blessing to say that God did answer their prayer. By the next time we went to the doctor, my hearing had been totally restored! From that day forward I never had any trouble hearing again!

Lord of all healing, let all our prayers be prayers of faith.

Mike Stoltzfus gives leadership to the Lancaster Micro Church Network.

Saved From Despair

"He lifted me out of the pit of despair, out from the bog and the mire...." *Psalms 40:2 (The Living Bible)*

I've had a kidney disease since I was about eleven years old. I also contracted herpes in my twenties, being promiscuous. In December of 2003 my kidney function decreased and I also broke out with a horrible case of herpes.

During this terrible outbreak, I started crying out to the Lord. I was desperate. At this point I was not saved. God heard my prayers, and He first started healing me spiritually. Approximately a month later, a pastor prayed for physical healing for me. A few nights later I was awakened in the middle of the night by hearing myself blurting out, "I'm healing you!" This was the Holy Spirit speaking through me.

What I can tell you is that my kidneys are being healed! Prior to my healing I've always had blood in my urine because of the disease. Recently one kidney doctor said, "Your urine is like a baby's urine!" How's that for healing!

As for the herpes, it's virtually gone! God has done what the doctors could not do with medication. I'm talking about permanent healing!

The most awesome thing about all of this is that beyond the healings, I've developed a true relationship with God!

Lord, I'm so thankful for my salvation and for our awesome relationship. Thank you also for the inherited right of healing through Jesus!

Efrain Torres, Jr. is a recording/mixing engineer and entrepreneur. He is being discipled at *In The Light Ministries* in Lancaster City.

August 25

Power-filled Words

"On the same day, when evening had come, He said to them, 'Let us cross over to the other side.' Now when they had left the multitude, they took Him along in the boat as He was. And other little boats were also with Him. And a great windstorm arose, and the waves beat into the boat, so that it was already filling. But He was in the stern, asleep on a pillow. And they awoke Him and said to Him, 'Teacher, do You not care that we are perishing?' Then He arose and rebuked the wind, and said to the sea, 'Peace, be still!' And the wind ceased and there was a great calm." *Mark 4:35–39 (New King James Version)*

Peace, be still." These words were spoken to the disciples in the midst of a situation that caused them great concern and fear. Circumstances that are beyond our control provide the opportunity for God to reveal Himself and His awesome mighty power in greater and more tangible ways.

We were on a flight to Guatemala some time ago. Many on the plane were sleeping when the plane started to jolt, bump and roll. The sudden notable turbulence caused everyone to wake up, and the reactions of a number of passengers revealed that they had become quite concerned. I spoke out loud, saying "Peace, be still!" A few short minutes later the turbulence completely subsided. What an awesome testimony to the power, reality and faithfulness of God when he is called upon!

Lord, please cause us to remember and be assured that nothing is impossible with you, no matter how violent the storm, nor how big a sum is needed. Regardless the diagnosis, hurt or disappointment—You are God and with You nothing is impossible. You have power over all and every created thing!

Reyna Britton, RN, is the director of accreditation and quality standards for Lancaster General Hospital and is the wife of Duane Britton, senior pastor of DOVE Christian Fellowship Westgate Celebration.

Setting High Expectations

"Then as I looked, I saw a door open in heaven, and the same voice I had heard before spoke to me with the sound of a mighty trumpet blast. The voice said, 'Come up here, and I will show you what must happen after these things.' And instantly I was in the Spirit, and I saw a throne in heaven and someone sitting on it!" *Revelation 4:1–2 (New Living Translation)*

When John received the invitation to "come up here," he was ushered into the brilliance and supernatural glory of heaven. Instantly he saw the throne and all the hosts surrounding it—worshiping in ways beyond what John could humanly grasp. John must have been changed forever by that moment when he got a glimpse of the wonder of God!

Undoubtedly it changed his entire perspective of everything he had experienced in his earthly life. After that, John most likely never settled for anything less than the very presence of God. The bar had been set far too high for him.

May we not accept substitutes for God's presence in our midst—or lower our bar of expectation for His power to transform lives, churches, and communities.

Pray for Lancaster County is our weekly prayer focus for the individuals, families, churches and communities of our region. Please carry this emphasis in your heart and your prayers throughout the week.

Organized Living

"Above all else, guard your heart, for it is the wellspring of life."
Proverbs 4:23

I recently shopped at a store called "Organized Living." It was going out of business. Maybe people don't really want to get organized after all! Or maybe they've discovered that stuff like boxes and files and shelves aren't the answer.

This store was dying because they promised something they could not deliver—an organized life. Cool stuff only makes us *feel* organized. And we think that if we feel organized, all of the pieces of our lives will somehow fall into place.

The downside of life in the 21st century is its organization around feelings and technology. I thought that having a Personal Digital Assistant (PDA) was going to get me organized. It didn't. Have you ever looked at some new product and thought, "this is just what I need for…," only to find it a year later sitting on a shelf somewhere, or in a box out of sight so you won't feel guilty or stupid for another failed attempt to get your life in order?

Here's why this stuff rarely works for us: it's the human *will* which gets someone organized, not efficiency. It's in the heart, in the choices that you make, that God can organize a soul. The heart is the first "room" in the house that must be organized before all others. *"Life can only be pulled together from the inside. That is the function of the will, or heart, to organize our life as a whole, and indeed to organize it around God."* (Dallas Willard).

Do you want to get organized? Pay attention to the choices you are making minute by minute.

Ancient wisdom says, "Guard your heart, for it is the wellspring of life."

Lord, forgive me for my ego-centered efforts to organize my life with energy and technology. May Your kingdom come through my life, my heart, my will.

Robert Woodcock is with Robert Henry Consulting, LLC.

Tee Time

"Live such good lives among the pagans that, though they accuse you of doing wrong, they may see your good deeds and glorify God on the day he visits us." *1 Peter 2:12*

One day my father-in-law and I went to the golf course. It was one of those courses where they like to keep every tee time filled. Pairs of players or solos are a nuisance. So when the two of us arrived at the tee box, we were partnered with a single.

The man playing with us obviously wanted to be alone on the course. He kept the conversation to a minimum and pretty much ignored us the best he could. But about the third hole, my father-in-law asked him what he did for a living. The man responded. Then Dad said, "I'm retired from Western Electric and my son-in-law here is a pastor."

Probably the wrong thing to say. Not the Western Electric part. The pastor part. The man gave me a funny look. He barely spoke another word. Two holes later, as he went in search of an errant ball, we lost him. I guess not everyone likes pastors.

Most of us wrestle with the fact that not everyone likes Christians. To some, Christians are moral busybodies working to impose their will on the rest of society. To others, Christians are strange people. Some think that Christians look at life all wrong. For lots of reasons, not everyone likes Christians or wants to be one.

Peter reminds us that we are different. We need to be clear about our values in Christ and let those values drive our behavior. We must be careful how we live among our neighbors. The key is to always honor God in our lives—to make sure our behavior reflects the Savior.

Lord, help me to be more concerned about being like Jesus than being liked.

Dr. Stephen Dunn is senior pastor of the Church of God of Landisville. He is a member of the Board of Trustees of Lancaster County Council of Churches.

The Sin

"…I have set before you life and death, blessings and curses. Now choose life…." *Deuteronomy 30:19*

I became a Mennonite Christian in my early twenties. When my mother came to visit me, she brought beer to drink since we, of course, had none. Then my mother would leave her beer in my refrigerator for her next visit. This caused me some distress. She claimed she did it as a matter of her convenience. As a practical matter, I did not like having beer taking up space in my refrigerator. But, I also didn't want beer in my house, period. I had already been convicted by the Lord to pour out my almost full bottle of premium aged Jack Daniels. I suspect that this was yet another instance of my mother's and my on-going battle of who was going to control my life, which I did not win until she died. I complained to her and she did nothing; we argued, and I threatened to pour it out. I struggled with what it meant to "Honor Thy Father and Thy Mother" in this and every other situation.

A friend of mine (a former alcoholic and drug addict), told me that I was participating in my mother's sin by having beer in my house. Shortly after that, the Lord dropped this concept into my spirit: My mother's sin was not drinking beer. Her sin was rejecting Jesus. It did not matter how much she drank. It did not matter how many other things she did. The only thing that mattered was her relationship to Jesus.

The purpose of the law, the tree of knowledge of good and evil, is to point us to the Savior, the Tree of Life. From the beginning of time, we have had the choice of which fruit to eat—judgment or life. Too often, I choose judgment. Today, I purpose to choose life.

Lord, be my help.

Karen Boyd is a small group leader at ACTS and serves on the board of the Pennsylvania Homeschoolers Accreditation Agency.

August 30

The Work of God

"The weapons we fight with are not the weapons of the world. On the contrary, they have divine power to demolish strongholds."
2 Corinthians 10:4

In his book, *Evangelism, A Biblical Approach*, A.D. Dixon wrote, "When we rely upon organization, we get what organization can do; when we rely upon education, we get what education can do; when we rely upon eloquence, we get what eloquence can do, and so on. Nor am I disposed to undervalue any of these things in their proper place, but when we rely upon prayer, we get what God can do."

When Charles Spurgeon was asked the secret of his spiritual power, he responded by saying, "Knee work! Knee work!" Spurgeon was simply realistic; the only way lives are transformed is through the work of God's Spirit. We join with God in His fight for the souls of men and women when we fight on our knees.

Many church leaders are advocating approaches to work in the church that incorporate many of the concepts utilized by the organizations Dixon cites. These approaches are not bad in themselves. In fact, they may be very necessary. But we cannot get the results of God without the work of God. Certainly, we ought to use the tools God has given us in order to get the gospel out to people who are living in the darkness of this world. But those tools are only the technical means and only technical results will follow. The church must rely on spiritual means to accomplish spiritual ends. Heart transformation is the spiritual goal. It can only be accomplished through spiritual work.

We tend to want to see that our work has produced something. We want some kind of response that indicates what we have done has been worthwhile. Schools give grades. Employers give raises and promotions. God gives grace.

Let us persevere in prayer that the work of God may be accomplished in our world.

Jim Gambini is the former pastor of the Mount Pleasant Brethren in Christ Church.

Fear or Faith?

"We live by faith, not by sight." *2 Corinthians 5:7*

S teve, you have to hold still and keep your eye open," my doctor commanded. "I'm trying," was my reply. Ever had a needle stuck into your eyeball while you were every bit conscious with your eyes open? I have. And it hurts!

So what could possibly be accomplished from such sadistic torture? Well, for one thing, healing for a retinal tear and detachment. For another, to be able to make a decision in the midst of this test that spiritual sight is far superior to that of physical sight, and to realize that there is only so much medical science can do. I further learned that I must fully, totally and completely trust God for his wisdom, His method and His timing for healing. I discovered, also, that there is a huge difference between faith and fear. Faith is founded in the unseen, while fear is based upon the realm you and I can see. When we are in fear, we cannot be in faith. Fear and faith do not abide together.

Now faith is not that I never have doubts. It is, however, that my belief is stronger than my doubt. I personally feel that one of the scariest questions in the New Testament is found in Luke 18:8, "…when the Son of Man comes, will he find faith on the earth?" Is your faith stronger than your doubt? Or stated another way, how forceful is your faith?

When you or I give into a spirit of fear, we will lose faith. Fear will, in fact, immobilize us as Christians. Let's fall out of fellowship with fear and "…with that same spirit of faith we also believe and therefore speak…(2 Corinthians 4:13)." When faith comes and we speak through a spirit of faith, fear must go.

Heavenly Father, I declare faith over any fear found within my life. Your Word tells us that fear has torment. I will not be intimidated by fear. I chose to "live by faith and not by sight."

Steve Prokopchak serves on DOVE Christian Fellowship International's Apostolic Council.

*Art by Luke Hershey, grade 5
Locust Grove Mennonite School*

September

God speaks!

"Then you will call upon me and come and pray to me, and I will listen to you." *Jeremiah 29:12*

One time as I was ministering at the women's unit of a county prison, the Lord gave me a word on "hearing God." I noticed that a middle-aged woman sat quietly and listened intently. The following week she revealed that God spoke to her. She had been in prison for three months and was "lost in the system." She had not even been before the judge to hear her charges. She said the Lord told her that when she did go before the judge she was going to receive the sentence of "time served" and she was going home!

I almost panicked. "Did she really hear from God on this?" was my first thought. Then I looked into her face at the supernatural serenity that covered her. We prayed and agreed together that the word the Lord had spoken would come to pass. The following week, the woman told us this story: "I went before the judge and he sentenced me to 12 years in prison! I said, 'No! My Father told me that I was going to get time served and I was going home.'

"The judge inquired, 'Who is your father?' In response, I just looked up to acknowledge my heavenly Father. Two female deputies came and led me out of the courtroom. As soon as we stood under the exit sign of the door, the judge shouted to us, 'Wait!' We stopped instantly and looked at the judge a bit puzzled. The judge continued, 'I have no idea why I am doing this!' He changed my sentence to *time served*. And then he told me, 'You may go home.'"

On my next visit to the prison, my friend was not there. She had been released and gone home. The Bible Study increased from its previous 3-5 women to 35 at the very next session. Word traveled very quickly through the prison that there was a God who heard prayers and answered by miracles!

Thank you, Jesus, for hearing and answering our prayers!

Sharon Weaver is the seminar coordinator for DOVE Christian Fellowship International.

God Stories

Handyman or Lover?

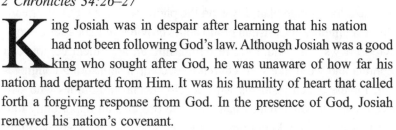

Pray for Lancaster County

"...This is what the Lord, the God of Israel, says concerning the words you heard: Because your heart was responsive and you humbled yourself before God when you heard what he spoke...and because you humbled yourself before me and tore your robes and wept in my presence, I have heard you, declares the Lord."
2 Chronicles 34:26–27

K ing Josiah was in despair after learning that his nation had not been following God's law. Although Josiah was a good king who sought after God, he was unaware of how far his nation had departed from Him. It was his humility of heart that called forth a forgiving response from God. In the presence of God, Josiah renewed his nation's covenant.

In the same way, we need to invite God to examine our hearts and motives. Why do we want God to come and transform us? Is it because we want Him to be our "handyman," ready and available to fix all our problems or is it because we are desperately seeking the One who desires an intimate relationship with us? Do we want God as a handyman who comes at our convenience, or do we want Him as a lover who saturates our lives with His presence?

We will hinder transformation if we view God simply as one who can mend our relationships, keep us out of financial crisis, or make us successful. He is the ultimate searcher of the heart. Are you willing to allow Him to shine the searchlight of His love into your life and search out the real intentions of your heart?

Pray for Lancaster County is our weekly prayer focus for the individuals, families, churches and communities of our region. Please carry this emphasis in your heart and your prayers throughout the week.

God's Time Frame

"Trust in the Lord with all your heart and lean not on your own understanding; in all your ways acknowledge him, and he will make your paths straight." *Proverbs 3:5–6*

Five years seemed like a reasonable time frame. After all, we were new at this. It would take time to equip the congregation for what we felt called to do. We'd had an informal ministry to people with disabilities for years, but now we hoped to become more intentional, focused and committed. In five years, our goal was to adopt a group home in the community. Yes, five years would be reasonable.

About five *weeks* after our Special Needs Committee met to formulate a long-range plan, I was on the phone with the CEO of Friendship Community, a Christian group home provider in Lancaster County. "Good news!" he said. "We're purchasing an apartment complex in Ephrata and we'd like your church to become a sponsoring congregation for the dozen residents with developmental disabilities who will live there!" It was obvious that God had dropped an opportunity into our laps that we could not ignore. At the same time, we were woefully aware of our inadequacy for the task—which is precisely where God wanted us, relying on His strength that is perfected in weakness.

Our learning curve was steep, God's provision was abundant and it has never stopped. Over the past six years, we have learned to "hold the steering wheel with a light touch" and enjoy the ride. We have experienced the thrill of watching God's handwork in ways beyond what we could ask or imagine. Our congregation of 350 now has about thirty individuals with all different types of special needs who regularly exercise their gifts of grace in our midst.

Dear heavenly Father, help us to remember that You want our committed hearts more than our "perfect" plans.

Stephanie Hubach is an author, speaker, and disability advocate who—in partnership with her husband Fred—leads the Special Needs Ministry at Reformed Presbyterian Church of Ephrata.

September 4

In Honor of Work

"Servants, in all things do the orders of your natural masters; not only when their eyes are on you, as pleasers of men, but with all your heart, fearing the Lord" *Colossians 3:22 (Bible in Basic English)*

For several years our extended family gathered at the Ressler farm to celebrate Labor Day—by working! My wife's father, Martin, always had a number of special new construction or repair projects ready for our muscles.

Aunts and uncles, brothers and sisters, cousins, in-laws, and friends put their hands to a variety of jobs. We prepared meals, cranked home-made ice cream, watched young children, sawed lumber, swung hammers, laid concrete blocks, drove tractors, unloaded hay in the barn, cleared trails in the woods, played imaginatively in the hay mow, petted cats, and swept the cow stables. Others chose to "supervise" the work.

God used our working together on those holidays to strengthen our family relationships. The adage, "many hands make light work," proved true and made the hours pass quickly. We joined in the spirit of this holiday to recognize the value of laborers who are the backbone of our national economy and free enterprise.

Work is honorable. God worked six days to create the world as we know it, and then He rested. Made in His image, our work in the marketplace can really be worship to Him. With reverence before God, we sincerely do our work well not to be seen by others but ultimately to please Him.

Father, by Your Holy Spirit, prompt us to work each day in honor of work and of You. Strengthen us to give a good day's work to those we serve. Lead those who desire to work but who lack a job to a place of gainful employment. Give us compassion to encourage those whose work is limited because of handicaps. Through Jesus, Amen.

Keith Yoder and his wife, **Marian**, have served as educators and in a variety of ministry roles throughout their 35 years of marriage.

To Preach Good Tidings

"The Spirit of the Lord God is upon Me, because the Lord has anointed Me to preach good tidings to the poor; He has sent Me to heal the brokenhearted, to proclaim liberty to the captives and the opening of the prison to those who are bound...." *Isaiah 61:1 (New King James Version)*

Last spring, I was blessed to be part of a medical team from Lancaster County which traveled to Haiti to serve with a missionary located in Mount Rouis, Haiti. We collected suitcases of medical and hygienic supplies: drugs, toothbrushes and toothpaste, and toys and treats to be dispensed at the clinics we would conduct.

The week turned out to be an adventure that was physically challenging. It was dangerous during open-bed truck rides to and from a remote mountain village where roads had been washed out by hurricanes, or during gunfire in the streets of the capital city. But it was totally rewarding, as many gave their lives to Jesus and hundreds were given medical attention in the clinics conducted by our team.

The children living in poverty and hopelessness captured our hearts. We visited schools where children are educated, served nourishing food, and taught about the God who loves them passionately. These little ones will break out of the generational curses to freedom in Christ and will be the nation changers that God intends them to be.

Being part of such an amazing team during this time of service impacted my life forever. We can go as the Word of God commands us, "Go into all the world and preach the gospel to every creature (Mark 16:15)."

Father, help us to obey Your Word and go to the lost, whether he is our next-door neighbor or someone in another nation. Give us a passion to reach the lost, poor, and needy with the Good News of Christ and give us compassion to meet the physical and emotional needs as well.

Mary Prokopchak is a nurse and serves with her husband, Steve, on the Apostolic Council of DOVE Christian Fellowship International.

The Best Way

"To all perfection I see a limit; but your commands are boundless." *Psalms 119:96*

It was another Tuesday as I was driving my teenage daughter, Rachel, to her class on the other side of town. The construction project on the bypass was in full swing, and every week I navigated the new traffic patterns. Every week the lanes switched from one side to another. Every week, what was the right lane for me became the "exit only" lane for another location.

Going there was not so bad, but coming home was. It wasn't uncommon to miss the new entrance for my destination and end up speeding toward a distant city. It wasn't uncommon to enter the highway traveling west and have the traffic force you to loop around underpasses and end up going east. Every week my daughter laughed at me as I wandered the maze that was called Route 30.

One week, my daughter recognized my extreme frustration and distress over this. She reached over and patted me on the back and said, "It's okay. We don't have to go the best way every time." What a relief.

In my head, I had been hearing the voice of my past. The voice said I must be the best every time; I must go the best, most efficient way. And I believed it. I don't know why. It was clear that the people who said that to me didn't live it. They weren't perfect. But I tried hard to be perfect so that they would love me. It didn't work.

2 Corinthians 12:9 says, "But he [the Lord] said to me 'My grace is sufficient for you, for my power is made perfect in weakness.' Therefore I will boast all the more gladly about my weaknesses, so that Christ's power may rest on me." I don't have to go the "best way" every time....

Lord, I am weak and imperfect; show Yourself strong in me. Amen.

Karen Boyd is a small group leader at ACTS and serves on the board of the Pennsylvania Homeschoolers Accreditation Agency.

Speak the Truth

"Therefore each of you must put off falsehood and speak truth-fully to his neighbor...." *Ephesians 4:25*

When Sharon and I were preparing to move to South America for missionary service, the organization for which we would work in Brazil asked us to bring several thousand dollars' worth of sophisticated audio/video equipment along. In order to save the high import tax on such items, they asked us to include the equipment as part of our personal household belongings. These were exempt from customs fees. We felt this would be a misrepresentation.

I respectfully told our employer that I would gladly bring the items, but I would not say that they belonged to us. The leaders were frustrated, believing that we would cost them many hundreds of dollars in customs duties. Nevertheless, we stood our ground. We believed that God would honor truthfulness. We flew to Brazil and were soon notified that our freight was at the airport for pick-up. Along with two men from the mission and a borrowed truck, I went to claim our items.

The customs officers looked over the list I had prepared. Each household item was listed and each expensive AV item was clearly marked as not belonging to us personally, but rather to the mission. Immediately he asked to see each one of these items. I opened the freight containers and pointed out each item. Then the officer walked away. A few minutes later he returned and told me to load up all the containers and leave. There would be no import tax, no request for a bribe (a common practice), no problems. A process that typically took several days was completed in less than an hour!

I was humbled and amazed at God's goodness and challenged again to obey His instructions, even when they might seem foolish.

Lord Jesus, I purpose to speak truthfully, even when it would seem easier to be deceptive. Thank you that I can relax, knowing that You will take care of the outcome.

John Charles is director of Abundant Living Ministries, a Christian marriage and family counseling organization near Lititz.

The Thirst For True Water

"...Everyone who drinks this water will be thirsty again, but whoever drinks the water I give him will never thirst. Indeed, the water I give him will become in him a spring of water welling up to eternal life." *John 4:13–14*

O f all the skills gleaned from my college experience, getting along with roommates was the most important. The comprehensive document I was required to submit before I left home appeared to suggest the college would exhaust every effort to match me with someone.

In a small study and sleep area, four eighteen-year-old males were expected to live in peace and harmony...without committing murder. By the time I arrived, Mike had already claimed a bunk. "Wait until you meet Ed," he greeted me. Ed, from the East, rumbled in with a stereo and records. Dick, from the Midwest, rolled in last. As we settled into our new life-style, I wondered, "Why did they have us fill out that form? These people are not like *me." We* were all sizes and shapes, with different socioeconomic backgrounds. Remarkably, we didn't kill each other that year. What I learned, as a scared boy far from home, was that people are not machines that behave, or computers that process, or organisms that feel. We are human beings who long deeply for satisfaction. The four of us, despite our differences, were thirsty for the water of a loving relationship and meaningful impact.

In reality, everyone longs for these two kinds of water, which only God can supply. Everything else is like a high-calorie, nutrition-void soft drink. It tastes good going down, but ultimately doesn't quench the thirst. That is what I started to learn my freshman year. I wouldn't trade that dormitory year and all the experiences that came with it.

Dear Lord, may we increasingly realize that it is You and You alone who gives us satisfaction. Help us to respond in gratitude and to demonstrate real concern for others. In Jesus' name, Amen.

Peter W. Teague is president of Lancaster Bible College and Graduate School.

The Pursuit of God

"One thing I ask of the Lord, this is what I seek: that I may dwell in the house of the Lord all the days of my life, to gaze upon the beauty of the Lord and to seek him in his temple." *Psalms 27:4*

David desired one thing—the presence of God. He wanted to dwell with the Lord, gaze on His beauty, and seek Him with his whole heart. David reached a place in his life where nothing else mattered more to him.

As we examine the motives of our hearts, it is not enough to apologetically recognize that perhaps we have come to view God as a "cosmic handyman" who can fix things for us. We must also realize the need to make a deliberate determination to turn our hearts back toward God with the same passionate pursuit that David modeled. A heart that is pleasing to God is one that says, "I cannot bear to live another day without Your presence. I need You; I need Your presence."

If that becomes the humble, pure, and sincere cry of your heart, God will respond. There is no substitute for intimacy. Look deep within and determine whether you are willing to pursue God.

Pray for Lancaster County is our weekly prayer focus for the individuals, families, churches and communities of our region. Please carry this emphasis in your heart and your prayers throughout the week.

Delight in Differences

"The body is a unit, though it is made up of many parts; and though its parts are many, they form one body. So it is with Christ." *1 Corinthians 12:12*

During the first year of marriage (especially), you learn to adjust to the differences between you and your spouse. While some of those differences can be annoying at first, others can be a refreshing change. For example, I cannot play a single instrument. I am the writer, while my husband is the musician. He plays the guitar and now is learning to play the piano.

Recently, we purchased a used keyboard. Now our house is filled with music. There's always music playing. This is one difference that I personally appreciate. I love to be sitting at home writing on the computer while my husband is playing music.

This reminds me that God has given each of us in the body of Christ a unique talent. But the key is that we need to be using it for His honor and glory. If we are just doing it to impress others and to look good, God will not bless it. And He may even take our gift away.

We also should not envy others' talents but accept what the Lord has given us.

Dear Heavenly Father, thank you that You have made each one of us different and with a special gift. May we not get jealous of others, but may we use the talents You have given us to further Your kingdom. Amen.

Jennifer Paules-Kanode is a writer, part-time DJ on WJTL 90.3 FM and an English as a Second Language instructor.

September 11

A Safe Landing

"...And surely I am with you always, to the very end of the age."
Matthew 28:20

In the spring of 1988, my wife and I and our two children were flying home from Ohio to Lancaster, PA, in a single engine plane. The pilot and his wife were friends of ours and he was a flight instructor. It was our 12 year old daughter's very first time flying, and we needed to take time to reassure her and to tell her flying was safer than driving.

We were flying for 45 minutes when there was a loud bang and the airplane lost all power. The crankshaft in the single engine had snapped in half. We could feel the loss of power and the loss of altitude. As the pilot radioed for help, the four of us in the back prayed for wisdom and mercy. The peace and presence of God filled the plane in a real and powerful way. There was no fear present. My daughter asked, "What will we do now?"

The pilot's wife looked out the window and saw the Akron-Canton Airport 10 miles to the north.

She said, "We are going to land at that airport." Eighty-five knots—the perfect glide speed for that model airplane, and riding on the wings of prayer and a strong southwest wind—we just made it over the trees at the end of the runway for a perfect dead stick landing. The fire engines were waiting for us, but they were not needed that day. Before we climbed out, we bowed our heads and thanked our heavenly Father for His mercy and wisdom. The first rescue person to reach us told us to go home and thank God tonight for saving us. We told him we had already taken care of that. I still remember the powerful presence of God even as we faced our own death.

Father, we thank you for never leaving or forsaking us, no matter what.

Gene Forrey pastors at East Petersburg Mennonite Church and enjoys telling stories of God in action.

All Your Diseases

"...Who forgives all your iniquities, Who heals all your diseases."
Psalms 103:1–3

I grimaced as I felt that stabbing pain once again. "That's crazy," I thought. This sharp pain that was so persistent was also very focused. It came only to the three middle toes of my right foot. It kept me awake at night and was a distraction by day.

I was doing what I knew to do. I was praising God for being so good. I was thanking Him for all of His provisions for His children. I was speaking His words into those painful toes (Isaiah 53:4; Matthew 8:16–17; 1 Peter 2:24; 3 John 2; Psalms 103:1–3, Psalms 107:20). I was choosing humility, grace and a pure heart by the power of the cross.

I would have the thought that this pain was just a small thing— three toes in the center of my right foot. Many suffer so much more. I should be glad it wasn't worse and be content to live with it. I would ask myself, "Is that thought from God? Did Jesus only pay the price for a harsh diagnosis?" God had been teaching me about His Father's heart. I had come to the revelation that attacks against my body do not come from my heavenly Father. Such things have a different source, and the provision for healing has been purchased at a high price. I would continue to stand and refuse to be robbed.

One Sunday morning, after a very worshipful service, a brother made this clear declaration: "There is someone here who has been having severe pain in your feet. Actually, it is your right foot. The pain is in your center three toes. God is healing you today." I leaped with gratitude and received this wonderful provision! That was three years ago. I've had no pain since that day.

Oh Lord, I worship You as the God of stunning power and as my loving Father.

Ann Gibbel serves in the areas of prayer and healing.

No Weapon...Anywhere

"No weapon that is formed against you shall prosper...." Isaiah 54:17 (New American Standard)

One of the darkest days of my life occurred when I was a young therapist working in the Midwest. One day, without warning, an ominous looking letter appeared on my desk, bearing the letterhead of a certain law firm. My hands began to tremble and my heart began to beat rapidly as I opened the letter. The opening sentence, "You are being sued in court," made me feel weak and limp.

I battled fear and depression over the next several months. I was concerned that the lawsuit might strip me of my earthly goods. I was also fearful that I might lose my license and professional reputation. I battled Satan, who gave me messages like, "You're a miserable failure as a counselor! Why don't you give up the counseling profession?"

Eventually, the fog began to lift and the scripture quoted above flashed through my mind. "No weapon formed against you will prosper in court," the Spirit seemed to whisper. The process continued, with many depositions and appearances before various attorneys. However, I now had a renewed confidence that God was going to see me through this difficult time.

Finally, an amicable settlement was reached. God preserved my earthly possessions and I wasn't robbed of my license to practice counseling. I am so glad I didn't listen to Satan's voice to turn my back on my profession, because I love my job as a counselor.

Father, many of us will face situations where the things we have worked so hard to accumulate may seem threatened. We may feel anxious and depressed, and want to give up. Help us to recognize that You walk with us through every dark valley, and You take us through the hard times. Teach us, once again, that no weapon formed against us will prosper.

James E. Johnson, LCSW, D.Min, is the executive director of Shepherd's Touch Counseling Ministry, a Christian counseling ministry in Leola. He has over forty years in counseling experience and has written two books.

Pour Out

"Therefore encourage one another and build each other up, just as in fact you are doing." *1 Thessalonians 5:11*

When I first became a pastor at the age of 37, I was in for a rude awakening. But these first years have been made better because of a couple of retired men who have more than 100 years between them and a couple of other men who are experienced pastors. These men continue to take time to answer my questions and pray with me when I have felt that I was getting in over my head. These times are invaluable to me as a "young" pastor just finishing his fifth year.

Many years ago, I was told by another pastor to find some young man and pour my life into his. At the time I was in single adult ministry and did not think I had time to do this. But I took his advice and started spending time with one of the young men at church. Over time, that young man went into full-time service with Wycliffe Bible Translators as a machinist. Another young man that I was able to mentor is now in his senior year at Liberty University and looking to become a pastor. Neither of these young men were my sons, yet I feel a bond to them and they have thanked me for the time I spent with them.

I encourage you to find someone younger to pour your life into in order to make a difference for the kingdom of God. It need not be your child. Instruct them in the Word of God. Preach it to them, not only with your mouth, but show them with your life.

Dear Lord, show me someone that I can pour my life into and affect for the kingdom of God like those who shared their lives with me.

Pastor Kevin Kirkpatrick is the pastor of Berean Bible Fellowship Church in Terre Hill. He and his wife Diane are former missionaries and have been together in the ministry for five years.

Perspective

"I lift up my eyes to the hills—where does my help come from?
My help comes from the Lord, the Maker of heaven and earth."
Psalms 121:1–2

When I was in Sinai for a Middle Eastern term, I first thought that the desert and the mountains were far away and huge. Then I realized that a tree in the foreground gave me this perception. What I thought was a tree like the ones at home—old and gnarled and 80 feet tall—was not that at all. On closer inspection, I realized that this "large tree" was only 10 feet tall. In the desert, the trees are small, for lack of water. When I stood next to that tiny and gnarled tree, the mountains were right in front of me and not large at all.

When life with its problems is like a desert, we shouldn't focus on how big the mountains are, or compare them to what is familiar around us. Instead, we need to focus on the Lord. The real question is, "How big is God?" "Can He help me in this situation?" Of course He can; He is the Maker of heaven and earth. The solution is not always a large miracle that takes us away or takes the problem away. At times, the solution is just finding the source of water that wasn't seen before. It's found by tapping into the peace that passes understanding and resting there. It is not the mountain ahead that wears us down; it is the grain of sand in our shoes.

Dear Lord, thank you that You gave us eyes to see You. Help us to focus our spiritual eyes on You and trust You to find the answers.

Lois Mishler is a nutritionist at WIC in Lancaster and a member of ACTS Covenant Fellowship.

September 16

Making Right Whatever Offends God

Pray for Lancaster County

"...A solemn fear descended on the city, and the name of the Lord Jesus was greatly honored. Many who became believers confessed their sinful practices. A number of them who had been practicing magic brought their incantation books and burned them at a public bonfire. The value of the books was several million dollars. So the message about the Lord spread widely and had a powerful effect." *Acts 19:17–20 (New Living Translation)*

When the name of Jesus is lifted up over a city or church, there is no place for things that offend God. In this instance, some of the people of Ephesus witnessed a dramatic display of demonic power that frightened them, and the story spread quickly. They immediately determined that only Jesus would be welcomed and honored in their city, which meant destroying everything that was offensive to God. Their occult materials, worth a phenomenal amount of money, suddenly became worthless in their eyes as they sought to find favor with God.

When they made things right with God Almighty, there was a powerful release of the gospel message throughout their city. If we desire to see change in the spiritual climate of our city, we must ensure that the name of Jesus is honored in all things through repentance of *whatever* offends God.

Pray for Lancaster County is our weekly prayer focus for the individuals, families, churches and communities of our region. Please carry this emphasis in your heart and your prayers throughout the week.

The Church, God's Solution

"Now I say to you that you are Peter, and upon this rock I will build my church, and all the powers of hell will not conquer it."
Matthew 16:18 (New Living Translation)

The church (body of Christ) is the only solution to the maladies of our society. In his book, *Strength to Love,* Dr. Martin Luther King Jr. makes this observation:

"The church must be reminded that it is not the master or the servant of the state, but rather the conscience of the state. It must be the guide and the critic of the state, and never its tool. If the church does not recapture its prophetic zeal, it will become an irrelevant social club without moral or spiritual authority."

Father, awaken Your church to its divine purpose. May the wind of Pentecost blow a fresh anointing of prophetic authority that will expose darkness and bring hope to our nation; and Father, let it began in Lancaster. Father, I pray that You will stir the hearts of many as they read this devotion. In the mighty name of Jesus Christ!

Rev. Emanuel J. Oliver is an urban ministry director at the Light Of Hope Community Service Organization.

Help Them Find The Gate

"I am the gate; whoever enters through me will be saved. He will come in and go out, and find pasture. The thief comes only to steal and kill and destroy; I have come that they may have life, and have it to the full." *John 10:9–10*

I have a close friend and brother in the Lord Jesus that was raised as a Palestinian Muslim. We talk occasionally on the telephone, keeping up our friendship and hearing each other's family news. His journey to know the Messiah included a vision, and then a simple, faithful believer who taught him to pray. This former revolutionary fighter has peace with God through Jesus. He found the gate.

At one point we talked about the raging war in Iraq. He told me that every Friday after the prayer time at the mosque is finished, vehicles filled with young Palestinian recruits drive off to die in Iraq. These young men do not expect to defeat the foreign armies; they are simply going to die. They live their lives without hope of decent employment, no hope of raising a family outside the squalor of their refugee camps, and no hope (it seems) to get God's attention. They reason, "Isn't death as a Muslim martyr and the reward of paradise better than this destitute life?" These are not insane people, but people whose only assurance of Paradise is dying for Islam.

All philosophies that circumvent Jesus steal, kill, and destroy. People's lives are stolen at an early age, death reigns all around the region, and destruction continues in many forms. These are the fingerprints of the Evil One, the Thief. Laborers are needed to communicate the truth of the Shepherd. There are still too few to get the job done. Jesus wants an abundant, full life for these people.

Lord Jesus, I pray You would send more workers into the world, especially into those places that have not had an opportunity to know You as I do.

Bruce Heckman serves with Immerge, training people for cross-cultural ministry.

September 19

Do the Math

"For God did not send the Son into the world to judge the world, but that the world might be saved through Him. He who believes in Him is not judged; he who does not believe has been judged already, because he has not believed in the name of the only begotten Son of God." *John 3:17–18 (New American Standard)*

What do you do when someone rips you off? I have worked and lived in Lancaster City for several years. There have been times when I have returned to a job site to find something missing. One time, a tool chest was completely emptied of its tools ($3,500 worth of useful equipment). When thefts like this happen, I need to quickly pray so I don't descend into a "woe is me!" attitude. After one such event, I asked God, very strongly, where He was, and why He let it happen. The response was a simple, "Do the math. Were your tools and equipment higher in value than the souls of the persons who did the stealing?"

My response was, "No, but they put me out of business once, shut down our day of work, cost me a lot of time to document the items lost, not to mention buying other tools."

The question returns, "Is your time more valuable than the person who did the stealing?" I have to say "no," and I need to begin to pray for salvation and not justice. John 3:18 is not very popular because it is so exclusive. There is only one way to escape the automatic sowing and reaping that was begun by God Himself. We can be agents of that release and freedom. Yes, I still hate the loss of time, but I am beginning to see from God's point of view; that is the beginning of a miracle. If we keep a lighter hold on our physical things and a greater hold on the gift of God, then we will see more release for other people and for ourselves.

Jesus, please forgive us for our tight hold on the material. Help us to see people, not from our human viewpoint, but Yours. Amen.

Brian Mishler is a construction supervisor for Lancaster Area Habitat for Humanity.

God Stories

September 20

Mustard Seed Faith

"...For truly, I say to you, if you have faith as a grain of mustard seed, you will say to this mountain, 'Move from here to there,' and it will move; and nothing will be impossible to you."
Matthew 17:20 (Revised Standard Version)

I always wanted to know how big a mustard seed of faith is. I knew that a mustard seed was tiny, but how much of that is measured in faith? How much faith does it really take to move a mountain? When I was a teenager, my father left the family for nine years. For nine years I was angry at God for letting Dad leave. By God's grace, a man befriended me and shared with me the true love of the heavenly Father. That inspired my passion for more of God. One night, as I was driving into the city, I heard a voice in my head. The voice I heard told me something that was going to happen to me five minutes later. Five minutes passed, and that exact series of events came true. At that point, I came to a crisis of belief. Either there was a God in heaven who spoke to me, or I was psychic. Well, that night, before going to bed, I got down on my knees and prayed like I never prayed before. I prayed with a mustard seed of faith—because for the first time in my life, I believed, beyond the shadow of a doubt, that there was a God in heaven who loved me enough to talk to me personally. Looking back, I believe that I could have asked for anything that night, and God would have given it to me. What did I pray for? For the first time in nine years, I prayed that my Daddy would come home. That very minute a series of events started to unfold in my Dad's life. Six days later, through no intervention of my own, my Dad rededicated his life to God and was back living with us, his family, again.

Father, thank you for being an all merciful God who still talks to Your children personally. You amaze me with Your power and tenderness. You astound me with Your words of grace and hope. You awe me with Your touch of restoration and healing. Come, Dad, let's walk together in the garden of life today. Amen.

Rod Redcay serves as youth leader at DOVE Westgate.

Look At My Face

"When You said, 'Seek My face,' my heart said to You, 'Your face, Lord, I will seek.'" *Psalms 27:8 (New King James Version)*

I learn so much from my kids. When they are distracted, frantic, or simply not heeding, I direct them to "look at my face" and I literally point to my face. This brings out of the spotlight the selfish desire, distraction, or fear and brings into focus:

- My words (whether instructive or comforting)
- My nature (I am Mom—I'm in control, taking responsibility for you. Trust my love for you in this situation.)
- My presence (I am here)

This brings order, comfort, and redirection to the situation. Directions can be fully heard, emotions can be allayed.

So it is with my Father when I fall into spiritual ADHD (Attention Deficit Hyperactivity Disorder), running to and fro, distracted by many things, serving my own interests, or anxious and feeling my lack of strength and faith to carry through. It is His face I need to seek. His countenance is toward me, His eye upon me to encourage, instruct, correct, and guide. With His face toward me and mine lifted toward His, directions can be fully heeded; all else "grows strangely dim."

As a parent of a child with autism, I often show my son various facial expressions because he cannot "read" meaning and emotion from faces. He loses much of the non-verbal communication, so we drill him. He also shies, from eye contact, so I need to remind him how important it is. It shows honor to the one he's either speaking or listening to. It also denotes importance of the message.

So, too, the Father delights when I leave behind the distractions of the world and devote my attention to His face and His words, His nature and His presence.

Lord, let us fix our eyes on Jesus, the Author and Perfecter of faith; not just Your hand, but Your dear face. Amen.

Cindy Riker, a contributing editor to *God Stories*, is a wife and mother, involved in Teaching the Word Ministries.

God is Mission-Hearted

"…You will be my witnesses in Jerusalem, and in all Judea and Samaria, and to the ends of the earth." *Acts 1:8*

My wife and I recently spent time with a couple from Lancaster, Pennsylvania, who are sponsored as "missionaries" from a local church. He is the pastor of a large church (1,000 plus members) in Asia, yet lives in the USA. He travels to Asia for weeks at a time to provide pastoral leadership and occasionally to do ministry in other Asian countries. Traditional paradigms say he is not a missionary but a pastor; yet not a true pastor, because he does not live in geographic proximity to his church; and definitely not a missionary, because he is serving people of his own ethnic background.

I was impressed with this couple's humble demeanor, their spiritual wisdom and passion, and their deeply-held faith which came to them through years of sacrificial ministry. They told stories of miracles of healing and of divine provision. I realized that I was experiencing an invigorating conversation with a truly "contextualized missionary" whose faith caused him to break through boundaries that would have kept others back from ministry.

I left that evening's experience with a new appreciation for the work of the Holy Spirit who desires to craft in each of us a definition of *missionary* that is uniquely ours! This does not happen to the faint-hearted and distracted, but to those who say, "Lord send me." It is for those who go and do not limit the call of God. We are *all* sent into the world because God is fundamentally mission-hearted.

Father, today show us who needs to hear of Your Love. Help us to be missionaries no matter where we serve. Show us how to expand our borders to think and act beyond what seems normal so that Your good news can reach around the world.

Glen J. Yoder serves as pastor of Ephrata DOVE Christian Fellowship and as Missionary Care Coordinator for DOVE Mission International.

Restoring Broken Covenants

"I prayed, 'O my God, I am utterly ashamed; I blush to lift up my face to you. For our sins are piled higher than our heads, and our guilt has reached to the heavens. Our whole history has been one of great sin…O Lord, God of Israel, you are just. We stand before you in our guilt as nothing but an escaped remnant, though in such a condition none of us can stand in your presence.'" *Ezra 9:6–7, 15 (New Living Translation)*

Ezra was appalled when he realized how much the nation of Judah had sinned against God in broken commandments and covenants. His prayer of anguish reveals his heart of deep sorrow. As Ezra confessed the sin of his nation with great weeping, the people (men, women, and children) joined him in weeping bitterly over their own sin. They chose from that day on to obey the law of God. When Ezra realized the depth of God's feelings about unresolved corporate sin, he sought to make complete restoration with Him.

Time doesn't always heal wounds; past iniquities must be dealt with in a way that is honoring to God. We must humble ourselves and make all things right in His sight.

Pray for Lancaster County is our weekly prayer focus for the individuals, families, churches and communities of our region. Please carry this emphasis in your heart and your prayers throughout the week.

Sons of the Creator

"The earnest expectation of creation eagerly waits for the revealing of the sons of God." *Romans 8:19*

Anyone in farming knows that nature is one of the key ingredients in production. While overseeing the family fruit farm we witnessed the privilege of being sons of the Creator time after time.

One year when the orchard was in full bloom, we listened to severe frost warnings. As we retired for the night, we prayed, "Lord, we declare the canopy of Your protection over those trees." We awoke to discover that an unexpected cloud cover had canopied over our hill, totally sparing our trees from frost.

In a year of desperate drought, Al prayed for the trees to be watered from below. Inexplicably, our harvest was unaffected by drought.

One night in the midst of peach harvest, I was awakened to the sound of distant thunder and the words, "Killer storm." Wind could seriously damage our ripened crop. Hail would be devastating. We prayed earnestly for protection as the violent storm approached rapidly. Suddenly we realized that the storm we had heard approaching from the west was now receding to the east. The next day confirmed severe wind and hail damage within miles to west and east, but our God heard our cries.

When we followed God's call to leave the farm and we gathered our last autumn harvest, we literally were unable to contain what God poured out. We scrounged bushel baskets from the barn that had never been used, sold bulk bins retail, and still we were running over.

Father, thank you for revealing Yourself through Your creation. Thank you that Jesus is before all things in heaven and on earth. All things consist and are held together in Him. Amen.

Ruth Ann Stauffer serves in prayer, counseling, and teaching. Husband Al joins her in OASIS Streams Ministries, an associate ministry of Teaching The Word Ministries.

September 25

Transforming Power

"And my speech and my preaching were not with persuasive words of human wisdom, but in demonstration of the Spirit and of power, that your faith should not be in the wisdom of men but in the power of God." *1 Corinthians 2:4–5 (New King James Version)*

Over the years, I have often prayed that God's power would be made known as it was in the days of Jesus—where healings would happen, and demons would leave because of His presence.

One evening as I was leading worship with a team, I saw a woman enter the back of the sanctuary. I noticed that she didn't seem to be comfortable with the worship. Not knowing who she was, I thought she was uncomfortable with the style of contemporary worship that we were doing. We continued to worship, and as I remember, the room was filled with expectation of meeting with God. There was a hunger for the presence of God, not just from the worship team, but from the majority of the people there. Before I realized what was going on, the woman was lying on the floor. I saw a few people gather around her to minister to her. I hoped she was all right. It was a little distracting for me, but I managed to continue to lead the worship.

Later, I found out that as the presence of God filled the room, she was unable to stand. While on the floor, she was delivered of strongholds that had haunted her for years. She got up a free woman, not because of the ministry of a person, but because of an encounter with the Lord in her life that night.

Father, make Your manifest presence known in Your church and in my life each day. May Your transforming power mold us and form us into Your image so that we can partner with You in changing lives and transforming our communities. Amen.

Mark Ulrich is associate pastor of youth/worship at Ephrata Community Church.

September 26

One Penny

"Truly, I say to you that this poor widow has put in more than all; for all these out of their abundance have put in offerings for God, but she out of her poverty put in all the livelihood that she had."
Luke 21:3–4 (New King James Version)

T*hree pennies.* During a walk along a busy street I found three pennies along the pavement. I reflected and I remembered what Jesus taught about the widow.

Two pennies. All that she had. The Lord measured the impact of giving not by the monetary amount, but by the extent to which she devoted what she had to God. In sacrifice, up to the full extent of what one has, God is honored. This is true worship.

One penny. It was a bright sunny morning as the congregation gathered around a temporary platform on the parking lot of the property they were purchasing. The contract had been signed, and now they were dedicating themselves to the work of renovating the former department store as their new congregational home.

As the celebrative time began, one of the leaders saw a penny on the pavement. She rejoiced as the Lord stirred faith in her heart that He would provide the hundreds of thousands of dollars needed to complete the project. Seventeen months later, the congregation moved into their new home with a wonderful spirit of dedication and celebration. That one penny remains a testimony that the Lord will continue to provide unto the completion of the project—and future expansion.

Two mites or a penny represent the smallest units of monetary measurement. Yet when they are joined with largeness of heart, trust, and even sacrifice, they may become great expressions of worship.

Father, even the smallest thing of value is not beyond Your notice. We invite Your Spirit to direct us in worshiping You today with all that we have.

Keith Yoder is founder of Teaching The Word Ministries and a member of the Regional Council of the Regional Church of Lancaster County.

Fruitful

"I am the true vine, and my Father is the gardener. He cuts off every branch in me that bears no fruit, while every branch that does bear fruit he prunes so that it will be even more fruitful."
John 15:1–2

Not too many years ago, our church went through a crisis. There was hard preaching from the pulpit. There was resistance from the congregation. Both the leaders and the congregation were deeply hurt and angry. People were leaving in droves. Was this the cutting and pruning of the Lord? Most of the rest of us looked for a good reason to leave. We asked God to please release us from that place of pain. Things seemed hopeless. As attendance and offerings dropped each week, we wondered if the congregation would even survive. Much of what was happening seemed like, well, let's say *manure*.

But we stayed. An outside consultant, a godly man, led the congregation to pray and talk through almost every aspect of congregational life. Week after week, month after month, we worked. We learned to trust God and His pruning. We began to trust each other. New leaders were discerned, and a pastor was found. New people began to come. After many months, we walked through a symbolic door out of the past and into the future. We had survived.

What we had lived through was stinking, unpleasant, and hazardous to our spiritual health. But in the end, it had helped us to grow. One evening, as our small group reviewed the past, the truth hit us. Manure is fertilizer. Verses 7 and 11 of Hebrews 12 say, "Endure hardship as discipline...later on, however, it produces a harvest of righteousness and peace for those who have been trained by it."

Lord, help us to stay rooted in You. Help us to receive Your fertilizer and become fruitful for Your kingdom and in Your time. Amen.

Karen Boyd, a contributing editor to *God Stories*, is a small group leader at ACTS and serves on the board of the Pennsylvania Homeschoolers Accreditation Agency.

Compassionate Hospitality

"Then Jesus said to his host, 'When you give a luncheon or dinner, do not invite your friends, your brothers or relatives, or your rich neighbors; if you do, they may invite you back and so you will be repaid. But when you give a banquet, invite the poor, the crippled, the lame, the blind, and you will be blessed. Although they cannot repay you, you will be repaid at the resurrection of the righteous.'" *Luke 14:12–14*

As a Lancaster County farm kid growing up in the early 1950s, I'll never forget the homeless men who roamed the countryside during the summertime. Every couple of weeks we'd get a knock on the door and there was a bedraggled man, often reeking of alcohol, asking for a hot meal. As a kid, it was easy to turn up my nose and say, "Ugh, he's stinky!" but mom never gave me that option. She'd say, "You never know, he could be an angel," as she went to work heating up a plateful of food presented on a tray, complete with a doily and neatly folded napkin.

Hebrews 13:2 says, "Don't neglect to show hospitality to strangers for by this some have entertained angels unaware." Showing hospitality really means to show kindness to strangers. Having compassion in our hearts causes us to impart the presence of Christ to all who cross our threshold. We are called to practice compassionate hospitality, not only in our homes, but at our jobs, in the grocery store, or pushing the kids on the swing in the park. Compassion comes from sitting at the feet of Jesus and then taking steps to open up our hearts to reach out to people as we practice unconditional love.

Father, we know that You are at work in our lives helping us make those heart adjustments to be compassionate people. Help us to be hospitable people and open up our hearts to others.

LaVerne Kreider serves with her husband Larry giving oversight to DOVE Christian Fellowship International. She also serves on the leadership team of a micro-church near Lititz.

The Watering Hole

"Are not two sparrows sold for a penny? Yet not one of them will fall to the ground apart from the will of your Father. And even the very hairs of your head are all numbered. So don't be afraid; you are worth more than many sparrows." *Matthew 10:29–31*

The morning air was crisp and cold as I made my way through the meadow to "Ann's Ridge," so titled by my dad and brother in reference to the two elk I had shot there. After several hours of hunting and enjoying the beauty of the mountains of Montana, I trudged through the snow back across the meadow to meet up with my family. As I did, something caught my eye. A large flat rock that had earlier that morning been home to a thin sheet of ice now held a puddle of water. On one side, there were squirrel tracks leading up to the rock and continuing in the opposite direction. Picturing the squirrel scampering to the rock, pausing for a drink, and continuing on its way, I was struck with the realization that God had provided a watering hole of sorts for none other than a *squirrel!* Marveling at the wonder of such provision, I was reminded of the verses in Matthew that speak of our worth to God. Now when I think of those verses, I can't resist adding, "Don't be afraid; you are worth more than many squirrels!"

God, thank you that I can trust You to provide everything I need. Thank you for my worth in Your eyes.

Ann Weldy is the administrative secretary at DOVE Christian Fellowship Westgate, in Ephrata, and serves as a worship leader at DOVE Elizabethtown.

Things That Separate

Pray for Lancaster County

"Then a voice told him, 'Get up, Peter. Kill and eat.' 'Surely not, Lord!' Peter replied. 'I have never eaten anything impure or unclean.' The voice spoke to him a second time, 'Do not call anything impure that God has made clean.'" *Acts 10:13–15*

When Peter received a vision of animals that were unclean (according to Jewish law) being lowered in a sheet from heaven, he thought he was being true to his religion by refusing to eat what was offered to him. But God used this vision to show Peter that *all* believers are valued in God's eyes.

Those who have been made clean through Jesus Christ are equally a part of the church, regardless of ethnic or denominational background. Biblical unity is a priority with God. Because we understand that to a degree, we make attempts toward unity with inclusive programming and cooperative meetings.

But at the same time, we can be like Peter when we continue to allow our theological disagreements, worship preferences, or exclusive denominational associations to keep us apart from one another in heart relationships. God's presence will be manifested when we value biblical unity as He does.

Pray for Lancaster County is our weekly prayer focus for the individuals, families, churches and communities of our region. Please carry this emphasis in your heart and your prayers throughout the week.

October

October 1

The Eyes of Faith

"But as for me, the nearness of God is my good; I have made the Lord God my refuge, that I may tell of all Your works." *Psalms 73:28 (New American Standard Bible)*

Last October we went to Austria to do children's ministry at a missionary retreat. One of the assignments for the retreat was to spend some time meditating as we walked through a labyrinth. As I walked through this labyrinth I was reminded of my own personal journey. No matter where I am on the journey, I am never really alone. The Lord is walking beside me, guiding me. Sometimes along the journey, I step aside for others to pass. Sometimes others step aside for me.

Traveling along the labyrinth, I noticed various views. In one direction the awesomeness of the Alps stretched upward before me and met up with a cloud of fog right in front of me. When I turned, there was the green of a nearby hillside. Yet another turn revealed the very ordinary if not rustic rooftops of the ancient castle in which we were staying.

As I continued to make my way around the labyrinth, I noticed that a cross appeared in the midst of the cloud. With each successive pass, the fog began to clear, and little by little I was able to see some activity below. I stopped to watch what was happening. The longer I stood and watched, the more I could see what was going on beneath the fog. I was reminded again how our journey is like that. Things are happening, even though we may see none of it in the midst of the fog.

Thanks, Lord, for Your hand that guides me through the fog of life. Father, I want to live with my hand in Yours—with my eyes, my ears, my heart in tune with You each moment of the day. Amen.

Mike and Liz Ingold are founders of a satellite ministry of Petra Christian Fellowship, New Holland which encourages and strengthens missionaries.

Photos by Rachel Boyd, recent graduate of Millersville University

October 2

Connection

"And I thank Christ Jesus our Lord who has enabled me, because He counted me faithful, putting me into the ministry." *1 Timothy 1:12 (New King James Version)*

According to U.S. Labor Department statistics, the average American worker stays at a job for three and one-half years and will change jobs nine times between the ages of eighteen to thirty-four. Home mortgages, though taken out for thirty years, are changed in seven years. People move, on average, every seven years! We've lost our sense of connection in this society.

Have you noticed that those around you do not seem to have anything holding them in place? "Snap decisions" that have life-changing effects are made without regard to the consequences. Lives are ruined, huge sums of money are lost, and relationships are broken.

In November of 1987, at a Marilyn Hickey meeting in Philadelphia, God undeniably "put" me into ministry. I had been ministering in churches most of my life, fulfilling various roles as Sunday School teacher or superintendent, youth leader, church planter, usher, small group leader. I like to think that I was serving faithfully. When I took on the responsibility of becoming a pastor, I needed Him to enable me! Something else was vitally needed to sustain me—the knowledge that He had "called" me or "put" me into ministry. That November the connection was made. Like a locomotive engine coupling to a railroad car, I was forever hooked! It has been a tremendous ride. Many times I revisit in my spirit and mind that night when God literally shook me as I was "connected" with Him to serve as one of His ministers.

Whatever we are "called" by God to do, may we keep the connections firm. This will empower us to stay where we're planted.

Lord, may I stay where You want me to stay as I strengthen my connection with You and others. Thank you for Your enabling power. Amen.

Richard Armstrong serves on staff at The Worship Center as assistant director of Global Ministries.

It Pays to Trust the Lord

"Trust in the Lord with all your heart; do not depend on your own understanding." *Proverbs 3:5 (New Living Translation)*

I don't know about you, but I'd be a total nut case without God. I mean that the whole God package has "all of the answers" if you're willing to accept that God loves those who need Him the most and trust Him in everything. He actually wants us to depend on Him. Not a little bit—a lot!

I've tried to "make" things happen. For fourteen years I banged on doors and made phone calls and wrote letters trying to get enough gigs to make a living. It was frustrating and exhausting. At one point I really thought about giving up this whole "music" thing.

Then one day someone mentioned to me that I'd be good at teaching and performing for children and families. With that in mind, my wife Joyce and I talked about this possible shift in musical direction. At the time we were broke. Really broke. But we decided to knock on some new doors. The doors opened. People started calling me instead of me calling them! God gave us a glimpse of the potential, and we both decided to put all of our trust in Him. In May of 1991, I performed my first children's concert, and by the time August rolled around, it was a full-time job.

That was fifteen years ago. Today, thirty-five hundred concerts, two TV shows and nineteen albums later, I'm still answering the phone—and e-mails too! I still don't fully understand it all. But, I do know this: it pays to trust in God with all your heart!

Lord Jesus, help me to trust You completely. Turn my lack of understanding into true wisdom...to know Your goodness, Your direction and Your will. In Jesus' name, Amen.

Steven Courtney is an award-winning producer and performing songwriter who lives in Manheim with his wife Joyce and their two children.

Faithfulness in Adversity

"But thanks be to God who gives us the victory through our Lord Jesus Christ." *1 Corinthians 15:57 (New King James Version)*

A number of years ago, our family went through a time of real financial hardship. We were within thirty days of losing our house. Some of this was brought on because we lost sight of God's plan for our lives, and some of it was due to being hit with medical bills and some other things.

As we were falling deeper into debt, we were afraid to share our need with others. We were afraid of what others would think, and we isolated ourselves from sharing.

One of the things that we did right was that we never lost sight of our God, who has the victory in all things. We were careful about the words we spoke, making sure they were God's words—words of life that would see us through our situation instead of words that could hold us back or totally bring failure. We continued to tithe and give of our time and talents to our church and community. We also knew that if were going to come through this time, we needed to stay united in our marriage. Financial pressure can really take its toll in a marriage, but we knew that unity was key in pulling through.

God restored everything with amazing speed. It didn't take years and years. When we got our focus back on what He had called us to do, the abundance began to flow, and it has not stopped.

If you are experiencing any adversity in your life, bring it into the light. Let others walk with you through the fire. We had to be broken before we could be set free.

Father God, we thank You for Your presence in our lives. For it is in You that we find our strength and have the victory.

Ed Garner is president of Garner Construction, Inc. and a leader in the small group ministries at The Worship Center.

Keeping Commitments

"...Let your 'Yes' be 'Yes', and your 'No,' 'No'...."
James 5:12 (New King James Version)

When I was a young man I was in a partnership with my father-in-law and two brothers-in-law on a large dairy farm. Because we were one of the largest farms in the county, we were well known by the equipment dealers. One time we bought three high horsepower tractors at one time. Needless to say, we had a reputation and dealers wanted our business.

One particular time we were planning on purchasing a specific piece of machinery. We looked at a number of dealers and received quotes. A decision was made, and we verbally told one dealer that we would purchase from him. A few hours later, another dealer dropped by and offered the exact piece of machinery at a much more discounted price. We would save hundreds of dollars if we bought it from him.

I will never forget what my father-in-law told me. "We can save a lot of money by buying the piece from this company, but we gave our word that we would purchase it from the first dealer, so we will be men of our word and buy it from him." It had a profound impact on my life. I adopted this policy and have tried to apply it to every area of my life.

I am amazed that many people will so easily change their word or make another decision when something better comes along. This happens in business as well as in everyday life. An honorable man keeps his commitments and follows through on his obligations.

Lord Jesus, I pray that I would be a man / woman of my word. Grant me integrity of speech so that my "yes" would be "yes," and my "no" would be "no." Help me to follow through on commitments and honor the words of my mouth, that Your name might be honored and glorified. In Jesus' Name.

Ron Myer serves on DOVE Christian Fellowship International's apostolic council.

"Shhh, Said the Angels"

"...Like seed sown on good soil, hear the word...and produce a crop...." Mark 4:20

When I began to direct the J. P. McCaskey High School Gospel Choir as a college student at Millersville University, I had no idea of the power of God's Word in song.

Marianne was a senior in high school with dreams for the future. She was bright, talented, and she loved Gospel Choir. It was rare to see her without a smile, so it gave me great concern when she came to me one day after school wearing something other than her brilliant smile, as she tersely stated, "I am pregnant."

I listened and allowed her to talk out her pain and tears. She spoke of the hurt that her family would feel and the changes she would have to make to her life and her hopes for the future. And then she spoke about another option—to terminate the pregnancy.

Within me, I could feel the passionate desire to give her my opinion. I wanted to throw a verbal "life-line" to save the child who was growing in her. But I felt muted by a power far greater than the rules that separate church and state in my role as her teacher. It was as though angels were surrounding me, each one with his finger to his lips. "Shhh," they appeared to be exclaiming.

In the spring of the next school year, I got a knock at my classroom door. Marianne was standing there with her signature smile. She was not alone. She held a precious baby boy in her arms. Once again the angels seemed to appear. "Shhhh," they proclaimed softly. "You did not need to say anything nine months earlier because she was carrying two seeds—the child and the Word." As the child grew, so did the Word that was placed in Marianne through the songs she sang in Gospel Choir. In the end, all three—Marianne, the child and the Word—nourished and gave life to one another.

Thank you that the seed of Your Word always produces a bumper crop!

Irvin L. Scott is principal of McCaskey East High School, Lancaster.

October 7

Pursuing True Unity

Pray for Lancaster County

"...But God has combined the members of the body and has given greater honor to the parts that lacked it, so that there should be no division in the body, but that its parts should have equal concern for each other." *Corinthians 12:24–25*

Pursuit of true biblical unity starts with the understanding that we cannot "do unity." Unity is a by-product of the relationships we build with one another, and that can only come as a result of heartfelt humility. In humility, we must be willing to lay down our agendas, our ministries, and even our own desires in order to give ourselves away to one another and to our city. It does not mean that we stop doing what God calls us to do, but it means that we stop pushing our ministry agendas by seeking to get others on board with *our* programs.

The valuable lesson of this scripture passage is that we need each other, and we need each other's ministries. Another ministry or church is not your competition; it is your complementary partner in God's kingdom. God gave us diversity and different giftings so that only together can we understand His plan and purposes for our city. No one church or ministry, no matter how large or successful, will be used exclusively of God to build His kingdom in your city. It takes His church as a whole seeking God together. Building relationships through humility will result in pursing biblical unity—and that will attract the presence of God.

Pray for Lancaster County is our weekly prayer focus for the individuals, families, churches and communities of our region. Please carry this emphasis in your heart and your prayers throughout the week.

Delayed Gratification

"...hope that is seen is no hope at all. Who hopes for what he already has? But if we hope for what we do not yet have, we wait for it patiently." *Romans 8:24–25*

In our early years of marriage, money was *really* tight. But God helped our meager funds stretch. However, I wasn't always willing to wait patiently for God's provision. So, one year I guess He figured I needed to be taught an important lesson. In late August, I told John that our son, Justin, would need a new coat for the coming winter, and that I had seen one in a catalog at a greatly discounted price. John said, "Well, I guess you can order it. Although I think it might be better to wait. Maybe the Lord will provide one in some other way."

I wouldn't wait. I ordered the coat. When it arrived, Justin began wearing it, even before the weather was cold enough to warrant a heavy coat. One Saturday in October a friend from our small group at church called. "Sharon, I was wondering… does Justin need a winter coat this year?"

"Well, not really, but why do you ask?"

"Oh, I was praying for your family the other day and I felt like the Lord told me I was supposed to buy Justin a winter coat…but, I guess not." I was stunned and ashamed. My impatience had cost several people a blessing. Our friend would have had the joy of giving, plus the delight of being used by the Lord to meet a specific need.

It was a humbling lesson, but one that I remember often, especially when I'm tempted to "make things happen." God delights in giving good gifts to His children. And those good gifts are *definitely worth waiting for!*

Lord, help me to really *trust You for provision of my everyday needs! I want to learn to wait patiently, even if that means postponing "instant gratification!"*

Sharon Charles enjoys assisting her husband John, in directing Abundant Living Ministries, a Christian marriage and family counseling organization near Lititz.

Kind Words

"Death and life are in the power of the tongue." *James 3:8–10*

Recently, my three-year-old grandson was encountering a little boy in his Sunday School class who was hitting and exemplifying other naughty behavior. As my grandson would complain following these events, my daughter-in-law would repeatedly tell Preston, "You need to say kind words to him and maybe someday he'll be nice to you!" One Sunday morning as my grandson climbed into the car after church, he emphatically exclaimed, "Mommy, that boy was really mean today." After his mother again tried to explain the importance of saying kind words, Preston exclaimed, "But, Mommy, sometimes my kind words get all [gone]!"

How many times have we as grown-ups struggled with the same feelings? Kind words are an issue of the heart. For out of the heart the mouth speaks. My heart has been grieved as I listen to those who have been wounded by others' tongues, even within our churches. As I use my tongue, am I using it constructively or destructively? As Christians, we are called to speak life to others.

The story of my grandson has a great ending. Several weeks later, after the continual talks about kindness, my grandson was dropped off at his Sunday School room, and a little boy came running up to Preston, wrapping his arms around him to welcome him. Not knowing who the child was, my daughter-in-law later asked who his friend was that was so glad to see him. Preston told her it was the same boy who had been so unkind to him in previous weeks. Be kind to one another…it works!

Dear God, create in me a clean heart and renew a right spirit within me so that I can speak life to those I meet today.

Julie Heller is a pastor's wife who mentors women through "Apples of Gold." She also serves ladies in her Victorian Tea room.

Be a Child Again

"Jesus said, 'Let the little children come to me, and do not hinder them, for the kingdom of heaven belongs to such as these.'"
Matthew 19:14

We often hear the phrase, "Oh, to be a child again, to run free with no responsibilities or worries…" followed by a wistful sigh. Let's stop dreaming and become what we desire. Jesus wants us to come to Him as children—innocent, pure and trusting. People grow up so fast these days, and their focus becomes paying bills, putting in more hours at work, and achieving happiness through stuff. What happens instead is worry, frustration and emptiness.

As a child, I never worried about life. I can remember looking up at the clouds and thinking about what it would be like to sit on them and what they would taste like. As silly as this sounds, this is the pleasure of God. He delights in us enjoying His creation. He wants us to cast all worries upon Him. He wants to speak to our little boy and little girl hearts, and minister grace, peace and healing.

We live in a stressful world, and it can damage our hearts; but there is a place where we can still run free, and enjoy the day. Find this place in Jesus. Come sit on His lap as He shares His heart with you and lays His big, strong, soft hands on you, praying a blessing. Live in the purity and innocence of a child…for therein lies the kingdom of heaven.

Dear Jesus, let me climb into Your lap today and worship You. Tell me You love me and that I am Yours. Let me bathe in Your glory and there find rest and peace. I need Your touch and Your security. I give all my worries to You and rest in knowing that You are in control and that in Your arms I am the safest I could ever be. I love you, Daddy. In Jesus' name, Amen.

Mike Wenger is director of TNT Youth Ministry.

Keys To Satisfaction

"The fear of the Lord leads to life, and he who has it will abide in satisfaction; He will not be visited with evil." *Proverbs 19:23 (New King James Version)*

God initially used sales to prepare me for the pastorate, and when God led me to lay down ministry last year, He again led me into sales, which will help prepare me for any future ministry. It has become clear to me that our "success" in life is determined by our inner development. One result is my growing conviction that the fear of the Lord, the fruit of meekness, and God's favor are closely linked together, and play a key role in the fruitfulness of our lives.

According to Proverbs, the fear of the Lord is the key to finding fulfillment and satisfaction in life. The more we fear God, the more meek we become. Jesus said the meek will inherit the good things of this earth (Matthew 5:5). It is the fruit of meekness, being humble enough to obey God's voice, which brings God's special favor to manifest His blessings in our lives. It all happens by grace as we catch a greater revelation of who God really is and how He views us—and then in faith, respond accordingly.

O loving Father, thank you for Your favor. Give us a hunger for an accurate revelation of You. Help us to seek You with all our hearts, and fill us with the fear of God. Amen.

Dean Witmer, a former pastor, now works for Rohrer's One Hour Heating and Air Conditioning.

October 12

Avoiding the Trap

"A man's wisdom gives him patience; it is to his glory to overlook an offense." *Proverbs 19:11*

Satan has devised a trap with bait that is so effective that multitudes of people are caught in it. I have seen people overcome addictions and sins of many kinds, but this one thing causes more people to stumble than anything else the devil throws at us.

The trap? Offenses that come our way.

We can't keep people from doing things and saying things that are hurtful, but we can control our response to it. We can avoid the trap surrounding the offense.

If you are in the place God wants you, the devil will try to offend you to get you out of that place.

Most of us will be treated unjustly at times. But if you and I can stay free of offense, we will stay in God's will. If we become offended, we will be taken captive by the enemy and thwart God's plan and become dull in our spirit.

How can we stay out of the trap when we are offended and hurt by someone?

First, ask whose offense it is—mine or someone else's?

Admit that you might not see the whole picture—intent, context, assumptions.

Take it to the cross and forgive—instead of taking it into your heart. Take it as an opportunity to join in the suffering of Jesus and to die to self. Let Him absorb your pain.

Choose the high road—bless and pray.

Heavenly Father, I bring those offenses to You that I have been carrying in my heart. I choose to forgive and release the person who hurt me. I ask that You bless them and give me love for them. In Jesus' name, Amen.

Lester Zimmerman is senior pastor of Petra Christian Fellowship, overseer of the Hopewell Network of Churches and serves on the council of the Regional Church of Lancaster County.

The Breakthrough Pig

"David said, 'God has broken through my enemies by my hand, like the breakthrough of waters.' Therefore they named that place Baal-perazim." *1 Chronicles 14:11*

L ike David, we too have enemies that hear of us and come out to war against us. It is at the *"Place of Breakthrough"* that our enemies are defeated. The Hebrew word for "breakout" here is *parats* meaning to *burst out, to increase or to be opened up.* The implication is that somebody has been *closed off, shut up, restricted, or confined.* Do you ever feel that way? If so, you need a breakthrough!

Let me tell you about our "breakthrough pig." On our farm we used electric fences to keep our pigs in a pasture. After a few mildly uncomfortable experiences, the pigs would learn where they were allowed to roam. In fact, we could eventually turn the electricity off because they would stop challenging the fence.

That's a lot like we are. We remember when we once challenged our boundaries, and we don't want to go there anymore. So, we live very contented lives inside the area where we feel we are "allowed to go." But, we had one pig that would always break out. She would approach the fence. When she saw where it was, she would back up, then let out a loud squeal and charge it. The wire would slide over her back for a short second and then it was all over. She quieted down and began to eat the grass "outside the fence." She was willing to experience momentary discomfort in order to break out of the barriers.

What boundaries do you need to challenge? God is a gate-crashing, wall-breaking obstacle-removing God. He wants us to become like Him, so that we pass through barriers too.

Father, forgive me for letting the enemy confine me inside this comfort zone where I live. I want to break out and walk in all that You have created me to be.

Barry Wissler, senior pastor of Ephrata Community Church, leads HarvestNET, a resource ministry linking churches and ministries, and serves on the executive team of the Regional Church.

Pray for Lancaster County

Extended Time With God

"Teach us to number our days aright,
that we may gain a heart of wisdom."
Psalms 90:12

The simple concept of time is a monumental obstacle when considering hindrances to revival and transformation. Lack of time has become an epidemic blight in Western society. We fill our calendars with multiple things that become driving priorities in our lives. However, if asked to spend an extended time in prayer seeking the face of God, most will revert to the "I don't have time" excuse. But the reality is that we make time for what is important to us—and, sadly, we rarely have time for God.

Our actions say that He belongs in His proper time slot on Sunday mornings or in a quick morning devotional. We need a significant shift in our thinking and priorities. A heart-cry for revival cannot be "fit in" whenever convenient. We must ask God to teach us to order our days and allot our time so that we revere and desire extended time with Him. It is in that extended time that God can begin to speak to us, transform our hearts, and align us to His purposes.

Pray for Lancaster County is our weekly prayer focus for the individuals, families, churches and communities of our region. Please carry this emphasis in your heart and your prayers throughout the week.

An Unlikely Answer to Prayer

"I know that you can do all things; no plans of yours can be thwarted. Therefore, I despise myself and repent in dust and ashes." *Job 42:2,6*

The couple with a troubled marriage had been having many highs and lows in their relationship. But this time the wife's desperate voice on the telephone indicated they had really hit a new low and were at rock-bottom. With considerable persuasion from his wife, the man finally got on the phone and emphatically told me their marriage was over. He was proceeding with divorce. I appealed to him in several ways, but to no avail. I didn't know what else to do but pray for a miracle.

The next morning I called to talk to his wife to see how the night had been. I thought he would be at work but she said, "Oh, things are much better. He's here; do you want to talk with him?" He sounded like a different person and quickly apologized for his attitude the evening before. And then he proceeded to tell me what happened.

After our conversation, he had gone to a secular bookstore to read up on how to go about getting a divorce. To his surprise, two different authors started their books by challenging the reader to reconsider their intentions to get a divorce! They bluntly said that whatever your spouse has done is not so terrible that you cannot forgive them. This advice from a secular source confounded him. He became convinced that the voice of God was loud and clear. God had spoken to him in an unexpected way. In his words, "I was shocked. This is not what I was expecting. Since Christ forgave me, I must forgive all others. I immediately went home to my wife to make peace and repent."

Gracious God, we praise You that You can do all things. Help us to believe that Your ways will not be thwarted.

Jim Myer is part of the ministry team at the White Oak Church of the Brethren, Manheim.

October 16

Armored With Prayer

"Finally, be strong in the Lord and in His mighty power. Put on the full armor of God so that you can stand against the devil's schemes." *Ephesians 5:10–11*

P aul, writing to the Ephesians, encourages them to put on the full armor of God in order to withstand the attacks of the enemy. Today in our society, with all its trappings and the deceitfulness of our enemy, the devil, it is becoming more difficult to be a consistent disciple of Jesus Christ. Walking into each new day unprotected can produce uncertainty and give the devil a foothold in our lives. Scripture encourages us to be people of prayer; doers of the Word; and to be sensitive to the needs of those that we come in contact with as we go about our daily activities. One way of praying is to daily put on each piece of the armor, picturing each piece visually as you pray, placing it in the appropriate location.

The Apostle Paul, as he wrote this letter to the saints in Ephesus, was in a Roman prison, chained to a wall, somewhere deep in the bowels of a place filled with stench and misery where we cannot even imagine being. But he had a calling on his life. He had a Damascus road experience that he could not deny. If he, being in this position, could be Mr. Eternal Optimism, how can we miss being what God wants us to be? How can we function as His people if we are bogged down with our own flesh and personal desires?

To stay on track takes a daily commitment to prayer and devotion to Jesus Christ, as well as being sensitive to the Holy Spirit, each and every day.

Lord, help me to concentrate on a life of prayer and to seek the protection of Your armor, daily. In Jesus' precious name. Amen.

Jim Bednar is a financial adviser, political leader, and a member of several prayer organizations in Lancaster County.

God's Faithful Provision

"Even the sparrow has found a home, and the swallow a nest for herself, where she may have her young—a place near your altar, O Lord Almighty, my King and my God." *Psalms 84:3*

In the fall of 1996, the Lord was leading my wife and me to take a significant step. After years of serving as a self-supported pastor of a small congregation, He made it clear that we were to give ourselves to full-time ministry. It was an exciting time as we considered what God may have for our future, but our faith was tested as we would have little income and no place to live.

As I expressed my concern to Bishop Warren Hoffman, my overseer at that time, he shared Psalms 84:3 with me and assured me that God had a specific place that He would prepare for us. I held onto that verse for the next two years as we rented houses on a short-term basis, keeping the faith that God had a place for us to settle.

By the spring of 1998, our situation had become somewhat desperate as we struggled to raise our support for the on-campus ministry in which we were serving. A critical time came when we needed to find other housing, but we just didn't have the means to do so. As I prayed about this (with some desperation) the Lord gave me a picture of a house, complete with details on the brick exterior and the woodwork interior. I left that prayer time with a renewed faith in God's provision of a home.

It would be another nine months before the God-given picture in my mind became reality. God's fatherly concern for our provision is real, practical and refreshing. Our home is just what we needed. It serves as a constant reminder and testimony of His provision.

Father, I pray with faith according to Your Word, knowing that You will meet all my needs according to Your glorious riches in Christ Jesus (Philippians 4:19).

Kevin Eshleman serves as executive pastor of Ephrata Community Church.

October 18

"...And All These Things"

"But seek first His kingdom, and His righteousness, and all these things will be given to you as well." *Matthew 6:33*

I was a graduate student at the University of Colorado in the early 1970s. It was the end of my first year, and I had decided to hitchhike with two friends to see the Grand Canyon. (This is not something I would recommend these days, but as I tell my daughter, *things were different then.*) After spending a couple of days there, my friends and I were back on the road, headed home to Boulder. We had spent most of the day outside of Flagstaff, hoping for a ride, when a guy in a small Austin stopped. Before he could say, "I don't have enough room for everyone," Art, Dave and I were packed in. That night the four of us camped out in Albuquerque, New Mexico.

Long after my friends had gone to sleep, our "ride" and I stayed up talking. In fact, we talked the whole night. Maybe because we thought we'd never see each other again, we were extremely open and honest in our conversation. Whatever it was, it left an impact on both of us, an impact so strong that a year later he came to Boulder to visit me, and we were married on top of a mountain a few months later.

Inscribed on Chip's wedding ring were the words from Matthew 6:33. All my life I had prayed for a Christian husband, but in all honesty, I thought I knew better than God about who would be best for me. So, I would get involved with someone, *then* ask God to bless the relationship. This time was different. It was the first time I had ever really put God first in something important, and He added to me the greatest gift I could have ever received.

Father, help us to always seek Your kingdom and righteousness first, even as You add all these things.

Becky Toews leads the women's ministry at New Covenant Christian Church.

God Stories

October 19

Comfort Zone

"Now therefore, go, and I will be with your mouth and teach you what you shall say." *Exodus 4:12 (New King James Version)*

My husband and I were flying to Fiji for our first mission trip together. His "job description" was clear, and he was prepared to teach the adult evening school as well as some additional speaking engagements. Though I'm comfortable when things are spelled out, my mission was to help out "wherever needed" at the Christian school. "Okay, Lord," I prayed silently on the plane. "Whatever they ask me to do, I'll do in Your Name." I can organize books, check over their curriculum, do secretarial work, even clean the toilets.

After settling in on Saturday, we toured the facilities with the director. Turning to me, he stated that the new school term began Monday and asked if I would deliver the "kickoff" message. Stand in front of the whole school and speak? Anything but that! How do I decline? I could buy some time and say I'd pray about it. But in my heart I knew I already had prayed, and I had committed to doing whatever they asked. I heard myself say, "I'd love to."

After praying throughout Sunday, I knew exactly what the Lord wanted me to speak. Amazingly, I had no paralyzing fear, no racing pulse, no stumbling. In fact, I experienced just the opposite. I felt a connection with the kids right away. I had such fun and really enjoyed hearing apt truths flowing out of my mouth! When the director asked me to speak again the following week, I had no hesitation. It wasn't about me doing what I could comfortably accomplish. It was God at work in me, His strength being perfected in my weakness.

Thank you, Lord, for giving us opportunities to show Yourself within our willing vessels. Thank you for not letting us stay comfortable, but stretching our borders so that Your purposes will be accomplished. Amen.

Cindy Riker is a contributing editor to *God Stories,* a wife and mother of four, and involved in Teaching the Word Ministries in Leola.

October 20

Trust in His Sovereignty

"...His sovereignty rules over all." *Psalms 103:19*

God is sovereign. This we know. But what does it mean? To quote R.C. Sproul, it means "there are no maverick molecules." It means that He is in absolute control of all that He has created, and there is nothing outside of His control. Such power and control create some very real difficulties for us. How did evil enter into the world? Why is there pain and suffering? Why did the fall occur, causing all of creation to groan (Romans 8:22)? I could go on, but the point is clear: it seems that maybe God is not sovereign, yet scripture is clear that He is.

The most puzzling questions might be, "Did Christ die for everyone? Is God powerful enough to save everyone? Then why is everyone not saved?" We must conclude that the atonement Christ offers on the cross is limited. It is either limited in its power (because not everyone is saved) or in its extent, that is, it is not intended for everyone. Or, does human response make a difference?

Of course these are intriguing and important questions. We don't like questions we cannot answer. Yet we are simply forced to conclude that His ways are beyond our ways. We must conclude with Job that God's ways are "too wonderful for me (Job 42:3)." Whether we like it or not, we don't and can't know everything. We are finite beings with limited understanding. But I've got some good news. This sovereign God we serve is not capricious. He can be trusted. He loves His people, us, more than we love ourselves.

Almighty Father, I confess great discomfort in not being in complete control of my circumstances. Teach me to trust You in everything. Help me to realize that You are trustworthy in everything. I ask this in the meritorious name of Jesus Christ, Amen.

Marlin Detweiler is an elder at All Saints' Presbyterian Church and president of Veritas Press, an educational materials business for children in kindergarten through 12th grade.

October 21

Consumed by Distractions

Pray for Lancaster County

"But Martha was distracted by her many tasks; so she came to him and asked, 'Lord, do you not care that my sister has left me to do all the work by myself? Tell her then to help me.' But the Lord answered her, 'Martha, Martha, you are worried and distracted by many things; there is need of only one thing. Mary has chosen the better part, which will not be taken away from her.'"
Luke 10:40–42 (New Revised Standard Version)

Although Martha was in the very presence of the Lord Jesus Christ, she was distracted by the sense of urgency of things around her. She had so many good, wonderful things to accomplish, but she lost sight of the simple truth that her Lord wanted nothing more from her than her time.

Likewise, we can give assent to the truth of how distracted we are, but we continue allowing the distractions to consume us and keep us from intimacy with the Lord. The concerns or tasks that are engaging our minds in the moment will overtake us without fail. And even beyond the immediate, we are thinking ahead to the next thing that will soon consume us. The distractions become a constant, driving force in our lives.

We must intentionally deal with the many distractions. We must ask the Lord to help us choose "the better part" of preparing the way of the Lord.

Pray for Lancaster County is our weekly prayer focus for the individuals, families, churches and communities of our region. Please carry this emphasis in your heart and your prayers throughout the week.

True Fulfillment

"So I hated life…man has no advantage over the animal. Everything is meaningless." *Ecclesiastes 2:17; 3:19*

For years, this passage of scripture was the only passage that connected with me. I could find no relief from depression. I had extensive knowledge of scripture, a wonderful network of support from fellow sojourners, numerous experiences of watching God's hand at work, an amazing young lady who loved me…but for some reason I was chronically unfulfilled. I wanted desperately to be full of love and joy but found myself consumed with a dictating selfishness. Finally, in desperation I approached the leadership of my church asking for help in healing. They prayed and anointed me. They told me that they were confident of God's desire to heal me and encouraged me to walk in faith that healing would come. One month following that gathering, God opened my eyes to see the truth. I was in the process of comparing Solomon and David, when I came across David's writings:

"He said to me, 'You are my son; today I have become your father' (Psalms 2:7)." "Those who look to Him are radiant; their faces are never covered with shame (Psalms 34:5)."

"For the King trusts in the Lord; through the unfailing love of the Most High he will not be shaken (Psalms 21:7)."

At that moment, I began to understand why David had joy despite turmoil and Solomon experienced despair in the midst of unparalleled wealth and wisdom. David knew God in relationship, not theory. It was then that I began to see myself through eyes of faith, through the eyes of God. I knew I was beautiful. That was all I needed to bring joy in my heart. I was free to look past my need for validation. I could now live in joy and selfless love.

God, thank you for shedding Your blood in order to make me beautiful in Your eyes.

Tim Doering is pastor of Discipleship Ministries at Ephrata Church of the Brethren.

God Stories

Mechanically Minded

"Do not be anxious about anything, but in everything, by prayer and petition, with thanksgiving, present your requests to God."
Philippians 4:6

No! *Not another car problem!* I thought, when the air-conditioner compressor gave out. *We haven't finished paying off the last repair bill on this old car.*

Breathing a prayer of thankfulness that at least this was the end of such a hot summer, I informed my husband. He reminded me that we'd still need the compressor for the defroster in the winter. Driving in the above-average heat the next day, I gripped the steering wheel. "God, I know You heal people, and that all things in heaven and earth are subject to You. I know that includes all natural and man-made things. You know our needs. Please fix this car, in Jesus' Name. Amen."

I flipped the switch on. Hot air came streaming through. The next day I flipped the switch on. Hot air. On the third evening, I switched it on. Cool air—*could it be the cooler evening air?* The following day, I flipped the switch on. COLD AIR came forth! It had not been touched by human hands! I laughed aloud and wept, thanking the Lord for His grace toward us as I enjoyed the coolness. Throughout the week, even on cooler days, I'd flip the switch and giggle, glorying in the goodness of the Lord. Praise God from Whom all blessings flow!

In many ways, the air-conditioner is a luxury, not a need. Yet, I am daily aware of the tender refreshing love of my Father, caring about both the big and the small areas that concern me. He wants to be the Provider and Protector in my life. To Him be the glory!

Lord, thank you that You know the number of hairs on our heads and that nothing escapes Your notice. We bring all our concerns to You and rest in Your love for us. Amen.

Cindy Riker, a contributing editor to *God Stories*, is a wife and mother, involved in Teaching the Word Ministries.

Broken Pieces Made Whole

"Anyone who belongs to Christ is a new person."
2 Corinthians 5:17

Humpty Dumpty sat on a wall, Humpty Dumpty had a great fall. All the king's horses and all the king's men couldn't put Humpty Dumpty back together again. I was in a million broken pieces like the poor character in the nursery rhyme. I loathed myself for the things I'd done and the person I'd become. I was tired of trying to hide all my broken pieces, pretending to be a perfect egg, I tried to keep it all together on the outside so they wouldn't know that I was empty, hollow and dying on the inside.

And now my marriage was crumbling—just one more broken piece that couldn't be put back together again. "All the king's horses and all the king's men" had failed me.

I knew in my heart that it was the end of my life when I woke up that cold 28th day of February in 1989. I had lost all hope, but I did know one other thing that morning. It was a matter of life or death that I get to church.

And that day my life did end. I gave up! I surrendered my life, every broken piece of it, to Jesus Christ and His Lordship. My pastor prayed with me that I would never be the same again. And I never was!

Healing and personal growth happened when I stepped out of my pain and isolation. Out of my broken pieces came new life, purpose, strength and dignity. I no longer live for myself, but serve as a wounded healer to help others on their journey to find the hope and healing and transforming love of Jesus in those very areas that the enemy had meant to rob, steal, kill and destroy.

Father, help us to remember that sometimes the end is just the beginning as we surrender our broken pieces to You who loves us.

Sharon Blantz serves the Worship Center as regional pastor of Single Adult/Support Ministries.

God Stories

These are My People

"My heart is changed within me...." *Hosea 11:8*

L et's get this over with!" I grumbled to myself as I helped the church chorus set up equipment to sing at the prison. The smile on my face didn't match the thoughts clamoring through my mind. "What *are* we doing here? These men have gotten *exactly* what they deserved," I murmured silently. Such was the condition of my heart as I climbed the risers to begin singing praises to our Lord.

We were halfway through the first song when the Lord addressed the hypocrisy of what was occupying space in my heart and what was being proclaimed from my mouth. As I sang, I saw an image of Jesus out of the corner of my eye. He was standing in the midst of the prisoners with his left arm extended out as if embracing the shoulders of the men. *"These are my people—I love them. Can you love them too?"* He asked with gentleness and love. His words pierced my heart deeply and I wept uncontrollably throughout the performance. "Oh God, I have been forgiven of so much! You took a broken, ugly life of sin and freely offered compassion and hope," I cried. I ached from brokenness as He brought conviction regarding the judgment coming up out of my heart towards others who had been imprisoned by the deceit of the world.

After the program, with tear-swollen eyes and quivering voice, I shared what had happened. I told them how Jesus held them in His arms and proclaimed His love for them. And from a changed heart, I asked them for forgiveness for my condemnation and judgment. But God wasn't finished with me! Jim and I began ministering in the prison every Friday night. We were blessed over and over again by the very men I had deemed as unworthy!

Lord, forgive me for my hardened heart! Enable me to see as You see and to love as You love.

Judy Meador ministers with her husband, Jim, pastor at Willow Street Mennonite Church.

Obstacles

"These troubles and sufferings of ours are, after all, quite small and won't last long." *2 Corinthians 4:17 (Living Bible)*

Obstacles in life are always present, sometimes for a season, sometimes for a lifetime. What are the obstacles in your life? Are you a single mom or dad? Are you feeling trapped in a situation that you cannot fix? Do you have health issues?

The Lord showed me an illustration in nature that reminded me of my need to keep trusting God day by day, even when I don't see progress.

One day I was driving, traveling east on Route 30, when I gasped. On the highway was a box turtle, just ready to step from my lane of traffic onto the stone shoulder of the right-hand lane. His head was held high and his neck was stretched out, looking straight ahead to his goal. Those little legs were as far out of the shell as I had ever seen. He had overcome many obstacles going to his destination. He crossed four lanes of busy Route 30 traffic and a grassy median strip. He was probably aware of some of the obstacles, like stones and wind from the cars.

That turtle may have been oblivious to some of the certain dangers, yet he kept plodding along through the obstacles of his life until he got to the far side of the road.

God, in His mercy, allowed that turtle to be there at that precise moment when I could see him and be encouraged to keep plodding along through life's obstacles! I must remember to take all of life's obstacles to the Lord.

Dear Lord, Jesus, I yield my fears and obstacles of life to You. Help me to trust You more, and help me to keep plodding along as You give me strength for each new day. Amen.

Peg Waller lives in Lancaster City with her husband John and two sons. She attends Living Hope Community Church, Lancaster.

Dispelling Darkness

"When He had disarmed the rulers and authorities, He made a public display of them, having triumphed over them through Him." *Colossians 2:15*

A number of years ago when my three children were living at home, something extremely unusual happened to me one midnight as I was camping with my family. We were all sleeping soundly in a tent, packed in like sardines. I was abruptly awakened, startled by a profoundly sinful urge which caught me guarded, but greatly astonished at my heart's wicked desire. It was overwhelming. The spiritual oppression in that dark tent was such that I could feel the physical darkness. The urge of my heart was uncharacteristic of anything I ever experienced before. The evil presence was so strong that I physically had to lay on top of my hands—one holding the other as I repeated the precious and powerful name of my Savior. Again and again I spoke the name "Jesus." I pleaded His blood to cover and protect me.

This went on for what seemed to be an eternity as I continued to cry out. Finally, the oppressive darkness was soon replaced by a peace and serenity that I had never before or since experienced. God transformed that spiritual darkness into light. I sensed the presence of Jesus. The battle was over! Triumph was mine, by the power of the One who was nailed to the cross.

Satan and all his cohorts have been defeated. In our spiritual warfare experiences, we must remember that the battle belongs to the Lord. While Satan sneaks around seeking to devour the called of God, we do well to claim the promise of Jesus, that "not even the gates of hell will prevail against His church, the elect of God."

Lord Jesus, thank you for disarming the rulers and authorities, and for the promise of the evil one's future absolute containment and failure. Glorify Yourself in all our struggles as You continue to renew us.

Leon R. Shirk is senior pastor of Bethany Grace Fellowship, East Earl.

Squeeze Play: The Pressures of the World

"Don't copy the behavior and customs of this world, but let God transform you into a new person by changing the way you think. Then you will know what God wants you to do, and you will know how good and pleasing and perfect his will really is." *Romans 12:2 (New Living Translation)*

Although we are warned in scripture not to copy the behavior and customs of the world, the sad truth is that there seems to be little noticeable distinction between the church and the world. Apart from the religious activities that fill our lives, researchers tell us that the life-styles and values of Christians differ little from those who do not profess a faith in Christ.

As George Barna states: "We buy into the world's system, and we become so busy pursuing the stuff of the world that we don't have time for God. Or as we're juggling it all, God is just one of those balls that we're trying to keep in the air."

As the people of God, we are increasingly faced with the challenge of whether we want a "comfortable Christian life," or if we hunger for the all-consuming presence of God. Pursuing God comes at the price of not conforming to the pressures of the world. He will not come to a compromised Bride; He is looking for transformed hearts.

Pray for Lancaster County is our weekly prayer focus for the individuals, families, churches and communities of our region. Please carry this emphasis in your heart and your prayers throughout the week.

My God Story

"...a great multitude which no one could number, of all nations, tribes, peoples, and tongues, standing before the throne and before the Lamb, clothed with white robes, with palm branches in their hands, and crying out with a loud voice, saying, 'Salvation belongs to our God who sits on the throne, and to the Lamb!'"
Revelation 7:9–10 (New King James Version)

My family has deep roots in the Mennonite church, coming from the eastern part of Lancaster County. But when I was four, my parents were influenced by the Jesus movement and had a charismatic experience that led them to New Haven, Connecticut. There they assisted my grandfather in establishing the first Mennonite church in the New England states (Bible Fellowship Mennonite Church).

We lived in a racially diverse area, far from family roots and in the midst of inner-city social and racial turmoil, which consequently shaped my perspective of God's kingdom. I chose the verse in Revelation because of its vision of heaven being a place where all people worship in their own language and culture.

In my teenage years I spent a lot of time drinking and doing drugs, having lost the faith of my parents and becoming very cynical of church. When I returned to faith in Christ, it was authentic in leading me to a relationship with God who accepted me.

I still struggle with doubts. I can still be cynical because of the disparity between church life and the reality spoken of in Revelation. The testing of my faith has led to a conviction that no matter what today's reality reveals, tomorrow is a new day. God's vision in Revelation calls us to be the body of Christ where we commune with one another and God, no longer divided by race and economics.

Shape us, Holy Spirit, into the body of Christ where people from every nation and tribe can have communion with the Giver of Life.

Rodney A. Martin is an associate/youth pastor at Lititz Mennonite Church.

Fatal Flaw of Post-Modern Christianity

"You...know all about my teaching, my way of life, my purpose, faith, patience, love, endurance, persecutions, sufferings...continue in what you have learned...." *2 Timothy 3:10–11, 14*

As we contemplate evangelical Christianity today, we face a struggle—whether or not we should embrace fully the postmodern Christianity movement which calls for transformation of both the context of ministry and content of message to fit cultural demands of this generation. One major flaw in some postmodern Christian thought is that there is little appreciation for those in the faith who have gone before. Those elders and statesmen who stand as a "cloud of witnesses" are completely marginalized. Although mature in wisdom and knowledge, they are viewed as out of touch. Those who have wrestled with scripture and have a history of faithfulness are called "dogmatic old-timers," instead being valued for the insights they have gained on how to approach the Sovereign. When the Apostle Paul addresses this problem, he commands Timothy (the postmodernist of his day) not to try to make a new kind of Christianity, but to embrace the faith of his trusted older friend in the faith, Paul himself. We should not try to reinvent spirituality, but learn from saints that have gone before—mature men or women from whom we can glean understanding in issues of faith. Don't forsake the wealth of resources in older believers' hearts and minds. Can you ask God to bring to mind an older person of faith that would become your mentor? Pray for the opportunity to develop that relationship, and for openness to what they share with you.

Lord, thank you for those who have walked with You long before. Help me not disregard or discount what I could learn from their years of loving and serving You.

Jamie Mitchell is the pastor-teacher of NewSong Fellowship Church, Lancaster, and an adjunct faculty member at Lancaster Bible College.

Gospel Brings Joy to the City

"Those who had been scattered preached the gospel wherever they went...so there was great joy in that city." *Acts 8:4,8*

One evening, I was with a friend in downtown Lancaster City sharing the gospel with a group of people who were involved in Santeria, or witchcraft. It was a rainy, cold night, and some of them look so tired and desperate that I asked the Lord, "What future do they have?"

Then I heard His voice saying, "There is no future without Me."

There is no hope, nor future apart from Jesus Christ. If there is no hope, no future apart from Jesus Christ, we have to preach the gospel to bring hope to people, to families, to cities, to all.

Immediately, the Holy Spirit reminded me of the passage in Acts 8:1–8. My friend and I were able to share the gospel, and three people received Jesus as their personal savior. That evening, not only were they filled with joy, but we, the messengers, were filled with joy too.

What happens when the gospel is preached in a city?

1. When we preach the gospel, **Christ is proclaimed.** He is the power of salvation. He is the One we need.

2. When we preach the gospel, **signs and miracles happen**. Not only Philip, but all the apostles did miracles too; and all of us have the power of God within us to do the same.

3. When the gospel is preached, **there is great joy in that city**. There is joy when a person repents and renounces witchcraft. There is joy when cancer leaves a person. There is joy when a husband comes back home. There is joy when a drug addict is delivered. There is joy when a sinner repents.

Lord Jesus, our city needs You. Our city needs to see signs and miracles. Our city needs joy. Please pour Your Spirit on the city in a new way. Amen.

Marta Estrada is an author and the director of New Life for Girls of Lancaster. She is a member of Petra Christian Fellowship.

November

Where God Guides, He Provides

"The Lord is my Shepherd, I shall not want." *Psalms 23:1 (King James Version)*

I was the oldest of six children. As a young boy, I was taught hard work and was hired out to a farmer to help supplement our household expenses.

My father was a full-time pastor, but he served the church without any wages. This required that he work full-time at another job during the day to meet the family's financial needs. He spent evenings and weekends at the church. At times, I resented the church and my father's absence in our home because, on many occasions, I was put in the position of acting as the man in charge. In later years, I began to understand the Lord's call on my father's life and his obedience to serving the church. My father taught me, by example, to live an exemplary life and to take a call on one's life seriously. He knew the Lord was His Shepherd and would lay down His life for his sheep, so my father followed his Shepherd's example in his home and his flock (church). I grew to respect my father's commitment to the Lord. Late one evening when I couldn't sleep, I went to my father to ask him how I could ask Jesus to come into my heart. While kneeling by his bedside, he led me to the Great Shepherd, which changed my life forever.

My father's faithfulness to serve God is an example that is etched in the very depth of my own heart today. I take great comfort in knowing that I am one of the Lord's sheep and that He holds me in His hand, where "He guides and provides for me."

Dear Lord, thank you for being my Shepherd, for guiding me, and for providing for me. Lord, "I take, therefore, no thought for tomorrow, for tomorrow shall take care of itself." I love You and worship You today. Amen.

Herb Fisher is CEO of Fisher Companies.

Art by Lindsey Martin, 9th grade
Lancaster Mennonite High School

Pieces of the Puzzle

"As the heavens are higher than the earth, so are my ways higher than your ways and my thoughts than your thoughts." *Isaiah 55:9*

God reveals Himself to us in many ways. Sometimes God leads us to a deeper knowledge of Him not through intellectual understanding, but by faithfully taking us through the dark times of our lives. Sometimes God doesn't give us the answers. Sometimes life simply doesn't make sense.

During these seasons, I often picture my life as a jigsaw puzzle. The first thing I do when putting a puzzle together is prop up the box lid so I can look at it as I work. It helps to know exactly what the puzzle will look like when completed. When I occasionally get stuck, I'm not at a complete loss. I'm confident I will have the ability to figure out where all the pieces fit. I already know what the answers are.

But sometimes God asks me to work at the puzzle of my life without letting me see the picture. He asks, "Do you trust Me? Will you let me shepherd you even if you cannot see where we are going?" So much rests on how I answer. If I must be in control, if I must know exactly how many pieces are in the puzzle and where they will fall, then I will miss much of the journey to which the Lord calls me. I may miss getting to know His character and trusting Him in a new way. I may even assign meaning to events that He doesn't intend. I'm learning that the answers cannot become more important than the process.

I can't pretend that life is filled with easy answers just because I'm a follower of Christ. The Lord invites me to join Him on a journey that is far beyond a picture on a box. He asks me to trust Him to hold the answers. And He is not afraid of my questions.

Father, help me to trust You as You piece together the story of my life.

Joan Adams is an events fundraiser for Susquehanna Valley Pregnancy Services. She serves on the drama, media, and planning teams of Hosanna Christian Fellowship, Lititz.

November 3

God's Appointment

"In his heart a man plans his course, but the Lord determines his steps." *Proverbs 16:9*

The medical receptionist was unyielding. "The *only* appointment available is for 8 a.m. on Wednesday, April 1." Begrudgingly, I accepted the time slot. Such an early schedule was extremely inconvenient for my family as we lived almost an hour from Hershey Medical Center. But, somehow, we managed to get to the hospital on time. Hurry up and wait...nine o'clock...ten o'clock...eleven o'clock. Timmy, my infant son with Down Syndrome and a severe cardiac anomaly, was scheduled for the first appointment of the day. Yet, we had to wait three hours to be seen. When our cardiologist finally arrived, he marveled at how well Timmy was responding to treatment. We discussed modifications to his medication dosages. And then I went back to the receptionist's desk to check out, pay my bill, and schedule our next appointment.

While I was standing there, Timmy began to act agitated. I was overcome with a sense that I shouldn't go home. So I sat down to wait for...what? Within several minutes, his coloring turned gray, and his respirations became labored. Events rapidly spiraled from bad to disastrous. Timmy was admitted to the hospital and ultimately diagnosed with bacterial spinal meningitis. It ravaged his body for weeks. But in God's providence, we were in the right place at the right time when calamity struck. What if the receptionist had not been so insistent about the appointment? What if the physicians had not been so far behind schedule? What if I hadn't listened to that still, small, insistent voice that said, "*Don't* go home"? Timmy is now thirteen years old and a constant living, breathing, smiling reminder of God's providence.

Help us to remember that You are the blessed controller of all things— from the big events of our lives to the inconveniences in our schedules.

Stephanie Hubach is an author, speaker, and disability advocate who— in partnership with her husband Fred—leads the Special Needs Ministry at Reformed Presbyterian Church of Ephrata.

That Constant Buzz!

"Step out of the traffic! Take a long, loving look at me, your High God, above politics, above everything."
Psalms 46:10 (The Message)

We live in a culture that is filled with the buzzing of a myriad of voices calling for our time and attention. It is comparable to standing in the middle of the freeway and not noticing the rushing traffic because you have grown accustomed to the constant background noise.

Psalms 46:10 is normally translated as "Be still and know that I am God." The word in the Hebrew has the idea of *to be quiet, idle, to let drop*. In the cacophony of the noise of our culture, the voice of God is drowned out. If we are not able to actively listen when the Lord wants to speak, we will eventually lose the ability to discern His voice from the background noise. His whispers will seem to grow silent.

We must "step out of the traffic" and put aside the noises that drown out His voice. Quiet intimacy is needed for God to come in His transforming power.

Pray for Lancaster County is our weekly prayer focus for the individuals, families, churches and communities of our region. Please carry this emphasis in your heart and your prayers throughout the week.

Pray for the Persecuted Church

"Who shall separate us from the love of Christ? Shall trouble or hardship or persecution or famine or nakedness or danger or sword? As it is written: 'For your sake we face death all day long; we are considered as sheep to be slaughtered.' No, in all these things we are more than conquerors through him who loved us." *Romans 8:35–37*

In the 20th century, more believers were martyred for their faith than in all the previous centuries combined. An estimated 200 million Christians currently live in areas where their faith in Christ means the daily threat of discrimination and persecution. From Eden to Eritrea, Satan has always been at work to stop the gospel and stamp out belief in Jesus Christ.

A simple renunciation of Jesus could ensure a release from prison, reduce threats to their family, save their son or daughter from taunts and teasing in school or save the wage earner the shame of losing his job. With one word of denial, family unity could be restored and community festivals to the local gods could be enjoyed with the rest of their neighbors, friends and relatives. However—beyond compare—life and love in God has been discovered in the daily reality of "knowing Christ and the power of His resurrection and the fellowship of sharing in His sufferings, becoming like Him in His death (Philippians 3:9)." On this *International Day of Prayer for the Persecuted Church*, we join with our brothers and sisters around the world to pray for those under tremendous pressure to give up their faith!

Father, today we pray for the suffering church. We pray that the armor of God will enable those under persecution to stand firm and through their testimony many others will come to know You.

Jane Fasnacht is on the DOVE Mission International team, Lititz. For more information on the International Day of Prayer go to www.opendoorsusa.org

Let God Turn It To Good

"And we know that God causes everything to work together for the good of those who love God and are called according to his purpose for them." *Romans 8:28*

God works in everything for our good. During my first 24 years of life, motorcycles and I have not had the best track record. I was involved in two separate accidents, one almost costing my life, and the other my right leg. But I have learned that when I stand upon the Word of God, what the enemy meant for evil, God turns to good. Not only does my perspective on how I see things change, but the reality starts to change.

During my recovery from the second accident, I was faced with some additional hurdles—infection, tissues dying, additional skin grafts and a blood transfusion. During these obstacles, I had a choice to either look at reality and become bitter and discouraged, or believe the words of Christ that say everything that occurs in my life is used to benefit me. I cried out, "Lord Jesus, I am getting all the good out of this situation!" As I declared the Word of God, I saw not only my perspective change, but also the reality.

I can honestly say that I can see, in part, how the Lord has used this accident to impact the rest of my life. It has enabled me to step into the next season of life better prepared. I cannot say that I always see the benefit in every situation, but I do trust and know that God's Word is true in my life. Whether a flat tire, car accident, loss of money, or death of a loved one, I have a choice to make. I am going to receive all the good, for it will benefit me.

Lord Jesus, I ask You to give me the strength to apply Your Word to every situation in my life. I want to see life through You, and reap the good of every circumstance.

Keith Myer serves on the DOVE Christian Fellowship International youth team.

You Will Have Trouble

"In this world, you will have trouble. But be of good cheer! I have overcome the world." *John 16:33*

So spoke Jesus to His disciples near the end of His ministry on earth. They could not have realized the trouble they would experience throughout the remainder of their lives; and most of them died martyrs' deaths.

Jesus' message extends to us as we go through trials, the solutions for which seem beyond us. Recently, a very severe illness took me to death's doorstep and kept me in bed for several months. It was a time for pain, frustration, despair, and hopelessness. And a time for prayer. Each day, my dear wife sat with me in the hospital, reading from Psalms and praying with me. And each day, the Lord made me stronger.

He does this for each of us in our darkest times. We suffer, but God is there. In *Just Give Me Jesus,* Anne Graham Lotz, says, "...if you never have any difficulties that are greater than you can bear now, how will you ever know the awesome greatness and personal availability of His infinite power? It's when the Red Sea is before you, the mountains on one side of you, the desert is on the other side, and you feel the Egyptian army closing in from behind that you experience His power to open up an escape route."

God has given me back my earthly life. He can carry you through every trial as well. William Barclay's commentary on 1 Corinthians tells us: "...life has its dark places where there seems to be nothing to do but to hold on. Faith is always a victory, the victory of the soul which tenaciously maintains its clutch on God."

Today, maintain your clutch on God. Remember how Jesus ended his message to His disciples: "But be of good cheer! I have overcome the world."

Father, give me the faith today to maintain my clutch on You throughout my life; to remember that You will carry me through every trial.

Bob Weaver is the area director of Joni and Friends, the disability ministry of Joni Eareckson Tada.

November 8

Faith in Action

"Suppose a brother or sister is without clothes and daily food. If one of you says to him, 'Go, I wish you well; keep warm and well fed' but does nothing about his physical needs, what good is it? In the same way, faith by itself, if it is not accompanied by action, is dead." *James 2:15–17*

This passage elucidates a key component to a true Christian lifestyle, namely, that a true Christian, motivated by faith, will be spurred on to physical action in response to faith. Additionally, it tells us that words alone, in the face of a situation that requires a physical response, are insufficient. I believe that it would be a justified extrapolation from the passage above to propose that even if a Christian responded to a hungry person by praying for him or her (instead of just "well-wishing"), this still would be insufficient unless the Christian also took the action to feed the person. My point is this: While we cannot and must not do "good deeds" that are not covered in prayer, we must not simply pray and then wait for God to "sovereignly" act. We must demonstrate our faith through our action.

Today is Election Day. After you pray for our government leaders today (as is your Christian duty), put some action to your faith and prayer, and go vote. Voting is a way that we can put action to the prayer "Your Kingdom come, Your will be done, on earth as it is in heaven."

Father God, thank you for the country that we live in, and we ask that You would give us wisdom today as we choose our nation's leaders. We pray in faith, asking that You would establish competent men and women of integrity and moral clarity, and we commit to give action to our faith today by voting in a manner that will support Your kingdom coming to this earth. In Jesus' name, Amen.

Justin Harnish is member of Ephrata Community Church and serves on the Board of Supervisors for the Township of Clay.

Finishing Well

"I have fought the good fight, I have finished the race, I have kept the faith." *2 Timothy 4:7*

I have come to the conclusion that finishing well has a lot to do with how we live our lives now, not just how we live the last few years of our lives. Let me highlight a few checkpoints.

Establish healthy boundaries (Exodus 18:13-18). The people in the Bible who did not finish well struggled with boundary issues in their lives.

Grow in endurance (Colossians 1: 10–11). The Christian life is compared to a race, and a race is won by endurance. People who finish well are resilient and spring back quickly when they are knocked down.

Listen to godly advice (Proverbs 15:22). Many of the mistakes we make in life can be attributed to not listening to wise counsel or not seeking it. Listen to those God has placed as authorities in your life. The real purpose of authority is not to control but to protect.

Keep your spirit clear with people (Hebrews 12:15). Don't carry offenses, and don't pick up other peoples' offenses. I think this is one of the biggest limiters to the grace of God in our lives.

Nurture your relationship with God and His Word (2 Timothy 3:14–17). God's Word provides strength for us to make the journey. Paying attention to spiritual things now affects your tomorrow.

Nurture your relationship with your spouse, children, parents, friends and church family (Ephesians 5:21–6:4). You can't put your family and key relationships on hold while you pursue your dreams. If you don't nurture them now, you won't have them later.

Father God, show me the areas of my life that I need to pay more attention to now so that I can finish well. In Jesus' name, Amen.

Lester Zimmerman is senior pastor of Petra Christian Fellowship, overseer of the Hopewell Network of Churches and serves on the council of the Regional Church of Lancaster County.

Check it Out

*"…they listened eagerly to Paul's message. They searched the
Scriptures day after day to check up on Paul and Silas, to see if
they were really teaching the truth." Acts 17:11 (New Living
Translation)*

Turn to Moses 3:12," I would say, flipping through the Old Testament. As I watched, my fourth and fifth grade camp girls would promptly begin searching their Bibles for the ever-elusive book.
One by one they would stop and look up at me with puzzled expressions. Inevitably, as I waited, one would suddenly say, "Wait a minute!
There *isn't* a book of Moses, is there?"

Most of us probably wouldn't fall for such a ploy, unlike the young
girls I was counselor for. But the point I was attempting to make in
their impressionable minds is one that we need to be reminded of as
well. Just because someone presents something to us as biblical *doesn't
mean it IS!* Even well-intentioned believers are not infallible in their
teaching. Let's pattern our lives after the Bereans of which Paul spoke
in Acts 17:11: "They searched the scriptures day after day...to see...the
truth."

*God, please make me a truth-seeker. May I never allow myself to be too
busy or too lazy to dig into what Your Word says about each topic that
comes my way. Thank you for blessing me with Your written Word in a
language I can understand. May I never take that for granted.*

Ann Weldy is the administrative secretary at DOVE Christian Fellowship
Westgate, in Ephrata, and serves as a worship leader at DOVE
Elizabethtown.

Our Intimate God

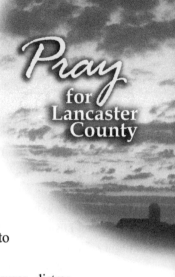

for Lancaster County

"Let him kiss me with the kisses of his mouth—for your love is more delightful than wine. Pleasing is the fragrance of your perfumes; your name is like perfume poured out. No wonder the maidens love you! Take me away with you—let us hurry! Let the king bring me into his chambers…." *Song of Songs 1:2–4*

As we free ourselves from the time pressures, distractions, and the ways of the world and its noise, we will be drawn deeper into the intimacy that the Lord longs to have with His bride.

When the people of God are so in love with God for who He is, they will discover that having His presence is worth more than anything else in this world. This kind of intimacy does not come without intention or cost, but it is desperately needed. Intimacy is the red carpet for inviting the manifest presence of the Living God into our midst. He is not attracted to programs, lofty goals, or gala celebrations. He is attracted to a love-starved bride who desires Him more than all the treasures, acclaim, and busyness of this world. Where intimacy is lacking, we must confess our lack of desire and ask Him to increase our appetite for His presence. There is no substitute!

Pray for Lancaster County is our weekly prayer focus for the individuals, families, churches and communities of our region. Please carry this emphasis in your heart and your prayers throughout the week.

Finding the Lord and His Ways

"You are holy, enthroned in the praises of Israel." *Psalms 22:3*

C indy, if you don't ever stop praising the Lord, we won't get to the important items on our prayer list." I didn't say it out loud, but I was irritated at the amount of time my co-worker was spending in worship. I understood the concept of praising the Lord in prayer, but I usually limited mine to a few words, "Dear Father, You are mighty, You are awesome, and now I have some serious requests for You...." Cindy went on and on, worshiping the Lord in the most adoring tone I'd ever heard.

Suddenly, and because the Lord is enthroned on our praises, the Lord drew near. His presence, manifested as holiness, flooded our room. And we were undone. Speechless. Paralyzed in awe. Like Isaiah, we felt our depravity in contrast to the Lord's holiness and said, "Woe is me."

That event, eight years ago, began to transform our ministry. In short, God taught us that He is worthy of our active worship, that it's our highest calling as His children, and that it's the best way to honor Him as a ministry and receive His wisdom for serving others.

Now, worship defines our ministry. The first hour of the morning is given to the Lord in corporate worship, planning meetings are filled with worship and prayer, and board meetings center on the Lord through worship and prayer.

As we're faithful to seek Him, He is faithful to fill us with more of Himself, more of His wisdom, more of His ways. His ways are higher. We want Him, and we want His ways.

Father, whether at work, at home, with friends, or with children, I will worship You. As I seek You, my greatest reward is to find You.

Lisa Hosler serves as president of Susquehanna Valley Pregnancy Services and is a member of the council of the Regional Church of Lancaster County.

Bonding Through Vulnerability

"We loved you so much that we shared with you not only God's good news but our own lives, too." *1 Thessalonians 2:8 (New Living Translation)*

The vote was a tie—two in favor, two opposed. It was a discussion my support group was having about whether or not people in leadership should be vulnerable with their staffers—you know, admit their struggles, their weaknesses, their fears. I sided with the two against such vulnerability, using arguments like, "You need your staffers' respect, and how can they respect you if they see that you're struggling?" So with my vote, three of us thought leaders should be more private, and two thought they should be more open.

Meanwhile, God initiated a life-style of worship and prayer in the ministry where I serve, and an incredible love and safety began to blanket our work environment. Before long, during the worship times, I would feel myself welling up with tears about a sensitive area in my life. But I held them inside. I could tell, though, that God was asking me to be vulnerable with my staffers, so I promised Him that the next time I would allow myself to cry. Sure enough, a few days later the tears came. As if on cue, my staffers gathered around me, prayed for me, and even cried along with me. That was the day God began an amazing work of vulnerability among us. Since then, tears have become a normal part of our working relationships. Who knew that God would bring such strong bonding through vulnerability? God did, and that's what He wanted for our ministry so we could more effectively build His kingdom as co-laborers who know and love each other deeply.

God, help me to love those I'm working with so much that I'm willing to share my own life with them in vulnerability and transparency.

Lisa Hosler serves as president of Susquehanna Valley Pregnancy Services and is a member of the council of the Regional Church of Lancaster County.

Be Joyful Always

"Be joyful always; pray continually; give thanks in all circumstances, for this is God's will for you in Christ Jesus."
1 Thessalonians 5:16–18

B e joyful always." Now there's a tall order! It doesn't just mean "be joyful" when I get a new job, or when my grandson excels at school, or when I'm on vacation. Those are all fine times to be joyful. But so are the times of trial: the times of illness, the times of personal tragedy, the times when we begin to wonder if God is really there. But how?

God tells us how in this simple verse. First, "give thanks in all circumstances." Thank the Lord that He is carrying you through your trial. Thank Him that, no matter how dark the situation seems or how far away that light at the end of the tunnel seems to be (is that light really there at all?), He will not test you beyond what you can endure, and He will work all things together for good for those who love Him. Thank Him that, no matter how difficult life becomes, we, as believers, can always look forward to eternal peace with Him.

"For this is God's will for you in Christ Jesus." God has a plan for you. It's far beyond our finite minds to understand the sublime complexity of His will, but the plan is there. "Oh, the depth of the riches of the wisdom and knowledge of God! How unsearchable his judgments, and his paths beyond tracing out! Who has known the mind of the Lord (Romans 11:33-34)?" "Has not God made foolish the wisdom of the world (1 Corinthians 1:20)?" So in every one of those continual prayers, we should be praying for His will tobe done.

Give me the faith, dear Lord, to be joyful always—to pray continually and to trust in Your perfect will.

Bob Weaver is the area director of Joni and Friends, the disability ministry of Joni Eareckson Tada.

Are You Giving What You Have?

"...You give them something to eat...." *Mark 6:37*

Mark 6:37 and the verses following could be paraphrased this way. **Jesus**: "You meet their needs (in this case, hunger)." **Followers**: "We are not able." **Jesus**: "What do you have?" **Followers**: "Not much." **Jesus**: "That's all I need. Give it to me and watch."

Whether it is the broken home next door or the rising divorce rate, we look at the problems and needs around us and wonder in despair, "What can I do?"

God replies, "Just give Me the little you have, and watch."

We are tempted to believe that we have little to offer God, but most of us have more than we think. We each get 24 hours, every day. Martin Luther spent several hours of each day praying on his knees. He then changed the world when he rose to his feet. We all have some measure of material wealth—not much compared to billionaires, but still more than most foreigners will ever see. We each have unique talents, experiences, knowledge, passions and intelligence.

Instead of focusing on those with more, God tells us to focus on birds and flowers and trust that He will meet our needs in the same way that He meets theirs. He tells us to use all that we have to "seek first His kingdom (Matthew 6:25-34)."

"To whom much is given, much is required (Luke 12:48)." No one has been given more than us. How much of all that we have are we freely giving away? How much are we giving up to seek Him?

Father, we live in a society rich with more than we need. Remind us that all of it will someday vanish, and the only thing that will matter is how much of what we had we gave to You. Teach us how to give You all.

Representative Gibson C. Armstrong represents part of Lancaster in the Pennsylvania House of Representatives.

A Sovereign Healing God

"For from Him and through Him and to Him are all things. To Him be the glory forever! Amen." *Romans 11:36*

In 1954, at age 12, something life-changing happened to me. I contracted a case of poliomyelitis. Due to a faithful mother and very dedicated chiropractor, I never experienced an iron lung, braces or even hospitalization. At the time I was living in Atmore, Alabama, where another missionary couple was faced with leukemia in their nine-year old daughter, Eunice Kling. Eunice and I were the sole focus of a simple, yet powerful prayer meeting one Wednesday night at the Freemansville Mennonite Church. This was long before all the emphasis of "divine healing" that you hear of today on TV. My prayer that Wednesday night as God's people assembled in my absence was, "Lord, if you heal me, I will serve you someday in full-time Christian ministry." That was it! Through the sovereign healing of the Great Physician who grants by His grace unworthy requests, I was marvelously healed.

Twenty years later, I pursued a path that led to my educational requirements at LBC and a long term (30 years) ministry at Bethany Grace Fellowship. We have witnessed God's gracious and merciful work in the hearts of His people. Years ago after being exposed to the doctrines of grace, I chose Romans 11:36 as my life and ministry verse. Little did I know then how refreshing this passage would be, which has caused my proud heart—time and again—to be humbled before the Ultimate Cause of it all.

Lord, I bless You and praise You because You are the Sovereign One of all the earth. You are building Your kingdom through those You call your own. Thank you for orchestrating my life. Thank you for salvation, for my call to the ministry, and for Your faithfulness through my thirty year tenure in Christian service. Please, Lord, use my experience for Your glory to encourage some young person today in his or her call.

Leon R. Shirk is senior pastor of Bethany Grace Fellowship, East Earl.

Are You Ready?

"I am the way, and the truth, and the life. The only way to the Father is through me." *John 14:6*

She was a beautiful woman, stunning in her middle years. She was a wife and mother, but she was mostly unhappy and restless. She was our full-time employee during the day, and a few nights a week she worked as a bar tender and waitress at a nearby restaurant.

I was especially drawn to Linda, taken by her empty, unfulfilled character. I knew I had the answer of God's love to offer her. But I also knew friendship evangelism is very important, having her respect me as her friend. One day after a distressful, full-blown argument with her spouse, she came crying to me for advice.

I did have the answer: I told her how God's love could heal her marriage and bring peace to her soul. She didn't seem interested. However, I told her about "Change of Pace" Bible Studies in case she wanted to know more about Jesus.

I was elated when she started to attend, even though sporadically. One day I invited her to attend a Christian Women's Club luncheon with me. She seemed so pleased to be my guest. I saw a smile on her face for the first time in a long time when the speaker invited those who asked Jesus into their heart to indicate by putting a cross on their nametag. Her cross was real! Together, we did a personal Bible Study, which gave her a depth of knowledge about God's Word.

Soon after our luncheon together, on her way home from her evening job, she was hit by a tractor-trailer head-on and was killed instantly! I knew Linda was in heaven, but her family hadn't gotten word of her conversion. A sad funeral turned into a happy praise celebration, knowing their loved one was home with the Lord.

My precious Savior, what a day that will be when we spend eternity in Your presence, praising You forever.

Dona L. Fisher is chairman of the local National Day of Prayer, and Change of Pace Bible Studies.

It Is Time to Seek the Lord

"Let us acknowledge the Lord; let us press on to acknowledge him. As surely as the sun rises, he will appear; he will come to us like the winter rains, like the spring rains that water the earth." *Hosea 6:3*

The call is crystal clear: "It is time to seek the Lord!" Hosea exhorts us to "*press on* to acknowledge Him." To press on means to not give up, not back down, and not be satisfied with anything less than God's very presence. Perhaps you have been faithful to pray and earnestly seek God. But this is still the time for decision and commitment. Will you determine that the presence of Almighty God is more desirable than whatever it might cost you? If so, then it is time to seek the Lord!

Pray for Lancaster County is our weekly prayer focus for the individuals, families, churches and communities of our region. Please carry this emphasis in your heart and your prayers throughout the week.

November 19

A Sheep Among Wolves

"I am sending you out like sheep among wolves. Therefore be as shrewd as snakes and as innocent as doves." *Matthew 10:16*

Doesn't Jesus create a vivid word picture for His disciples as He gives them their "marching orders?" The thought of being a sheep among a pack of wolves is pretty unnerving. Do you ever feel intimidated by a fast-paced world that operates under a different set of rules? How are we to be effective Christians while protecting ourselves and not harming others?

In the second part of Matthew 10:16, Jesus paints another word picture containing an unlikely and yet wonderful combination of animals. The serpent has always been an emblem of wisdom and cunning while the dove reminds us of innocence, almost to the point of weakness. In Matthew 10, Jesus gives His disciples the power to drive out evil spirits and heal illness and then tells them to "go to the lost sheep" and share the message.

Jesus has given us a guideline to follow as we interact daily with the world. The traits of the serpent or the dove can become faults when one is employed independently of the other. But by combining wisdom *and* innocence we're better equipped to be salt and light in a fallen world without becoming part of it.

I'm not sure how today's wolves stack up against those the disciples encountered, but I know that Jesus is still sending us out to engage the world for His sake.

Equip yourself with the wisdom God offers you by reading His Word every day. To wisdom, add love as you grow your relationship with Him through prayer. A steady diet of the Bible and prayer is a sure way to convert those wolves you encounter into sheep.

Dear God, prepare me to meet today's challenges with confidence, knowing I am not alone; You are by my side in every step I take. In Jesus' name. Amen.

Mike Heisey serves as lay pastor at Grace United Methodist Church in Millersville.

God and a Zucchini

" I am not ashamed of the gospel, because it is the power of God for the salvation of everyone who believes: first for the Jew, then for the Gentile." *Romans 1:16*

"...I have become all things to all men, so that by all possible means I might save some." *1 Corinthians 9:22*

Long before Veggie Tales, there was the Zucchini Festival. Every year thousands flock to Hayward, California, to experience zucchini almost any way imaginable. There are even zucchini races where the oblong vegetables are raced down a pinewood derby-like track. I once thought that this was a unique occurrence, but I've since learned that many locales celebrate this grand summer squash in similar fashion.

What brought me to this event was the unique privilege of running an evangelistic multimedia show. The event almost didn't take place. Plans were in the works for months, but the doors kept closing. First there wasn't enough space at the festival, and then the financial supporters seemed to disappear. Reluctantly, we canceled. God had other plans. A phone call came one day before the event was to begin. Miraculously, everything had come together. Getting ready on less than 24 hours notice was a challenge, but soon we were on our way. We had no idea what God was doing, but we trusted Him. The festival was a little rowdier than we were used to, but we boldly set up our tent and went about the Lord's work, sharing the gospel. When all was said and done several days later, nearly 100 people had trusted Christ as their Savior. Whoever said vegetables weren't good for you?

Heavenly Father, thank You for Your patience with people and that Your desire is that not one person should perish (2 Peter 3:9). Let me never be ashamed of the calling You have given me. Help me to seek after lost sheep as You once sought after me.

Brad Hoopes, an ordained minister, serves as Director of Development at Dayspring Christian Academy, a Principle Approach school utilizing America's classical, biblical model of education.

The Fear of the Lord

"To fear the Lord is to hate evil; I hate pride and arrogance, evil behavior and perverse speech." *Proverbs 8:13 (New King James Version)*

During the last year of my pastorate, God had me study and preach only one thing—the fear of the Lord. We saw God meet us in some powerful ways, and it impacted many of our lives significantly.

Proverbs 8:13 was one of the first scriptures God impressed upon me. He asked me, "Do you *hate* evil? Do you *hate* disobeying God? Do you feel *disgusted* by even the smallest sins in your life? Would you do *anything* to get rid of them?"

This scripture explains it in more detail. Evil is anything contrary to God's truth and character. Pride and arrogance speak of sinful attitudes. Anytime I choose my way over God's, there is a pride and arrogance issue. Evil behavior speaks of sinful actions. Perverse speech speaks of sinful words. Psalms 34:9–14 is more specific. It is speaking lies (anything contrary to God's Word), and being hurtful to others—doing or saying anything that sows strife in relationships, instead of pursuing peace. But that is not all.

To fear God is to reverence Him with the highest respect (Psalms 33:8) and it is hoping in God's unfailing love and mercy (Psalms 33:18; 147:11). It is not being afraid of His punishment. His perfect love casts out that kind of fear (1 John 4:18; 2 Timothy 1:7). But we realize that apart from His love and mercy, His holiness would destroy us. Yet because of His unfailing love and mercy we have hope! We can trust Him, and that hope is what gives us the energy and strength to continue to resist evil and fully obey Him! Hope keeps us from compromise.

Dear God, Your secret and Your covenant is with them that fear You. Fill our hearts with hope and the intense desire to be free from every hint of evil. Search our hearts. We want to fear You. Amen.

Dean Witmer, a former pastor, now works for Rohrer's One Hour Heating and Air Conditioning.

Finishing the Race

"I have fought the good fight, I have finished the race, I have kept the faith." *2 Timothy 4:7*

The apostle Paul compared his life to a marathon when he wrote this farewell to Timothy. When I completed my second marathon, just before my sixtieth birthday, God taught me some very valuable life lessons.

In order to run a successful race, you must keep your eyes on the goal. The closer I came to the goal of twenty-six miles, the more difficult the challenge to keep going. By mile twenty-two, I became disoriented, asking my son when our next walk break would occur when we had just finished one. But I never once considered quitting. Life confronts us with many hurdles: discouragement, weakness, defeat, failures, and struggles. As the finish line, the thrill of winning a medallion and the cheering crowds spurred me on, so in life, we "press on toward the goal to win the prize for which God has called us heavenward in Christ Jesus (Philippians 3:14)."

As I completed the grueling race and saw the thousands of spectators cheering us on, my heart almost leapt out of my chest. The tears began to flow as I realized my "race work" was finished. I can only imagine what it will be like when we cross the finish line of life and join the "great cloud of witnesses (Hebrews 12:1)" who will welcome us into heaven.

Today as you stay focused on Christ regardless of the hurdles you are facing, remember that it's always too soon to quit! It will be worth everything when we cross the finish line into the arms of our Savior, to the cheers of the multitudes in heaven who are waiting for us.

Lord God, be my strength today. Help me to be aware as I take each step of the race that You are holding me in Your eternal grip. Keep my focus on Christ, my goal, so that in everything He will be made greater in my life.

David D. Allen is associate pastor of Calvary Church, Lancaster.

Miracle—Africa

"For the Lord is good; His mercy is everlasting; and His truth endureth to all generations." *Psalms 100:5*

Miracle one—The Lord sent me to Africa for two weeks. I say the Lord sent me because, personally, I never wanted to go there. Reluctantly, I agreed to accompany my pastor, Allen Dise, to a church leaders' conference in Uganda. Afterward, we traveled to Kenya to visit with a pastor friend. Our original plans included a side trip to an orphanage outside of Nairobi, Kenya. Instead, we found ourselves flying 200 miles north to a very poor little village outside of Garissa. We went to attend the dedication of a new Christian school.

Miracle two—Almost everyone from the village was there. The chief of the region, the chief of the village and a government official, all sat with us at the head table. There were speeches, singing and much celebration. The amazing thing was, they were all Muslim! Desperate to have their children educated, they had invited Christians to build a school in their community. They even agreed that the children could be taught about Jesus.

Miracle three—Our van got stuck in the sand when we left Garissa to go back to our plane. It took six men to push it free. Then it would not start. The same six men tried for 15 minutes to get the engine running. Finally, Allen walked over and laid his hands on the top of the van, praying that God would intervene. Immediately, the engine started.

Miracle four—So why did God send me to Africa? He was doing a work in my sixty-year-old heart. He taught me to be thankful for more than possessions and to really celebrate what He is doing in the world. He showed me I must not be looking to the past, but I must actively pursue the plans He still has for me.

Lord, Your family has no geographical boundaries. Your mercy is for everyone. Your plans include every age group. Thank you!

Henry Bomberger is president of Bomberger's Store in Lititz.

Four Things God Does Not Know

"For God so loved the world, that He gave his only begotten Son, that whosoever believeth on Him should not perish but have everlasting life." *John 3:16 (King James Version)*

1 **God does not know any sin He does not hate!** "And the Lord said, 'Because the cry of Sodom and Gomorrah is great, and because their sin is very grievous, I will go down now and see whether they have done altogether according to the cry of it, which is come unto Me; and if not, I will know' (Genesis 18:20–21)."

2. God does not know a sinner He does not love. "But God commendeth his love toward us, in that, while we were yet sinners, Christ died for us (Romans 5:8)."

I am going to be honest with you; I do not understand how God could love a sinner like me. It blows my mind when I think about some of the things I've done when I was living without Him. However, He never stopped loving me.

3. He doesn't know any way we can receive salvation other than the way He has given us. "Neither is there salvation in any other: for there is none other name under heaven given among men, whereby we must be saved (Acts 4:12)."

There is no religion that will save you or me. "I am the door: by me if any man enter in, he shall be saved, and shall go in and out, and find pasture (John 10:9)." Jesus did it all; He is the only way!

4. God doesn't know of a better time than right now to be saved. "...Behold, now is the accepted time; behold, now is the day of salvation (2 Corinthians 6:2b)."

Lord, I pray that everyone who reads these verses could realize Your love toward them and know, without a shadow of doubt, they are saved through Your mercy and grace. Amen.

Davy Esh is owner of Solid Rock Gospel Internet Radio at http://www.solidrockgospel.com.

Commitment to Desperation: The Root

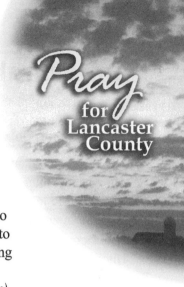

Pray for Lancaster County

"...O Lord, God of heaven, the great and awesome God who keeps his covenant of unfailing love with those who love him and obey his commands, listen to my prayer! Look down and see me praying night and day for your people Israel...."
Nehemiah 1:5–6 (New Living Translation)

Nehemiah was desperate when he prayed this prayer. He wept, mourned, fasted, and called out to God when he realized the seriousness of Israel's decline. We know very little of desperation in our culture of wealth and independence. We still have too many resources that we use to dig ourselves out of our situations. The root of desperation is the realization that there is no other place for us to turn. Nehemiah was willing to pray night and day until His great and awesome God relented and answered him.

When our desperation is greater than our fears and our excuses, we will begin to see the kind of breakthroughs being experienced in other places around the globe. Desperation is humbly saying to God, "You are our only hope. If You do not intervene, we are finished!"

Pray for Lancaster County is our weekly prayer focus for the individuals, families, churches and communities of our region. Please carry this emphasis in your heart and your prayers throughout the week.

Immeasurably More

"Now to him whom is able to do immeasurably more than all we ask or imagine, according to his power that is at work within us...." *Ephesians 3:20–21*

In 2002, I spent some quality time with a national-level pastor. Among other things, we talked about how to respond to the Spirit's big ideas. He told me: *Choose projects that are too large for the church to do by its own strength. That will drive you to your knees in dependence on God.*

His spiritual advice resonates with the wisdom of Ephesians 3:20. Paul calls us to a trust that is excessive.

I like words. In high school, I learned to diagram sentences, putting adjectives and adverbs in the right places. For emphasis, we use modifiers to add something to the subject, action verb, or object in a sentence. Sometimes, for great emphasis, we use more modifiers to add something to the modifiers already used. When that happens, we point to something extreme.

In this verse, Paul points to something extreme— God's power. He uses modifiers on top of modifiers to get his point across.

- God's power is not just *what we ask*, it's *all we ask*.
- God's power is not just *all we ask*, it's all we ask *or imagine*.
- God's power is not just *all we ask or imagine*; it's *more than* that.
- God's power is not just *more than all we ask or imagine*, it is *immeasurably more than* that.

Diagrammers may see Paul's sentence as a nightmare, but God's people are drawn to deeper trust in the extreme of God's power.

O God, it's too easy to settle for little things with You. By Your Spirit's mysterious work, awaken in me today a new capacity to trust You for abundantly far more than I could ask or imagine. In Jesus' name, Amen.

Kent Kroehler is senior pastor at First United Methodist Church in Lancaster.

Knocking Down Strongholds

"We use God's mighty weapons, not mere worldly weapons, to knock down the Devil's strongholds...we break down every proud argument that keeps people from knowing God...we conquer their rebellious ideas, and we teach them to obey Christ."
2 Corinthians 10:4–5 (New Living Translation)

A timid knock on my office door barely reached my ears. On the other side of the door stood my appointment, a young scraggly boy banned from the youth center until we had a talk. The easiest barrier that I removed from between us was that office door. The other barriers, spiritual in nature, would not be that easy. This young boy placed guards around his heart that showed in his hardened demeanor. He defended himself like an innocent bystander, oblivious to his crimes. My response matched his tone. Refreshing his memory, I highlighted his cursing, disruptive behavior and threatening comments. His bravado diminished.

Not wanting to crush his spirit, I transitioned to more light-hearted conversation, asking about his family and hobbies. The guards which stood watch on his heart retreated. My heart melted with the hardships this boy recounted as normal things.

God had taught me some things that I could impart to his life that would give him a promising future. My words seemed to captivate him. He turned from an antsy child to a sponge soaking in the passion of my testimony. Finally, I asked him if he would accept Christ into his life. After he prayed, I looked up and beheld a miracle. The hardhearted, stubborn boy sat crying as he embraced purpose. Hope permeated his being, as we talked a few minutes more. In the days to come, it would prove to be a genuine conversion as his behavior and life dramatically shifted. God's weapons are proven strong again.

Father, give illumination to my eyes that I might see that there are more for me than those that stand against me.

Jamie Centeno is an elder at In The Light Ministries and a field director Lancaster Teen Haven.

True Service is True Joy

"Keep the commandment and the law: to love the Lord your God, to walk in all his ways, to obey his commands, to hold fast to him and to serve him with all your heart and all your soul."
Joshua 22:5

For the past twenty-five years I have had the privilege to know and love a very special lady, my mother-in-law, Jacquelyn Meadors. She is a true servant of God, continually looking out for the needs of others, putting everyone else first in her life. She was an elementary school teacher who focused not only on teaching children academics, but loving and caring for the total child. She would bring clothes for the children in need, supply food for families, and take a personal interest in everyone. After teaching school, Jacquelyn would go to a Life Care Center to volunteer and help residents by reading to them, helping with letters, and praying with them. She has been recognized by the State of Virginia as "Volunteer of the Year" by the Virginia Health Care Association and has been designated as one of former President George Bush's "Points of Light."

When Jacquelyn receives a gift, her first instinct is to determine how she can share the gift with other people. Her true joy in life is serving the Lord and giving herself to the service of others. In all that she does, Jacquelyn does not expect or want recognition. My mother-in-law is a very special person, one who is humble, caring, and compassionate, and who serves the Lord with all her heart and soul. She has touched the lives of many people and has set an example for us all.

Father, help us to be good servants, looking to You for guidance and direction, and following the example of Your son, Jesus. Fill us with Your Holy Spirit, Your love, and compassion so we may truly make a difference in the lives of others.

William Worley is the superintendent of schools at Cocalico School District, and chairperson of the board of trustees at Evangelical School of Theology.

God's Mercy and Grace

"He saved us…because of his mercy. But by the grace of God I am what I am…." *Titus 3:5; 1 Corinthians 15:10*

A few years ago, I was traveling through a small Midwest town with my family. I was traveling 35 m.p.h., unaware the speed limit was 25 m.p.h. As I got to the other side of the town, I heard a shrill siren behind me. Sure enough, it was a policeman, signaling me to pull off to the side of the road. Now, if the policeman had been exercising mercy he would have said, "Look, I understand you didn't realize you were going 10 m.p.h. over the limit. I'll allow you to go free." If he would have been operating in a principle of grace, he would have said, "You are a really nice guy. In fact, I like you so much I'd like to give you a hundred dollars just for traveling on our streets." Unfortunately for me, he did not operate in mercy or grace, but he did allow me to receive *justice*—he gave me a ticket with a fine to pay!

I can remember, early in my Christian life, that I felt like God somehow owed me a nice family and a prosperous life, complete with a paycheck each week. After all, I thought, I had worked for it. I didn't realize how arrogant I was. If it were not for the grace of God, I would not have the physical strength or health to work in the first place. God didn't owe me anything. First He had shown mercy to me and delivered me from hell, then He showered His grace on me, giving me those things I did not deserve—God's wonderful presence in my life through Jesus Christ.

Lord, even though we do not deserve it, You offer us forgiveness, peace, eternal life, hope and healing—all because of Your wonderful grace!

Larry Kreider is the international director of DOVE Christian Fellowship International and serves on the executive team of the Regional Church of Lancaster County.

Stuck Together

"So we rebuilt the wall till all of it reached half its height, for the people worked with all their heart...half of my men did the work, while the other half were equipped with spears, shields, bows and armor...Those who carried materials did their work with one hand and held a weapon in the other." *Nehemiah 4:6,16–17*

In our family, we like to emphasize that we are a team that works together and helps each other, rather than competitors or loners. Our seven year old daughter, Elana, seems to have caught this message. Each time she prays at meal time, she ends the prayer with "our family will stick together like tape and glue!"

The rebuilding of the broken walls of Jerusalem by Nehemiah and his people paints a poignant picture how Christians can "stick together" and work together as families, small groups, churches, regions and around the world! Specifically, Nehemiah's "family" worked with all their might. There was no room for slackers; everybody did their job. Also, they worked together in unity toward a common goal and purpose. They practiced teamwork! Additionally, Nehemiah's people "stuck together" and protected each other's backs. They could distinguish between friends and foes and guarded each other against sneak attacks.

As a follower of Jesus, am I a team player? Do my teammates know we're playing on the same team? Or is my life alienated from others on the team? I seek to be a "Nehemiah-worker," one who works wholeheartedly toward the common vision, a team player who will protect and guard my teammates against attack. Imagine what our families, churches and regions would look like if Christians worked together as teammates. What a powerful team!

Lord, I pray that You would remove obstacles in my life that prevent me from working as a team player. May I display Christ-like attitudes and actions that would value, protect and build up those around me.

Allen Dise serves as senior elder of Newport DOVE in Elm.

Emily Weaver, grade 3, Doe Run Elementary School
Brooke Bunton, grade 5 and Wesley Bunton, grade 3
Veritas Academy

December

Message of Love

"And above all things have fervent love for one another, for 'love will cover a multitude of sins.'" *1 Peter 4:8 (New King James Version)*

We walked up and over a sand bank formed by prevailing winds. Mesmerized by the vast beauty of the ocean, the sounds of waves and seagulls, and the softness underfoot, we stood and just took it in. We noticed a woman in the distance, wearing a bright red sweater, walking slowly along the shoreline. Immediately, my heart received a message from the Lord: "Tell her I love her today." But the woman was far away, only a small patch of red visible a long way off.

Removing our shoes, we headed for the shoreline and began enjoying wet, cool feet and fresh shells tossed ashore by the power of the waves. We spent time exploring, exclaiming and exalting God's infinite creative ability. Up to our knees in the surf, we decided we wanted a photograph of us in the water. The camera was on shore and as we turned to go back, there the "red-sweater woman" stood in front of us! We asked her to take a picture of us out in the water. She smiled tentatively and nodded yes.

After the pictures were taken, I told her that the Lord loved her. Tears flowed like a river and deep sobs racked her body. We held her as she told us she had walked away from God. Addiction had owned her for three years. She had undergone treatment and returned to her husband and children just six weeks ago. She shared, "This morning I said to myself, there must be more, a better way." She spoke the words of repentance and received the restoration which only God can give.

Father, I thank you for showing us those who need Your comfort and compassion. Use me today Lord in any way that will touch someone and bring You glory. I commit to hear and obey in Jesus' name.

Diana Oliphant serves abroad with Global Missions of The Worship Center, Lancaster.

Commitment to Desperation: The Fruit

Pray for Lancaster County

"'All these I have kept since I was a boy,' he said. When Jesus heard this, he said to him, 'You still lack one thing. Sell everything you have and give to the poor, and you will have treasure in heaven. Then come, follow me.'" *Luke 18:21–22*

The rich young ruler was far too attached to his own possessions to rely completely on the Lord. What his life represented meant more to him than following Jesus. When the desperation for transformation really fills our hearts, the fruit will be abandonment to seek Him above all other things. A definition of abandonment is "the voluntary surrender of property (or a right to property) without attempting to reclaim it or give it away." When we are desperate for transformation, we will abandon all other priorities, all other privileges, and all other rights that we may legitimately have, in order to seek Him until He comes and brings that transforming revival. How often are we like the rich young ruler who could not let go of the temporal for the things that have eternal purpose? Time, resources, leisure, comfort, prestige, acclaim, success: all must be surrendered as we abandon ourselves to seeking the Lord for transformation.

Pray for Lancaster County is our weekly prayer focus for the individuals, families, churches and communities of our region. Please carry this emphasis in your heart and your prayers throughout the week.

Be Holy

"Wash yourselves, make yourselves clean; put away the evil of your doings from before My eyes. Cease to do evil, learn to do good; seek justice, reprove the oppressor; defend the fatherless, plead for the widow." *Isaiah 1:16 (New King James Version)*

An agnostic sociologist wrote a book on the condition of the church. He concluded: "Far from living in the 'other world' (the heavenlies), the faithful are remarkably just like the secular world...In practice, they are not the way they are supposed to be in their theology...The culture has trampled over them...Talk of hell, damnation and even sin has been replaced by non-judgmental language of understanding and empathy." Decades ago, C.S. Lewis said, "The greatest enemy to the church is 'contented worldliness.'"

What has happened to the church? Do we even use the word *sin* any longer? *Sin* is such an outdated word—not a nice word, definitely not a politically correct word. In our efforts to not offend, or sound condemning, we have compromised our standard of holiness.

I was delivered from sin when I accepted Jesus as my Savior and Lord. God still longs to save people from sinful life-styles, from addictions and habits that His Word calls sin. We all need an encounter with a holy God and His Holy Spirit who convicts us of sin. Then we need to walk in obedience to God's Word, "...not conforming yourselves to the former lusts, as in your ignorance; but as He who called you is holy, you also be holy in all your conduct... (1 Peter 1:14–16)."

Father, forgive us for walking in compromise. Help us to speak Your truth to the lost and those who are away from You, with compassion and love. Give us a passion for holiness and help us to be able to determine the difference between holiness and legalism. Let our lives radiate freedom from sin—and joy in obedience to You.

Mary Prokopchak is a nurse and serves with her husband, Steve, on the Apostolic Council of DOVE Christian Fellowship International.

The Nice Guy Syndrome

"Am I now trying to win the approval of men, or of God? Or am I trying to please men? If I were still trying to please men, I would not be a servant of Christ." *Galatians 1:10*

Several years ago, my wife and I attended a course on "Biblical Counseling." We were divided into lab sessions where we did some soul-searching and in-depth sharing. It was during this time that God showed me that I was overly concerned about acceptance and the approval of men, which could be called "the nice guy syndrome." This caused me to make decisions that were more people-pleasing than God-pleasing. It was a hindrance and a bondage that I needed to confess and forsake. It has caused wounds in my family, as well as in the church that I pastored. I was especially aware of this as I looked back on a very difficult situation in our congregation. In my attempts to find acceptance from persons on both sides of a particular issue, I failed to be definitive enough, which confused and frustrated me as well as those in my congregation.

Pursuing God's approval is so much better than being manipulated by man's approval. I am thankful that God is helping me to be more concerned about what He thinks than what man thinks. "He is my deliverer, and in Him will I trust."

Someone said, "A conformer is a person whose life is controlled by a person from without, while a transformer is a person controlled by a power from within." May God help me to be a transformer.

Dear God, may the thoughts and the decisions that I make today be centered around seeking to please You above all else, rather than seeking to please men.

Fred Heller serves on the pastoral team at Hammer Creek Mennonite Church.

Benefits Package

"Praise the Lord, O my soul, and forget not all his benefits."
Psalms 103:2

My newlywed co-worker lamented that she couldn't afford to see the dentist despite an increasingly painful toothache. With wedding expenses and the cost of furnishing a new household, there was no money left in the budget for unexpected emergencies.

"The company dental plan will pay for most of it," I reminded her.

She had completely forgotten about that benefit. To forget about such a major benefit seems odd, but her lapse of memory reminded me of how often I forget about benefits God offers to His children. Too often, I endure nagging condemnation for past failures. I live in fear of what might happen, not only to me, but to my children and grandchildren. I become tired and discouraged with too much to do and to little time to do it.

Amazingly, God's benefit package includes a cure for all those complaints. "Forget not all his benefits," the psalmist reminds us. In Psalms 103, nineteen benefits are listed for those who put their trust in God: He forgives all our sins, heals all our diseases, redeems our life from the pit, crowns us with love and compassion, satisfies our desires with good things, renews our strength like the eagle's, bestows His righteousness upon our children's children....

Like employee benefits, God's benefits are of no value if claims are not submitted.

Unlike many companies, which cut benefits packages in order to economize, God promises His benefits are from everlasting to everlasting. One can't find a better benefit package from any corporation.

God, thank you for Your outstanding benefits. Let me not forget Your benefits and the love You promise, not only to me, but to my children's children.

Lou Ann Good is the food and family features editor for the Lancaster Farming Newspaper.

Obeying God's Promptings

"...he goes on ahead of them, and his sheep follow him because they know his voice." *John 10:4*

In 1999, a team of seven, mostly from Lancaster County, made a commitment to pray for two weeks in several nations of Europe. We wanted to support the work of a church in Great Britain and of some missionaries to North Africans living in France.

One day we found ourselves in downtown London, open to whatever God would have us do that day. As we prayed, we felt the Lord show us that we should pray at the National Gallery, the large art museum right in the heart of London. It was one of those "It's either God or I am crazy" moments. Whoever heard of walking through an art museum in prayer? But we went. In fact, we spent about two hours walking through the rooms of the museum, praying for God to invade that place with His presence, and for there to be art which pointed people to Him. Then we left, still wondering if we were weird!

The following year, I returned to the same art museum to find a large banner with the words, "Seeing Salvation." Intrigued, I went into a number of rooms dedicated to paintings which showed different aspects of Jesus' life and ministry. There were scripture verses in large letters around the walls; the gift shop was selling Bibles and devotional books too! Amazed, I remembered our prayers—it was God after all! He had wanted to communicate Jesus to the people of London through a whole art exhibition—and we got to be a part of it through prayer.

After this experience, I tend to listen more carefully to those thoughts that come: they just might be God, communicating His heart for the peoples of the world.

Lord, help me to discern Your voice and to obey those promptings from You in my daily life.

Peter Bunton serves as leader for the work of DOVE Christian Fellowship International in Europe, as well as with DOVE Mission International, supporting the work of missionaries around the world.

Just Wait and See

"Yet the Lord longs to be gracious to you; He rises to show you compassion. For the Lord is a God of justice. Blessed are all who wait for Him!" *Isaiah 30:18*

Before becoming a first-time mother this year, I taught pre-K at a local Christian school. I really love this age group, the way they soak up every word you say and hand-draw sweet little pictures to display on your desk. Of course there are those times, as any teacher could tell you, that the questions of "when" and "why" can be a bit more numerous than you'd like!

One particular morning I was mixing up paint and preparing the materials for the activities that day. The children would come to me during their play time to ask me, "What are you doing?" "What are we going to do today?" "Why are you putting that paint on those plates?" I kept responding to those questions with, "Well, you'll just have to wait and see. This is your play time now...go enjoy yourself with your friends and you'll find out soon enough what I'm preparing for you." They went off to their play time and sure enough, they soon found themselves diving into the activities and having a good time.

Could it be the same way with our heavenly Father? So many times we can tend to question God with, "What are you doing with my life?" "Why is it taking so long?" And, all along, God is reminding us that He's in control, He knows what He's doing, and He is bringing about His best in our lives, all in His good timing. We need His grace to rest and enjoy the season He has us in.

Isn't it great to know that our God is an understanding and loving Father, and His patience with us is beyond our understanding? Wait and see how the Lord will work in your life!

Lord Jesus, thank you for being in control of my life. I choose to trust and rest in Your arms of grace today.

Cindy Zeyak worked with preschool children for 11 years and has recently become a mother. She is also a worship leader. She and her family live in Lancaster City.

December 8

Conquer the Darkness

"Thou shall tread upon the lion and adder: the young lion and the dragon shalt thou trample under your feet." *Psalms 91:13 (King James Version)*

I stared down the barrel of the gun and braced for the impact of the bullet. A single father on Christmas break from Christian college, I was spending my "vacation" working as a fuel delivery driver.

I started my morning that day with a devotion from Psalms 91, and the words in verse 13 had stayed with me. Their meaning became clear on my last delivery of the day. It was then that two gunmen appeared and demanded my money. One covered me from a few feet away, while the other jerked my wallet from my back pocket.

What happened next surprised all three of us. I heard myself speak. I said, "I have 50 dollars in my wallet, but that's all I have to my name. I'm in Bible college, studying for the ministry, and I'm trying to make some money to survive. In fact, I probably have less money than you!"

I'd spoken to them as "partners in poverty." There was an eerie silence. The eyes of one gunman changed and they locked with mine. He was a struggling human being, and so was I. He pocketed his gun and told his companion to leave me alone. My wallet was returned, with the money, and the two men walked away. As I stood there stunned, I sensed their remorse, so I called out, "Thanks. I'll be praying for you guys." They half-smiled and disappeared around the corner.

I learned that day that we can conquer the darkness with kindness, and tred upon lions and snakes with truth and integrity. As a police officer, I've applied the principles I discovered that day to every person I've dealt with on the job. I've even had people thank me for arresting them!

Lord, help me to remember that You are in control of whatever evil tomorrow holds.

John DePaul is a police officer and guitarist who shares his testimony with music.

Pray for **Lancaster County**

December 9

Begin at the Beginning

"Who is wise? He will realize these things. Who is discerning? He will understand them. The ways of the Lord are right; the righteous walk in them, but the rebellious stumble in them." *Hosea 14:9*

An understanding of the path of transformation means being able to discern "God's footprints." Where is He working in ways that we must follow? Where do we see clear evidences of His powerful hand at work—and how can we learn from that? God is mightily at work in the island nation of Fiji in the South Pacific.

Transforming revival is bringing change to lives, society, and even the ecology of the land. This amazing transformation began not with a conference or a seminar, but in the hearts of individuals who were desperate for God to come. They were not just looking for God to fix a problem; they wanted Him to search their own hearts. They embarked on an 18-month process of asking the Lord to reveal everything of wickedness and sin in their hearts. They took as much time as needed for God to do His thorough, heart-searching work. They did not stop until they knew God had dealt with everything. This is revival preparation 101.

If you ask God to reveal to your heart all that is displeasing to Him, it may take more than just a few minutes when convenient. It will likely take several weeks, as we live in continual openness to God's penetrating gaze. Are you willing and ready to begin such a process of allowing God intimate access to your heart and mind? You can start today.

Pray for Lancaster County is our weekly prayer focus for the individuals, families, churches and communities of our region. Please carry this emphasis in your heart and your prayers throughout the week.

About My Feet, God...

"...Shall what is formed say to him who formed it, 'Why did you make me like this?'" *Romans 9:20*

I don't like my feet. I believe God could have done a better job with them. For one thing, they're small compared to the rest of my body. I don't always like where God has taken my feet, either. When I was a youth pastor, my feet experienced eighty miles of the Appalachian Trail. God could have put my feet in a ministry where the kids loved to play computer games. But God led them into a ministry where a good time meant sleeping on the ground and carrying your belongings in a backpack. God, why did you assign my small feet to hobble over the Appalachians?

These feet haven't walked up any steps for an award or won any races. They're so ordinary, common and utilitarian. God, I'm just not happy with my feet.

Paul wrote, "Who are you, O man, to talk back to God? Shall what is formed say to him who formed it, 'Why did you make me like this?' Does not the potter have the right to make out of the same lump of clay some pottery for noble purposes and some for common use (Romans 9:20–21)?"

Created beings are often dissatisfied with how they are created, or where they are being used. Do I have the right to determine my fashion, function, or fortune? I must praise the Sovereign Potter for forming me to be used as He sees fit. He could have left me as a lump of clay. However, He chose to mold my small feet so that they're big and strong enough to carry me where He would have me minister—where He wants the Good News declared. He has let them be tired and sore so that I can draw upon His resources, not my own. These feet have fallen and His grace and mercy have picked them up.

Thank you God for my feet. They might be small, but You made them that way and they are Yours. Amen!

Robert Reid is the senior pastor of Calvary Monument Bible Church.

Patience for God's Timing

"Be joyful in hope, patient in affliction, faithful in prayer."
Romans 12:12

Many years ago I was working in Columbus, Ohio. I had a strong desire to move back to Lancaster County where I had grown up. I prayed about this frequently, but had trouble finding a job that compared to the employment I had in Columbus. During this time I was involved in teaching and leadership at my church and had a key role in a large project at work. Six months into my job search, I finally got a good Lancaster job lead sent to me by a friend. I was offered and accepted that job. I realized then that God had worked perfect timing for my move. My responsibilities at church had ended and other people were available to fill in for my roles at work.

Years later my employer asked me to move, and I decided against it. I went through another long period of searching for the right employment. After praying specifically for employment with a company that had Christian values, God led me to meet a friend and business owner in a shopping mall. He suggested that I talk with the information technology director at his company, even though they did not have an opening. I thought it was a long shot, but it ended up being a great match for me. I have been blessed by the great work environment at a company that honors God. This time of searching also helped me make important decisions about my relationship with a friend who is now my wife (Jeremiah 29:11).

Heavenly Father, we know that You care about us. You know our needs, and You know what is best for us. Help us to be patient when waiting for answers to our prayers. Your timing is perfect; and Your results are better than our desires.

Brad Sauder is employed as a computer programmer at Signature Custom Cabinetry and is a small group leader at DOVE Christian Fellowship Westgate Celebration.

A Life Mission

"The Lord will keep you from all harm—he will watch over your life; the Lord will watch over your coming and going both now and forevermore." *Psalms 121:7–8*

Years ago as a young man driving down a lonely stretch of highway in Kentucky, I was feeling quite uncertain about my next steps in life. Even though I was on my way back to Bible college, I truly felt alone and very uncertain about what I should do with my life. On impulse I reached out and turned on the radio. Immediately I heard the scripture noted above being spoken as a "sign off" message from a religious broadcast. My heart was deeply touched as I quickly realized this was much more than coincidence. It was a God encounter to touch me where I most needed to hear from God at that moment. Suddenly a random scripture became a promise, an anchor, and now a life verse that has nurtured me for many years.

This life experience, along with many others along the way, has left me with an unshakable conviction that Jehovah will watch over my life. And more importantly, He will guard a life mission deposited within. I also learned over time that a life mission is grown like a tree more than it is crafted like a blueprint and built like a house.

Just like a mighty oak grows from a little sapling to a large awesome tree, so it is with the life mission within you deposited there by the Almighty. Your job is to discover it, water it, feed it, nurture it in partnership with the Holy Spirit. Start by identifying what has already been revealed, and let it grow. Let God show you what He desires.

Heavenly Father, we thank you for the divine deposit within—a life mission. We seek to see more clearly what You have in mind for us. We commit ourselves to faithfully nurture and grow what You have placed in us. We reject our tendency to simply live day by day without thought to Your purpose for us. We commit ourselves to walking with You—to be led by divine appointments and divine mission. Amen

Glen J. Yoder serves as pastor of Ephrata DOVE Christian Fellowship and as Missionary Care Coordinator for DOVE Mission International.

December 13

Prayer: Our Lifeline!

"...My house shall be called a house of prayer for all nations...."
Mark 11:17

C orrie Ten Boom asked, "Is prayer your steering wheel or your spare tire?" Prayer is our power line to heaven. My travel shaver slows down and eventually stops if it is not regularly recharged. We will experience frustration as we pray lopsided prayers that focus only on pet prayer areas.

Jesus taught His disciples to pray with six major focuses (or spiritual rooms in which to pray) so they could experience a balanced prayer life. This prayer is not a law to follow, but a guide to pray by the leading of His Holy Spirit.

Adoration room: *Our Father in heaven, may your name be honored.* He is our Daddy who loves when we come to Him as we worship and adore Him in Spirit and truth. **Declaration room:** *May your kingdom come [soon]. May your will be done here on earth just as it is in heaven.* Declare His kingdom to come to your life, your family, your church, your city, your region, your nation, and in the nations. **Provision room:** *Give us this day our daily bread.* Be specific when you ask for provision. He wants to provide for us. **Freedom room:** *And forgive us our sins, just as we have forgiven those who have sinned against us.* God has called us to keep short accounts. Forgive those who hurt you so that no bitterness can develop a root in your heart. **Warfare room:** *And don't let us yield to temptation, but deliver us from the evil one.* We are called to spiritual warfare as soldiers of Christ. Regardless of the temptation that comes your way, God always provides a way of escape! **Exaltation room:** *For Yours is the kingdom and the power and the glory forever. Amen.* Building a personal house of prayer begins and ends with honoring and exalting the Lord and gazing upon Him.

Jesus, You are our source and our life!

Larry Kreider serves on the executive team of the Regional Church of Lancaster County and as the International Director of DOVE Christian Fellowship International.

Merciful God

"But in Your great mercy You did not put an end to them or abandon them, for You are a gracious and merciful God."
Nehemiah 9:31

For many years God has been patient with those who turn their backs to Him. The children of Israel heard the prophets, but would not listen, and paid no attention to God. They did just what they wanted to do. But God kept his covenant with them because He is an awesome God.

What mercy is God displaying in my life when I am not listening to his commands and words of advice? Each day, I search for new areas in my life that need a touch from God to heal, restore and refine. He is so awesome that if I am sincere, He shows me new ways to walk with Him that reflect His ways. God is faithful. May we find ourselves being faithful to Him.

Dear God, thank you for Your patience with me and Your faithful love and mercy. May I respond by loving obedience to Your commands. Amen.

Miriam M. Witmer is a wife, mother, grandmother, great-grandmother, and volunteer at Landis Homes Retirement Community and Mennonite Central Committee Material Resource Center.

Our Sufficiency is from God

"Not that we are sufficient of ourselves...but our sufficiency is from God...." *2 Corinthians 3:4–6 (New King James Version)*

I've experienced some insensitivity regarding my marital status. I'm here to set the record straight! Singleness isn't a sin, a disease to be cured of, or a curse to die of. Single adults are the same sensitive human beings as everyone else, with similar joys, hurts, cares and needs for God and His people.

We come to church to worship God, connect with others, and be part of a family. We wish to find more love, acceptance and concern among our family of faith than we get in the world. I would never ask my married friends if they are still married. When someone asks us if we are still single it can hurt and make us feel inadequate or inferior. If we are dating, you will know it—no need to ask!

God didn't create marriage first. He created humankind first. But it sometimes seems that marriage is the basis for a fulfilled life. Sorry, Jerry McGuire, no one else "completes me." A fulfilled life comes from a close relationship with Jesus and recognizing that I am unique, separate, whole and complete in Him.

I don't want to be consumed with a desire to be married or anything else for that matter. I want to seek Him first and His righteousness and believe marriage is one of these things that will be added to me. I want to live a fulfilled, satisfying life NOW. That doesn't mean I lose my desire to be married. I've merely surrendered it to Christ.

God created us with a need for relationships. We need each other! So let's make every effort to accept single adults without prejudgments or suspicions or non-biblical limitations. And single adults: don't limit yourself by feeling inferior or incomplete. Each of us was created to be single, unique and whole in Christ regardless of our marital status.

Father, we draw our sufficiency from You who satisfies our hearts' deepest need.

Sharon Blantz serves The Worship Center as regional pastor of Single Adult/Support Ministries.

Next Steps to Transformation

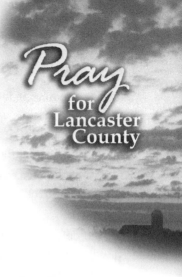

Pray for Lancaster County

"Finally, all of you, live in harmony with one another; be sympathetic, love as brothers, be compassionate and humble. Do not repay evil with evil or insult with insult, but with blessing, because to this you were called so that you may inherit a blessing."
1 Peter 3:8–9

After all personal sin and repentance issues have been dealt with thoroughly, God then moves us on to a corporate level. It begins with each of us dealing with issues we may have with others. After our own hearts have been cleansed, we must look to the anger, gossip, resentment, evil-speaking, jealousy, dissension, discord, envy, and anything else that has come between us and other people. We must approach others with an attitude of brokenness and humility. Again, this must be given as much time as is needed.

Continue to allow the Lord to bring up those issues that we must deal with, and don't minimize anything the Lord reveals. If He brings it to your mind, it is not minimal.

Following the individual-to-individual restoration, the next phase is to deal with corporate issues in families, as a church, and even as a city. This process must be bathed in continual prayer and immersion in the Word of God. In many cases this process ends with a period of fasting and prayer in anticipation of how God will answer. As the people of Fiji are experiencing, God does respond very powerfully and tangibly! Give yourself to this transformational process with anticipation of what will God do in answer to your obedience.

Pray for Lancaster County is our weekly prayer focus for the individuals, families, churches and communities of our region. Please carry this emphasis in your heart and your prayers throughout the week.

His Power Made Perfect

"Who is wise and understanding among you? Let him show by good conduct that his works are done in the meekness of wisdom. But if you have bitter envy and self-seeking in your hearts, do not boast and lie against the truth." *James 3:13–14*

"But with righteousness He shall judge the poor, and decide with equity for the meek of the earth." *Isaiah 11:4 (New King James Version)*

The definition of meekness is *having a patient, gentle disposition: yielding to others' actions and opinions.* This smacks right in the face of the American way, which says we have the right of free speech and assembly. We often assume people want to hear our opinion and so we espouse it whenever possible.

Humility is the act of being humble, but meekness is having the character and disposition to be humble all the time. Sometimes God must humble us for our own good and the good of others. However, God does not make us meek. I believe there are times we need to hold our tongue and just be an example of meekness. Yes, there are times when we need to speak up against something blatantly wrong, but there are probably many more times that we need to be quiet, be patient and be meek. Allow God and others to exalt you as the Word says, "Let the lowly brother glory in his exaltation, but the rich in his humiliation... (James 1: 9–10)."

"Blessed are the meek, for they shall inherit the earth (Matthew 5:5)."

Lord, I pray that You would help me to walk the road of meekness. Lord keep me from being humbled because of my own pride and selfish ways. Allow me to act in humility and adopt meekness as a life-style. Amen.

Eric Davenport is the owner of Davenport Design & Advertising and and attends a local marketplace ministry Bible study through Faith Connections at Work, which is devoted to raising up workplace evangelists.

Crushed

"...God opposes the proud, but gives grace to the humble. Humble yourselves, therefore, under God's mighty hand that in due time He might lift you up." *1 Peter 5:5–6*

As soon as I saw the deacon and the senior pastor walking to the door, I knew that something was up. I led them into the living room and almost immediately heard these words, "Doug, we've come to talk to you about your critical spirit."

In the week prior to this visit, I received two independent calls, one from another pastor and the other from a friend. Both expressed concern over my "critical spirit." The first I had blown off as coming from a man who felt threatened by me; the second was harder to dismiss. Now two more men came and spoke to me about this same issue. I was crushed.

Almost immediately, I fell to my knees in front of these men. I wept as I cried out to God to forgive me and cleanse me of this sin (and spirit) that was robbing me while polluting the very air of the saints around me. I knew God was speaking and I could not dismiss it. It was time for repentance. So I cried and prayed and confessed.

Some months later, my wife and I moved to Lancaster where I had the privilege of taking the role of a reconciler. Indeed, my life changed that day while on my knees; I went from always noting what was wrong to helping others find the good in one another. I had spent years noting people's faults; now I could spend years encouraging people in the grace of God in Christ.

Do not be afraid of God's heavy hand—even His crushing hand—upon your life. If you will humble yourself before Him, He will help you in time.

Lord, please do Your work in my life and use me as Your instrument of healing. Forgive me of my old ways. I pray in Jesus' name, Amen.

Doug Winne is the pastor of Evangelical Free Church, Lititz.

God's Perfect Orchestration

"Listen to this, O Job, Stand and consider the wonders of God."
Job 37:14 (New American Standard Bible)

During the summer of 1994, I went to Bolivia on a mission trip with sixteen others from Lancaster Bible College. Home base was the missionary's house, which made for some very cramped living. On one particular excursion, we took a rented van and the missionary's 4x4 vehicle, and traveled to Copacabana, a Bolivian city located on the eastern border of Peru. We had to cross Lake Titicaca with our vehicles, then travel about ninety minutes on a dusty road to reach Copacabana. The name of our ferry: "Titanic Two."

After about forty minutes of bouncing around on the dusty road, our van blew the right rear tire. As I got to the rear of the van, I heard a peculiar hissing sound. It was coming from the left rear tire. We only had one spare tire. Our missionary friend loaded up our tires in his vehicle, along with our driver, and headed to Copacabana to have the tires repaired. We, however, were stuck waiting for their return. We climbed the nearby hills to pray and explore.

As we were praying, we noticed sheep coming toward us, followed by two young shepherd boys. One, David, was carrying a soccer ball. He showed us an open field nearby that was level enough to kick the ball without it rolling completely down the hill. After fifteen minutes of playing soccer with David, one of our Spanish-speaking teammates shared the gospel with him and he accepted Christ as his Savior.

Fifteen minutes later, the repaired tires were on the van and we were on our way.

One flat tire, no problem; two flat tires, priceless. Sometimes the cost of a life being saved means inconvenience for a whole lot of people.

Father, give me the grace to be inconvenienced so that others may know Your Beloved Son.

Keith Hahn is an elder at New Hope Bible Fellowship Church and a staff member of Lancaster Youth Network of Churches.

Extra-ordinary Calling

"...Moses said to the Lord, 'O Lord, I have never been eloquent, ...I am slow of speech and tongue....'" *Exodus 4:10*

L ike Moses, I often allow the mundane and ordinary events of life to limit my perspective of God's awesome power. I become angry when the coffee maker breaks down first thing in the morning or one of our teen children takes off their dirty socks and throws them on the table in the living room. Also like Moses, even after I witness a miraculous show of God's miracles, I have the audacity to remind God of my inabilities rather than trust Him for His ability to perform a task. When I become discouraged or things aren't going as planned, I find it so easy to blame myself for the failure. When I tell myself, "I'm not smart enough," or "I don't have enough money," or "I'm not gifted enough." I'm not simply selling myself short, I'm short-circuiting the divine "trial by fire" method of purification (James 1).

I'm slowly learning it's not about me. Success can be defined as faithfulness to God's call. I have nothing to give someone else that I have not already received from the Lord myself. I am only as useful in God's kingdom as my ability to allow His grace to transform my heart at the deepest level. Religious jargon doesn't cut it. When I'm physically tired, emotionally spent, and made vulnerable by my physical limitations, my spirit is thirsty for a divine experience of tasting "living water." It's that point of desperation that most qualifies me to help others connect with the same source of extra-ordinary inspiration, hope, and relief from difficult circumstances.

Lord, help me not to despise days of desperation. Help me to receive Your grace and trust You to turn cursing into blessing. Help me to look past the ordinary in my existence and find the extra-ordinary power of Your transformational healing touch.

Ed Hersh provides counseling and healing prayer ministry, trains lay counselors, and helps leaders receive spiritual renewal.

Fighting the Current

"When you pass through the waters, I will be with you...."
Isaiah 43:2

I was a youth pastor on a mission trip in El Salvador. We had taken the day off to refresh ourselves and go swimming at a local beach. It was a little eerie, though, because no one was there. No lifeguards, no lifeboats, no one except us! This "alone-ness" became frightfully apparent when one of our students, Chris (who had never even *seen* the ocean) decided to go out a little too far.

Trained in lifeguarding, I arrogantly "shadowed" Chris, thinking I could take care of everything. I was resting in my abilities; I didn't even whisper a prayer.

All that changed when we both got caught in a dangerous undertow. Chris was a weak swimmer and began losing strength and panicking. Slipping out to sea, I began to fear for our lives as I tried to pull a heavy student in to shore. It seemed like a nightmare. No one was there to help us as we drifted further out! I seriously thought that this would be my last day on earth.

Until I prayed with great desperation: "Lord Jesus, help us!"

After praying, a thought struck me from the blue— "don't fight the current, swim sideways!" This was common sense, but I had forgotten it in the terror of the moment. I listened to that voice. Unbeknownst to us, within twenty feet was a sandbar. Chris and I stood in ankle-depth water hundreds of yards from the beach. We would live because we remembered that God walks with us through the disasters of life.

How many times have we fought the current on our own, even to the point of exhaustion? Are you in the midst of great trouble in your life and fighting the current? Perhaps your deliverance is only twenty feet away. Are you ready to let God lead you there?

Oh Lord, please help me to know You are in the midst of all my troubles; help me hear where Your voice is leading me.

John Wilkinson is the senior high student ministries pastor at Lancaster County Bible Church.

Christmas Giving

"Do not withhold good from those who deserve it, when it is in your power to act." *Proverbs 3:27*

Have you noticed that sometimes our agenda is not exactly the same as the Lord's? One day at the office where I work I heard about a committee which planned to come in early in the morning to work on a project. I thought to myself how nice it would be to bring in a breakfast treat for our faithful volunteers, especially because it was the Christmas season.

Later I dismissed the idea. I felt I had enough to do with Christmas just around the corner. I really didn't need anything added to my list.

Later on I picked up my Bible during personal time with God. I read through Proverbs 3. As I continued through the book, verse 27 really jumped off the page at me. I remembered my idea of blessing the office volunteers. I felt the conviction of the Holy Spirit to honor those who served us.

I did come up with some simple, festive munchies for the team to enjoy while they worked.

Much is said about giving around Christmas. It truly is more blessed to give than receive! Maybe your calendar and shopping bags are already full. But maybe, just maybe, there may be someone else you could bless this season as we celebrate Christ's birth. Ask the Lord to direct your paths this giving season!

Lord, thank you that we are able to give this Christmas. We are grateful to be able to share with others from the blessings we have received. We thank you for Your wonderful gift of our Savior, Jesus Christ. Amen.

Sarah Sauder serves as the director of House To House Publications, Lititz.

Holding to Heavenly Expectations

"Since you have been raised to new life with Christ, set your sights on the realities of heaven, where Christ sits at God's right hand in the place of honor and power. Let heaven fill your thoughts. Do not think only about things down here on earth." *Colossians 3:1–2 (New Living Translation)*

As followers of Jesus Christ, we have been granted an entirely new view of what is truly reality. We no longer need to settle for the things we currently see on earth as being "the best it gets for now." When Jesus instructed the disciples to pray "Your Kingdom come, Your will be done on earth as it is in heaven" (Matthew 6:10), He was encouraging them to go for the bigger vision!

When we realize that Christ is now sitting at God's right hand in a place of honor and power, the reality of revived churches and transformed communities—and even nations—is well within the grasp of those who will lay hold of God in prayer and not let go. Paul declares in Colossians 1:15 that Christ is supreme over all creation, so we can certainly live with a heavenly expectation that He will display His glory over all the earth!

Pray for Lancaster County is our weekly prayer focus for the individuals, families, churches and communities of our region. Please carry this emphasis in your heart and your prayers throughout the week.

God Stories

More Than Enough

"But God has surely listened and heard my voice in prayer."
Psalms 66:19

My most memorable Christmas was the year we had almost no money. My husband, Kevin, had been called into full-time ministry and was raising his own support, which was trickling in slowly. We lived in a run-down house, for which I was eternally grateful, because few landlords would rent to someone without a steady income. We dropped our health insurance, frequented a food bank, and bought clothes at Goodwill—anything to make ends meet. Our families would have "rescued" us instantly had we asked them, but we were making out okay. God was good to us.

But that December Kevin told me that we could only afford to buy one present for each of our children, Hannah and Daniel. I cried. I could not imagine giving them only one Christmas present. I knew they would receive many gifts from our extended family, but it wasn't the same. I prayed that Christmas would be really special for them in spite of our circumstances. I told my boss, Wendy Reasner, of my dilemma. She gave me the pep talk I needed, along with lots of inexpensive ideas for Christmas. I left work that day, full of hope.

That year we strung popcorn on the tree. We turned off the lights and chewed Wintergreen Lifesavers to watch them spark. We made a birthday cake for Jesus. We drove through fancy neighborhoods to see their fabulous Christmas light displays. We laughed a lot and were truly having a great time without all the gifts.

But the Lord wasn't finished. We came home a couple days before Christmas to find boxes of gifts, overflowing with toys, medicines and food on our porch. We were stunned and thrilled at the love and generosity of our anonymous donors. God had more than answered my prayer.

Dear Lord, thank you for always answering my prayers and for caring about even the smallest details of my life.

Stephanie Eshleman serves with her husband, Kevin, at Ephrata Community Church.

December 25

God and Santa Claus

"Truly, I say to you, if you ask the Father for anything in My name, He will give it to you." *John 16:23 (New American Standard Bible)*

I used to believe in Santa Claus. I still have a letter I wrote him when I was 6, requesting a toy army tank and a tool kit. He delivered the goods right on time (and returned my letter, too, I guess!). Today, my children know that Santa is an imaginary part of the fun of the Christmas season, and they don't write notes to the North Pole. But they sure do turn in a detailed Christmas wish-list to Mom and Dad each year! In the winter of 1999, I penned such a list myself for a local agency that had chosen to bless my family in a time of need.

I was asked to write suggested gift items for everyone in my family, including my wife and myself. So I did...and then forgot about it (well, almost...) until the phone call inviting me to pick up the presents.

I was amazed. "Santa" had delivered a laundry basket filled with dozens of colorfully wrapped gifts, each one labeled specifically for my family members. On Christmas, when we sat down for our annual gift-opening ritual, we had the biggest pile of presents we'd seen in years. When the last one was opened, I realized that *everything* I'd written on my wish-list—down to the John Wayne videos I'd requested for myself—was there. There was even a gift for our dog! Somebody (Santa's elves?) had done some intense and specific shopping!

And that's what our Lord is like. He knows our needs before we even ask, but He also knows our *wants*—and He *asks* us to ask. Sometimes (just because He loves us), He gives us every little thing on our list.

Thank you, God, that as I take my delight in You, You give me the desires of my heart.

Mark Ammerman, communications director of the Regional Church of Lancaster County, serves on the leadership staff of In The Light Ministries in Lancaster City.

God Stories

December 26

Like Father, Like Son

"Be imitators of God, therefore, as dearly loved children and live a life of love just as Christ loved us and gave himself up for us as a fragrant offering and sacrifice to God." *Ephesians 5:1–2*

I have heard it said, "You sound or act just like your father. I can see which family you belong to." Recently, I heard my wife say just that while I was standing and visiting with a small group of men. I had my hands in my pant pockets and there beside me stood our six-year-old son with his hands in his pant pockets as well. I have also taken him along on the truck with me different times and when we get home he imitates what he saw me doing while he was along with me. For example, he gets a clip board with papers and a map and pretends he is making a delivery, checking out his destination, marking where all his drops are located and so forth.

When people see or hear me, do they see a reflection of my Heavenly Father? Do they know I have been adopted into the family of God? Some people may not know, but my desire is that they would know I am a part of God's family as they learn to know me. I certainly do not want them to be surprised or shocked that I am a child of God if they find it out through someone else.

I also thank my Heavenly Father for His promise in Romans 8:29 which says: "For those God foreknew He also predestined to be conformed to the likeness of His Son, that He might be the firstborn among many brothers."

Heavenly Father, help me to be an imitator of Christ as one of Your dearly loved children.

Clifford Sauder is a husband, father and truck driver whom Jesus loves and who attends Weaverland Mennonite Church.

December 27

Nothing Too Difficult

"Is anything too difficult for the Lord?" *Genesis 18:14 (New American Standard Bible)*

The conviction deepened almost daily. After many years of renting, the Lord was leading us to declare that we were "wedded to the land" by purchasing our first house.

It sounded great, but there were several significant obstacles. We had just moved from out of state. Officially, the ministry I served employed me part-time. After years of serving in not-for-profit organizations, we had no down-payment. We were not prime candidates to qualify, according to any reasonable criteria, as homebuyers.

Yet, one by one, the obstacles were removed. We found the right house. The down-payment came together days before the public sale. Ours was the winning bid. A brother in the Lord provided an interest-free mortgage and asked us to set the terms so they would not be a burden to us.

There were several points in the process where we came very close to dropping out. Each time, the Lord spoke through people, scriptures, and other creative ways to remind us of Who He is. In each instance, we chose the path of faith rather than sight.

Two years later, I received a call informing me that our brother felt the Lord was directing him to return the mortgage to us marked "Paid in Full." We went from being non-qualifiers to fully owning our home in two years. Is anything too difficult for the Lord? I still struggle with life's obstacles. Yet at each point of testing, I remember the Lord's faithfulness and make the choice anew to embrace the path of faith.

What challenges and obstacles are you currently facing? Is anything too difficult for the Lord?

Mighty Father, You transcend every problem, need, obstacle or trial that I could ever face. Help me to hear Your voice today and place my trust in You.

Don Riker serves congregational, ministry and business leaders with Teaching The Word Ministries in Leola.

Not Afraid

"You shall not be afraid of the terror by night...." *Psalms 91:5 (New King James Version)*

The year was 1980, and I was spending a year of voluntary service with a prison ministry team. We traveled across the country singing in prisons and churches. Our team both traveled and lived in a converted motor coach.

This particular day we were in Dade County, Florida, and headed to a local church for an evening program. As we drove through a remote area, our engine stopped and would not start again. We made contact with the church, and they arranged to pick us up. We locked the bus and headed to the church.

After the evening program, instead of staying with folks from the church, we all decided to go back to our bus. As we approached the bus, it looked like the bottom bays were open. Then it looked like the front door was hanging open. As we drove closer, we saw a couple of people exit the bus and flee into the darkness. Two of our guys entered the bus expecting to find others. There was no one left, but the bus had been ransacked and one of the cupboards was burned, probably by the candles they used as they looked for loot. Needless to say, we were all scared. So we prayed and asked the Lord to start the bus and get us closer to town for the night.

The Lord answered our prayers and the bus started. As we drove toward the outskirts of town and passed under a bright street light, the bus quit and would not start again. We praised the Lord because we knew He had answered our prayers in a powerful way and protected us from further harm or injury that night.

Dear God, thank you for answering prayer, sometimes in a quick and powerful way. In Christ's name, Amen.

Tim Landis is pastor of Bainbridge Church of God in Bainbridge.

God's Repayment Plan

"I will repay you for the years the locusts have eaten...."
Joel 2:25

When I was five, I stepped on the scales and heard my sister say "she's getting too heavy." I remember feeling ashamed and worried that something was wrong with me. The resulting cycle of low self-esteem and comfort eating lasted for the next 18 years. A good day was one in which no one made fun of me. I prayed at night for friends, and later, for someone to love me. As a committed Christian, I felt incredibly guilty about my inability to manage food. Throughout my childhood, adolescence, and young adulthood, I dreamed of one day wearing pretty clothing, having friends, being able to run, and traveling to exciting places.

During graduate school, I wrote yet another self-analysis. Not expecting any revelations, I was stunned by an insight that changed my core belief about myself and allowed me to accept love from God and others for the first time. This began to tear down the wall of isolation and pain that had imprisoned me in the use of food as a coping mechanism.

Today, I am able to use my past to understand the pain, frustration, and loneliness of compulsive eaters in order to help them heal. This brings indescribable joy to me. I believe that God gave me insight into this disorder at a young age to answer my childhood prayer of helping many, many people. He has given me a precious gift in a life so fulfilling that if I had to choose the pain all over again, I would.

And by the way, God has blessed me with more friends than I can track, pretty clothing, and the excitement of running my second marathon in Louisiana in February.

Dear Jesus, I pray for all of Your children, that they will know Your power to turn sadness into joy, and that they will trust that You love them deeply.

Tricia Groff, M.S. is a counselor at Crossroads Counseling Center, Lancaster, and a cognitive therapist at ACADIA, Lancaster.

Beyond Imagination to Belief

"Now glory be to God! By his mighty power at work within us, he is able to accomplish infinitely more than we would ever dare to ask or hope. May he be given glory in the church and in Christ Jesus forever and ever through endless ages. Amen." *Ephesians 3:20–21 (New Living Translation)*

This prayer guide has been devoted to challenging you to think and pray beyond your normal expectations. It has been a call to go beyond *imagining* true revival and transformation, to actually *believing* that God wants to bring it about in our own lives—spilling over into our churches and communities. And because God is able to do mighty works beyond what we would ever dare to ask or hope—we have an invitation to hope for more than we have ever thought possible. What would you like God to do? What seems impossible to you right now? If we meet His conditions for answered prayer, He promises to accomplish infinitely more—for His glory. Dare to ask; dare to hope. Dare to believe!

Pray for Lancaster County is our weekly prayer focus for the individuals, families, churches and communities of our region. Please carry this emphasis in your heart and your prayers throughout the week.

December 31

Get Uncomfortable!

"As Goliath moved closer to attack, David quickly ran out to meet him." *1 Samuel 17:48*

Ever since I was a child, I have had a sense of wonder at who God is and what is my reason for being. God placed in me a sense of desiring Him. I was slow and ignorant on how to fulfill this desire, so it left for a while. Then my choice to pursue the college party scene began. It started a course of sin that led to many hurts and negative patterns. It wasn't until I found out about His word that things started to change.

My wife and I were married for about a year when we realized we needed God and relationships with people other then our party friends. We began looking for a church. At the leading of my prayerfully excited mom-in-law, Patty Pasquino, we decided to try the Worship Center. I remember feeling so uncomfortable.

After church, our discussion was something like "Wow, what was that?" Next week, we decided to "get uncomfortable" again. Within weeks the Spirit of God had us hooked! After giving our lives to Christ and receiving an outpouring of His Holy Spirit, we decided to try out a small group with other young married couples. When several couples asked us to dinner, learned about our life and didn't judge us, we were really hooked. The community we experienced propelled us to run after God because His love was shown in an awesome way.

Seven years later, I continue to be amazed at what God can do when we run after Him and His purpose for our lives, no matter how uncomfortable it may make us feel. For me, fighting through things that make me feel uncomfortable is necessary in allowing God to do all He wants through me.

Dear God, help me to always run after You and Your purpose for my life.

Joe Castronova is regional pastor at The Worship Center, serves in pastor care and leads Worship Center's Alpha program.

What is the Regional Church of Lancaster County?

A cooperative network of Christian leaders dedicated
to relational partnership in the growth of the
kingdom of God in Lancaster County.

Jesus prayed "...for those who will believe in me...that they all may be one, as you Father are in me and I in you—that the world may believe that you sent me (John 17:20–21)."

The Regional Church of Lancaster County believes that the most powerful witness of God's love is the relational biblical unity of His people. If the manifest unity of God's people can actually cause the world to believe that the Father sent the Son, then our disunity must be a major factor in the unbelief that is so prevalent (in spite of our best evangelistic efforts) in society today. This should move us to repentance and a renewal of our commitment to love one another in purposefully relational ways.

This unity cannot, however, be mandated by mission statement or manufactured through concerted effort. The unity of all believers— paid for at Calvary (Ephesians 2:14–16)—can only be imparted to us by the Father through the Holy Spirit. What we CAN do is position ourselves to walk in it, proclaim it as the Father's will, live it out as best we can through loving relationships within the body of Christ, and pray (as Jesus did) for the Father to manifest it in our midst.

The Regional Church of Lancaster County, as an organization, was formed to impart a vision for Christian unity and create a living, relational context for furthering that unity. But when we speak of the "regional church" as it pertains to all Christians in Lancaster County, we are speaking of the body of Christ in our region as seen from a "heaven's eye view." When God looks upon His Church in Lancaster, He sees more than our separate camps, communions, confessions and councils. He sees a "regional church," made up of believers in every community, church and walk of life. He honors our individual "wineskins," but He sees us in a much larger and more fully relational context. He sees His children—His family.

What is the vision?

- To encourage and help equip the whole church to grow and mature in Christ (Ephesians 4:1–16)
- To strategically work together to revive and revitalize the church in our region (Revelation 2:2–7)
- To serve together as a loving and united Christian witness to every resident of our county (Luke 10:25–37)
- To work and pray for the ultimate spiritual and social transformation of Lancaster County (2 Chronicles 7:14; 1 Timothy 2:1–4)

What is the mission?

Our mission is to help present the life-changing power of the gospel of Jesus Christ to every soul within our region—praying, planning, walking and working together to see the kingdom of God established in every Lancaster home, community and marketplace—including the media and the worlds of commerce, education and government. "Thy Kingdom come, Thy will be done on earth as it is in heaven."

What are the mission strategies?

- PRAY To blanket the region with continual prayer and worship
- WITNESS   To saturate the region with the gospel witness of Jesus Christ
- TRANSFORM To mobilize initiatives to transform our communities with God's love
- GUARD To guard the well-being of the church through reconciliation, relationship, accountability, intercession and spiritual discernment

No matter where God has placed you—whether in ministry service or in the marketplace—you have been called to embrace the vision of biblical unity and kingdom transformation for our region. Please check our website for current regional initiatives and ways to participate in the vision of the Regional Church of Lancaster County. Together let's embrace the life-changing power of the gospel of Christ. Let's devote ourselves to building relationships and cooperating in ways that position us for the answer to Christ's prayer that all God's people be one.

www.theregionalchurch.com

The Regional Church of Lancaster County

415 South Shippen Street, Lancaster, PA 17602

Phone (717) 293-9287